BUILD

THE
Successful

THEATER
COMPANY

THIRD EDITION

Lisa Mulcahy

ALLWORTH PRESS
NEW YORK

Allworth Press books may be purchased in bulk at special discounts for sales promotion, corporate gifts, fund-raising, or educational purposes. Special editions can also be created to specifications. For details, contact the Special Sales Department, Allworth Press, 307 West 36th Street, 11th Floor, New York, NY 10018 or info@skyhorsepublishing.com.

19 18 17 16 15   5 4 3 2 1

Published by Allworth Press, an imprint of Skyhorse Publishing, Inc.
307 West 36th Street, 11th Floor, New York, NY 10018.

Allworth Press® is a registered trademark of Skyhorse Publishing, Inc.®, a Delaware corporation.

www.allworth.com

Cover design by Chris Ritchie

Library of Congress Cataloging-in-Publication Data is available on file.

Print ISBN: 978-1-62153-524-9
Ebook ISBN: 978-1-62153-525-6

Printed in the United States of America

FOR MY FATHER, WILLIAM MULCAHY

3. Dad may be able to provide one get-out-of-jail-free card, but next time, it's going to be all up to you. Determine how much money you're going to need to stay solvent and make a profit, by calculating the number of seats you're going to have to fill per performance, to cover your expenses (plus make a little cash over, hopefully). Are you intending to sell concession items? You can project that potential profit into the mix if so. But please, be brutally realistic about what you can make.

4. No matter how little money you have, plan for the unexpected catastrophe expense. Even a little money can help cushion emergency financial blows. Try to put a little cash aside from your profits each week, just in case. Try, at least.

It's never too early to start projecting into the future, budget-wise. Surround yourself with other people who can take some of the load off your shoulders by keeping a clear head where planning is concerned.

Rick Lombardo (New Repertory Theatre) has this to say about business planning: "Keep three things in mind short-term. First, mission—why do we do what we do? Next, work out a realistic budget document. Then, manage on a day-to-day basis.

"A long-range plan means you ask where is the institution now, then ask what you see yourself becoming? To get there, you need a constant dialogue with your staff. Plus, you've got to keep your eyes open in terms of survivability—you must know the answer to, "Why does it matter?"

"I like a three-year planning process, from soup to nuts in terms of budget to production."

INSURANCE CONSIDERATIONS

Most rental spaces, not to mention unions, will require you to arrange for insurance. It's hard to paint an exact picture of what you'll need to take care of here, since every space will be different. Every production, depending on the number of personnel you're using per show, may have different insurance requirements as well.

It's a safe bet, though, to plan for adequate coverage in the event of a tornado inside the building during showtime. You definitely need to ask Actors' Equity about workers' compensation requirements as well. They vary according to the number of actors you're employing, and workers' comp is not a gray zone—if you need to provide it, you need to provide it, or Equity can penalize you financially and/or shut you down totally.

Even if you're not working with Equity, it's a good idea to take a look at insurance for your actors' welfare. How can you get the best deal on sufficient

Table of Contents

Acknowledgments

I want to thank the following wonderful people for helping me invaluably during my work on this book:

First of all, at Allworth Press, Tad Crawford and Nicole Potter for their support of me as a writer and their tremendous guidance, trust, and encouragement. To Kelsie Besaw and Kate Lothman for their professionalism, warmth, and assistance as well.

To all of the amazing artists and administrators who participated in interviews for this book, I give my utmost gratitude. Your honesty, the generosity you show in sharing your wisdom, and your immense skills inspire me and will no doubt inspire scores of readers. Seth Barrish, Lee Brock, Gilbert Cates, Lilly Tung Crystal, Aaron Davidman, Patrick Dooley, Terrence Dwyer, Sheldon Epps, David Fuller, Corey Fischer, Michael Gennaro, Leslie Jacobson, Dona Lee Kelly, Susan Kosoff, Rick Lombardo, Susan Albert Lowenberg, Kevin Mayes, Susan Medak, Richard Pletcher, Ralph Remington, Jack Reuler, Mitzi Sales, Robert Serrell, Harriet Sheets, David Zak, and Paul Zuckerman: each of you provided me with your valuable time, insight, and memories, and I'm honored to be able to pass what I learned from you on to others.

I also wish to thank the following theater personnel for their specific assistance in helping me arrange the logistics of interviews and for providing me with supplementary materials: Sheila Boyd, Brian Colvern, Kay Elliott, Elisa Hale, Terrence Keane, Emily Lister, Stacey Moore, Jason Raitt, Allison Rawlings, Jane Staab, Sara Truog, Shay Wafer, and Helene Sanghri York.

I would like to give a very special thank-you to Molly Smith, Artistic Director of Arena Stage.

For special technical assistance, I would like to thank Geoff Grammel and Johanne Cimon of the Most Office in Fitchburg, Massachusetts, whose work is excellent.

To my entire family, thank you for your support. To my posse of friends, you know who you are. To all of the phenomenal artists I've encountered throughout my long life in the theater, thanks for great times.

To the Brandeis University theater community, especially Ted Kazanoff, thanks for a great education. Thank you also to Edward Albee for giving me a wonderful break. To my mother, Joan Mulcahy, you mean the world to me and I can't believe I am lucky enough to be your daughter. Thanks, Mom, to you and Dad for instilling me with strength and confidence and standing by my side every minute. You're the greatest.

Introduction

What Makes a Theater Company Successful?

Passion. Blind faith. Talent. Naïveté. Focus. A burning desire to say something important.

These are some of the qualities possessed by those brave individuals who enter the incredibly challenging field of professional theater. It's been said by many, including me, that in order to take on a career in the dramatic arts, your need to do it must supersede virtually every other desire you could possibly have. To make it, you must make sacrifice your best friend: sacrifice of your time, sacrifice of your financial security, sacrifice of your personal life, sacrifice, many times, of every last shred of your peace of mind.

You must also be a very tough cookie. Your self-esteem had better be bulletproof, and not simply in terms of the endless professional rejection and struggle you will invariably face. You also need to know who you are and like who you are 24/7, because you can't measure success in the theater by any conventional business model yardstick. It's very, very hard to get rich running a theater company, for example, to be able to see those profit numbers pile up on paper, as one could if he or she was running, say, a Fortune 500 company (or nearly any other type of company, for that matter).

So why do it, then? Well, there's passion. Blind faith. Talent. Naïveté. Focus. A burning desire to say something important—and feel free to add your personal reasons to that list. The world is, indeed, fortunate and better off for the fact that there are those people who live to act, direct, write, stage manage, design for the stage, work tech crew for shows, and, perhaps the most daunting prospect of all, found and build their own theater companies.

This book will examine the processes and practicalities involved in running a professional theater company. I was privileged to interview at length the key personnel who run thirteen of this country's most successful, free-spirited, and artistically vital theater companies, and I learned more from them than I ever thought possible (even though I've worked in professional theater for many years myself). These folks do not pull punches. They're realistic, due to personal ideology as well as from hard experience. They're also as excited about their companies today as the day they started working on them. Their artistic and business perspectives are fluid and fresh, no matter how many years (in some cases, decades) their companies have been operational. They're survivors, both artistically and financially, and they're inspirations.

I choose to let these fascinating subjects tell their stories themselves in a series of directly quoted anecdotes that, to me, feel a lot like the type of discourse that might take place after a show, over a late, lingering dinner, when you—the hopeful, eager novice—are lucky enough to be seated next to a legendary elder who's in the mood to reminisce for a while. What will be discussed adds up to a full explanation of what factors make a solid theater company develop and persevere.

Diversity was a key component in my selection of the theater companies I wanted to include within this book. Some of the companies we'll be examining are traditional repertory organizations—that is, in terms of definition, a resident company of actors performing a number of different shows throughout a set season. Other companies are more concerned with a very specific artistic concentration—producing plays that speak to multicultural issues, for instance. Some bust all myth, expectation, and convention, and that is their mission statement.

So what makes a theater company successful? Primarily, it's the importance of combining a sharp artistic focus, a smart and objective business viewpoint, a fully operational approach to physical production in any given venue, and a big-picture plan.

It's also very crucial to understand that art and commerce do indeed walk hand in hand. Successful theater company personnel know when to be creative and when to take their heads out of the clouds and get down to the nitty-gritty of making the money they need to keep going. They know how to translate abstract artistic visions into clear and concise sound bites that attract funders. They know the importance of applying for grants. They know the value of networking and thinking out of the box about marketing and strategic planning.

Other vital aspects of what makes companies shine? Optimism and pride. The people behind the most successful theater organizations are universally can-do in their attitudes. Although they are realistic, they balance that with the knowledge that pessimism is an energy-drainer and, therefore, a big potential nail in a company's coffin. So they reject negative thinking. If these company heads want to do something, they figure out a way to do it, even if that takes a bit of time and brainstorming. They are not easily daunted.

Here now, in no particular order, is an overview of the theater companies whose stories we can learn from.

STEPPENWOLF THEATER COMPANY

Chicago, Illinois.

Established: 1974, initially organization. 1975, incorporation. 1976, reorganization and ensemble established. Nonprofit.

Founders: Jeff Perry, Terry Kinney, and Gary Sinise.

Key Current Personnel: Anna Shapiro, artistic director; David Schmitz, managing director.

Distinguished Company Members: Scores of respected artists are members of the Steppenwolf ensemble. In addition to Jeff Perry, Terry Kinney, and Gary Sinise, these artists include John Malkovich, Joan Allen, Laurie Metcalf, John Mahoney, Tina Landau, William Petersen, Alana Arenas, Frank Galati, Martha Plimpton, Kevin Anderson, Lois Smith, Jim True-Frost, Kathryn Erbe, Eric Simonson, Amy Morton, Gary Cole, Tom Irwin, Randall Arney, Kate Arrington, Robert Breuler, K. Todd Freeman, Ian Barford, Mariann Mayberry, Francis Guiman, Rondi Reed, Moira Harris, Rick Snyder, Alan Wilder, Tim Hopper, Ora Jones, Jon Michael Hill, Tracy Letts, Tarell Alvin McCraney, Austin Pendleton, Anna D. Shapiro, Yasen Peyankov, James Vincent Meredith, Sally Murphy, and Molly Regan, plus Artistic Director Martha Lavey.

Number of Plays Produced per Season: Five, mainstage; four, studio space; three, garage space; plus additional programs' productions.

Casting and Employment Practices: Employs a mix of resident company actors with jobbed-in performers. Casting is done by general audition, by casting director, and by invitation for specific shows. Does not hire outside technical employees.

Early Season Offerings: *And Miss Reardon Drinks a Little*, *Grease*, *Rosencrantz and Guildenstern Are Dead*, *The Glass Menagerie*.

Recent Season Offerings: *August: Osage County*, John Steinbeck's *East of Eden*, *Almost Atlanta*, *Bring Me the Head of James Franco*.

Awards, Citations, and a Few Notable Achievements: Steppenwolf has received numerous Tony Awards, Obie Awards, Drama Desk Awards, Theatre

World Awards, Joseph Jefferson Awards for Chicago Theatre Excellence, and Clarence Derwin Awards, plus the National Medal of Arts presented by former President Bill Clinton and First Lady Hillary Rodham Clinton, the Illinois Arts Award, and the Gradiva Award from the National Association for the Advancement of Psychoanalysis (to John Malkovich for the play *Hysteria*). The company's sterling artistic achievements include its esteemed productions of plays such as *The Grapes of Wrath*, *True West*, *Balm in Gilead*, *One Flew Over the Cuckoo's Nest*, *Burn This*, *Buried Child*, *The Libertine*, *The Glass Menagerie*, and numerous others. Many of the company's notable productions have played on Broadway, in the West End/internationally, and off-Broadway.

The Company's Mission: Steppenwolf was started with a deep commitment to ensemble work, and artistic risk. The company hopes to push forward the vitality and diversity of American theater work, while preserving the group's initial vision, in a collaborative, collective sense.

Speaking on Behalf of Steppenwolf: Michael Gennaro, the company's former executive director, worked as a performer both on Broadway and off-Broadway, and ran the Pennsylvania Ballet Company in Philadelphia; David Hawkanson, the company's former executive director, whose innovative leadership has brought the company further national/international acclaim, has helped build a blockbuster subscriber base of over 20,000 regular patrons.

THE GEFFEN PLAYHOUSE

Los Angeles, California.

Established: 1995. Nonprofit.

Founder: Gilbert Cates.

Key Current Personnel: Randall Arney, artistic director; Gil Cates Jr., executive director.

Distinguished Company Members: Many of film and television's most lauded luminaries have graced the Geffen's stages, including Annette Bening, Laurence Fishburne, John Goodman, Uta Hagen, Beau Bridges, Debbie Allen, Brenda Fricker, Carrie Fisher, Martin Short, Peter Falk, Jason Alexander, David Hyde-Pierce, Rebecca Pidgeon, Neil Patrick Harris, Alicia Silverstone, David Arquette, Matthew Modine, Brooke Shields, Dana Delany, Rita Wilson, and Roma Downey.

Number of Plays Produced per Season: Five, mainstage; three to four, second stage.

Casting and Employment Practices: Needs vary by current season.

Early Season Offerings: *Cat on a Hot Tin Roof.*

Recent Season Offerings: *Time Stands Still* by Donald Marguiles (Broadway transfer); *Wishful Drinking* by Carrie Fisher (Broadway transfer); the world premiere of the musical *Nightmare Alley* by Jonathan Brielle; the West Coast premiere of *Thurgood* by George Stevens Jr.; a staged reimagining of *The Exorcist*, directed by John Doyle.

Awards, Citations, and a Few Notable Achievements: Originally known as the Westwood Playhouse, the theater was purchased in 1993 by UCLA. UCLA's then-chancellor, Charles E. Young, strongly concurred with his associate Gil Cates (founder and former president of the UCLA School of Theater, Film, and Television) that their school's students needed a forum in which to see and learn from the very best stage work possible. Young then appointed Cates producing director of the theater. Enter legendary businessman and philanthropist David Geffen, who, in 2002, donated $5 million to the playhouse, one of the largest gifts ever made to an existing theater. The playhouse was subsequently renamed after Mr. Geffen as recognition for his generosity, and his support has paid off, culminating in a crowd-pleasing mix of classic productions and audacious new works.

The Company's Mission: To educate future theater leaders, as well as to expose the local community to world-class stage works.

Speaking on Behalf of the Geffen Playhouse: The late Gil Cates, founder and producing director, the theater, film, and television powerhouse known for his work as a director, a producer, and the force behind numerous Academy Awards shows.

LA JOLLA PLAYHOUSE
La Jolla, California.

Established: 1947. Nonprofit.

Founders: Gregory Peck, Dorothy McGuire, and Mel Ferrer.

Key Current Personnel: Christopher Ashley, artistic director; Michael S. Rosenberg, managing director.

Distinguished Company Members: Many film actors who wished to keep working on their stagecraft found the perfect sanctuary at the Playhouse in its early days. It was not uncommon to be able to see a show starring Eartha Kitt, Jennifer Jones, Joseph Cotten, Tallulah Bankhead, and many other movie stars treading the boards. The tradition of the Playhouse attracting wonderful performers, of course, continues to this day, such as Billy Crystal in *700 Sundays* and Matthew Broderick appearing in *How to Succeed in Business Without Really Trying* before those productions' hit Broadway runs. The Playhouse is also associated with groundbreaking works by Tony Kushner and Lisa Kron, as well as musical collaborations with Pete Townshend and Randy Newman. Respected directors Des McAnuff and Michael Greif served previously as artistic directors.

Number of Plays Produced per Season: Five, mainstage.

Casting and Employment Practices: Combines casting from its resident company with outside talent each season. Hires creative staff (directors, designers) plus tech staff from a mix of in-house and those jobbed in, depending upon current season specifics.

Early Season Offerings: A sample production from the 1947 season—*Night Must Fall*.

Recent Season Offerings: Recent years have seen lauded productions like *I Am My Own Wife*, *Jersey Boys*, and the Who's *Tommy* go on to acclaim on Broadway, off-Broadway, and around the world. The Playhouse also staged the West Coast premiere of *Rent*; other acclaimed productions include *Healing Wars* and *Up Here*.

Awards, Citations, and a Few Notable Achievements: The 1993 Tony Award for Outstanding Regional Theatre; over three hundred additional honors.

The Company's Mission: Originally, to give film actors the opportunity to do good work in the theater at a quality venue that was geographically close to the film studios of Los Angeles. Currently also to produce challenging, exciting, and innovative theater.

Speaking on Behalf of La Jolla Playhouse: Terrence Dwyer, who was highly desired by film and stage icon Des McAnuff to take on the managing director's position during a period of crucial growth for the Playhouse, following a search from 1990 to 1992.

GOODSPEED MUSICALS

East Haddam, Connecticut.

Established: 1963. Nonprofit.

Founder: William Goodspeed.

Key Current Personnel: Michael Gennaro, executive director.

Distinguished Company Members: Scores of the world's best composers, performers, designers, and directors have helped transform new musicals first produced at Goodspeed, including *Annie* and *Man of La Mancha*, into Broadway classics. Esteemed Goodspeed associates also include Norma Terris, star of Jerome Kern's *Show Boat*, for whom the company's Chester, CT, stage is named.

Number of Plays Produced per Season: Six.

Casting and Employment Practices: Needs vary per season.

Previous Season Offerings: *A Little Night Music, Brigadoon, Harrigan 'n Hart.*

Recent Season Offerings: Irving Berlin's *Annie Get Your Gun, Band Geeks!, Carnival!, La Cage aux Folles, It's a Wonderful Life.*

Awards, Citations, and a Few Notable Achievements: Too many to count—two Tony Awards to the company itself, plus more than a dozen Tonys for achievements within Goodspeed-associated productions. The company also established the Library of Musical Theatre, a rich research resource, on-site.

The Company's Mission: To foster the fruitful creation of new musicals while preserving and restaging classic material, all at the highest level of quality.

Speaking on Behalf of Goodspeed Musicals: Michael P. Price, who, as the company's longtime artistic director, spearheaded its success for nearly five decades through his tenacious talent and vision.

CHICAGO CITY LIMITS

New York City.

Established: The company's members came to New York from Chicago in 1979.

Founder: George Todisco.

Key Current Personnel: Paul Zuckerman, executive producer, artistic director, and original company member.

Distinguished Company Members: George Todisco passed away in 1982. Other members of the company from its early days, in addition to Paul Zuckerman, include Rick Crom, Carol Schindler, Linda Gelman, Chris Oyen, Bill McLaughlin, John Telfer, Denny Siegel, Carl Kissin, Andrew Daly, and many others. Current company members include Tony Carnevale, David Chernicoff, Jason Fletcher, Sharon Fogarty, Rachel Korowitz, Kobi Libli, Deb Racchai, Rob Schiffman, Rory Scholl, Ann Scobie, and Greg Tiggs. The company is also joined regularly by guest performers including Jerry Seinfeld, Jon Stewart, Bill Irwin, Rita Rudner, Paul Reiser, Brett Butler, and Larry Miller.

Number of Plays Produced per Season: Year-round improvised comedy shows for a total of over 8,500 performances.

Casting and Employment Practices: CCL casts only from its resident company. Outside tech help is hired, although directors and designers are culled from in-house talent only.

Awards, Citations, and a Few Notable Achievements: The company has performed for United Nations Delegates and at the Smithsonian Institution, Lincoln Center, and Super Bowl. Its TV appearances include *The Today Show, Entertainment Tonight,* and many other programs, plus the troupe had its own series on the USA Network, *Reel News.*

The Company's Mission: Pioneering comedy improvisation excellence; developing many of the most utilized and effective theater games, structures, and forms used widely today.

Speaking on Behalf of Chicago City Limits: Paul Zuckerman, one of the company's most vital early voices and its enduring visionary.

BERKELEY REPERTORY THEATRE

Berkeley, California/San Francisco Bay area.

Established: 1968. Nonprofit.

Founder: Michael Leibert.

Key Current Personnel: Tony Taccone, artistic director; Susan Medak, managing director

Distinguished Company Members: A huge number of fine, respected theater artists have flocked to Berkeley Rep. The company has also produced many notable and groundbreaking new works, including Tony Kushner's *Homebody/Kabul*, and has collaborated with artists ranging from George C. Wolfe to Anna Devere Smith to Nicolas Kent to Green Day.

Number of Plays Produced per Season: Seven plays in its two theaters, plus two to three special events.

Casting and Employment Practices: Directors, designers, performers, and techies all selected from company associates, plus jobbed in, depending upon current show/season requirements.

Early Season Offerings: Early works had a very literary thrust, including plays by Arthur Miller.

Recent Season Offerings: *Passing Strange, American Idiot, In the Next Room (or The Vibrator Play), Bridge & Tunnel, Amélie.*

Awards, Citations, and a Few Notable Achievements: Numerous, including the 1997 Tony Award.

The Company's Mission: A commitment to do ambitious work through strong dedication to its ensemble of talented artists and its desire to stay connected to its community in order to satisfy and challenge the audience.

Speaking on Behalf of Berkeley Rep: Susan Medak, whose credentials and associations include the Board of Directors for Theatre Communications Group, LORT, the National Endowment for the Arts Theatre Program Panel, the Massachusetts State Arts Council, and respected theaters including the Milwaukee Repertory Theatre. Also, Mitzi Sales, who joined Berkeley Rep as managing director under Michael Leibert in the early 1970s and was responsible for much of its early genesis and major success.

MIXED BLOOD THEATRE COMPANY

Minneapolis, Minnesota.

Established: 1976. Nonprofit.

Founder: Jack Reuler.

Key Current Personnel: Jack Reuler, artistic director.

Distinguished Company Members: Among the ranks of impressive, creative personnel who have acted, directed, and written for Mixed Blood is Don Cheadle, namesake of the company's Don Cheadle Apprentice Academy summer program for teenagers.

Number of Plays Produced per Season: Five, plus a number of educational touring productions, coproductions, and program events.

Casting and Employment Practices: Mixed Blood casts on a show-by-show basis, out of a resident/jobber pool. Directors and designers are jobbed in each season.

Previous Season Offerings: Among Mixed Blood's greatest hits: *Jackie Robinson*, *Eastern Parade*, *Daughters of Africa*, *Dr. King's Dream*, *Minnecanos*, *According to Coyote*, *Black Eagle*, and *Paul Robeson*. These productions have toured in educational venues for years, and are presented on an ongoing basis to the Minneapolis community at large.

Recent Season Offerings: *Colossal*, *Cedar Cypher*, *The Upstairs Concierge*, *Spinning into Butter*, *Love Person*, *Messy Utopia*, *Pure Confidence* (off-Broadway transfer).

Awards, Citations, and a Few Notable Achievements: A Pulitzer Prize nomination for *Love Person* in 2008, honoring playwright Aditi Kapil, is one of the jewels in the company's crown. Additionally, three Audelco Awards, three Twin Cities Drama Critics Awards, an Outstanding Achievement Award from the Minneapolis Commission on Civil Rights, the Actors' Equity Rosetta Le Noire Award, the Council on Black Minnesotans Dream Keeper Award, the Minneapolis Foundation's Diversity Award, the Martin Luther King Humanitarian Award, a Best New Play Award nomination by the American Theatre Critics Association, and the Actors' Equity Spirit Award to Jack Reuler.

The Company's Mission: To produce artistically risky work using culture-conscious casting, to provide a forum of expression for artists of color, to open up theater to a nontraditional audience, and to educate through its programs about issues of race and culture.

Speaking on Behalf of Mixed Blood: Jack Reuler, whose inspiration has always been the spirit of Dr. Martin Luther King's dream and philosophy.

WHEELOCK FAMILY THEATRE

Boston, Massachusetts.

Established: 1981. Nonprofit.

Founders: Susan Kosoff, Jane Staab, Tony Hancock, and Andrea Genser.

Key Current Personnel: Shelley Bolman, general manager, co-artistic director; Kay Elliott, administrative manager.

Distinguished Company Members: A long list of Boston's elite acting talent return over and over to the Wheelock stage. Alumni include Oscar winner Matt Damon, Julia Jones of the *Twilight* film series, and Broadway actors Wang Luoyong, Jessica Walling, Angela Hall, CeeCee Harshaw, and Jamie McKenzie.

Number of Plays Produced per Season: Three plays, including one musical, one children's production, and one adult drama or comedy. Staged readings throughout the season.

Casting and Employment Practices: Casts a mix of Equity and non-Equity actors per show. Hires outside management, artistic, and tech staff on an as-needed basis.

Previous Season Offerings: *Antigone, Anne of Green Gables, The King & I, Romeo & Juliet, Little Women, The Jungle Book*. All productions in the company's history have been concurrently interpreted in American Sign Language.

Recent Season Offerings: *Aladdin, The Secret Garden*.

Awards, Citations, and a Few Notable Achievements: The LEAD Award from the Kennedy Center for the Performing Arts and the Christopher Reeve Paralysis Foundation Award for Excellence in Accessibility Leadership; The President's Coming Up Taller Award; The Actors' Equity Rosetta Le Noire Award; Boston Parents Paper Family Favorite Award; Massachusetts Cultural Council's Commonwealth Award.

The Company's Mission: To serve children and family's entertainment and lifestyle needs, to educate budding theater professionals in the dramatic arts, to cast people of color in lead roles, and to be a theater for all people.

Speaking on Behalf of Wheelock Family Theatre: Susan Kosoff, cofounder, artistic directing force of nature, and distinguished Wheelock College professor.

LA THEATRE WORKS

Los Angeles, California.

Established: 1974. Nonprofit.

Founder: Susan Albert Loewenberg.

Key Current Personnel: Susan Albert Loewenberg, producing director.

Distinguished Company Members: A virtual who's who of the best artists working in film, television, and theater, including Oscar winners Helen Hunt and Richard Dreyfuss, Edward Asner, Michael York, director Gordon Hunt, and many, many others.

Casting and Employment Practices: Jobs in additional directors and staff as the need arises. Performers are hired through agent submission only.

Season Offerings: The company's work has spanned the gamut from its early cutting-edge workshop accomplishments in the California state prison system through its groundbreaking incarnation as a theater producing radio plays. Now its Audio Library collected works of more than 250 recorded plays is the largest in the country and is widely available to the public via bookstores, libraries, and satellite radio technology.

Awards, Citations, and a Few Notable Achievements: Almost too many to mention; of particular note has been the ARTS & Children outreach program, which is geared toward at-risk youth. Its educational programs are widely lauded as well.

The Company's Mission: To produce innovative theater and audio art, plus expand arts access to the community by using new technology.

Speaking on Behalf of LA Theatre Works: Susan Albert Loewenberg, known for her work as an actor and artist, as well as for being a keen businesswoman who has built her company through savvy diversification.

BAILIWICK REPERTORY/BAILIWICK CHICAGO

Chicago, Illinois.

Established: 1982. New entity established 2009. Nonprofit.

Founders: Initially an artistic enclave, which included David Zak. The company's second, separate incarnation was founded similarly by an artistic collective, led by Kevin Mayes.

Key Current Personnel: Lili-Anne Brown, artistic director.

Distinguished Company Members: Many trailblazing and fiercely brilliant theatrical visionaries have done great work under Bailiwick's original auspices, including Larry Kramer, artistic associate Cecilie D. Keenan, Claudia Allen, and many more writers and directors. Talented stage actors Greg Louganis and Tim Miller have been among the many performers who have appeared in Bailiwick productions.

Number of Plays Produced per Season: Currently varies, although the productions of Bailiwick Chicago have been critical and commercial smashes.

Casting and Employment Practices: Bailiwick Chicago is currently working exclusively in-house.

Past Season Offerings: *Corpus Christi*, *The Christmas Schooner*.

Recent Season Offerings: *The Wild Party*, Elton John's *Aida*.

Awards, Citations, and a Few Notable Achievements: Almost one hundred Jeff Awards, plus After Dark Awards citations. Bailiwick's production of *Corpus Christi* garnered stellar reviews and awards, plus the enthusiastic support of its author, Terrence McNally, who was in attendance for a performance.

The Company's Mission: A commitment to carrying out the vision of gifted artists.

Speaking on Behalf of Bailiwick: David Zak, the company's former leader; Kevin Mayes, Bailiwick Chicago's fresh visionary founder.

NEW REPERTORY THEATRE
Watertown, Massachusetts/Boston area.

Established: 1984. Nonprofit.

Founder: A small enclave of theater artists, specifically including Larry Lane.

Key Current Personnel: Jim Petosa, artistic director.

Distinguished Company Members: Austin Pendleton, who wowed Boston critics and audiences by codirecting an innovative production of *King Lear*. New Rep has also worked extensively with Brandeis University's professional theater training program, to provide work to its acting and design graduates, and to benefit from their talents.

Number of Plays Produced per Season: Five.

Casting and Employment Practices: Actors, directors, designers, and techies jobbed in, depending upon current positions available each season.

Previous Season Offerings: *Bus Stop, Blue Window, Spunk, Later Life, As You Like It, The Misanthrope, Sylvia, Skylight*, and many others.

Recent Season Offerings: *Topdog/Underdog, Quills, A Girl's War, A Number*.

Awards, Citations, and a Few Notable Achievements: Elliot Norton Awards, Best Of citations by the *Boston Globe, Boston Herald, Tab*, and *Back Bay Courant* newspapers, plus awards from the Independent Reviewers of New England.

The Company's Mission: To foster the production of challenging, high-quality writing and acting onstage where it otherwise might be lacking in the Boston area.

Speaking on Behalf of New Repertory Theatre: Rick Lombardo, former artistic director and the accomplished previous artistic head of both the Players Guild and the Stillwaters Theatre Company; Harriet Sheets, managing director.

THE ROUND BARN AT AMISH ACRES
Nappanee, Indiana.

Established: 1984. Commercial.

Founder: Richard Pletcher.

Key Current Personnel: Richard Pletcher, executive producer.

Distinguished Company Members: The company has enjoyed a long and productive collaboration with author Joseph Stein. Other associates include Stephen Schwartz, Scott Schwartz, and the York Theatre Company in New York City.

Number of Plays Produced per Season: Eight.

Casting and Employment Practices: Needs vary by current season. Holds auditions nationwide; in-house facilities include scenic and costume shops, plus ample rehearsal space, and all staff is housed on-site.

Previous Season Offerings: *Plain and Fancy, Damn Yankees, Cinderella.*

Recent Season Offerings: *The Taffetas, A Closer Walk with Patsy Cline, The Foreigner, Forever Plaid, The Miracle Worker, Crazy for You.*

Awards, Citations, and a Few Notable Achievements: The company now serves as the national home for the classic musical *Plain and Fancy*; it produces the show every season, to both audience and critical raves. What's more, within its commitment to producing good old-fashioned entertainment, the company has enjoyed great success from a commercial point of view. Located on a picturesque farm and surrounded by restaurant services, lodging, shopping, an arts and crafts festival, and a children's acting studio, the company has shrewdly positioned itself as a tourist must-see. Over ninety successful productions of Broadway shows tell the true tale.

The Company's Mission: To provide family-oriented entertainment for a wide audience.

Speaking on Behalf of Amish Acres: Richard Pletcher, an artist/businessman blessed with common sense, practical smarts, and a great eye for what works theatrically.

SHOTGUN PLAYERS

Berkeley, California.

Established: 1992. Nonprofit.

Founder: Patrick Dooley.

Key Current Personnel: Patrick Dooley, artistic director.

Distinguished Company Members: Andy Alaban, Nina Ball, Fontana Butterfield, Kevin Clarke, Valera Coble, Christine Cook, Kimberly Dooley, Mark Jackson, Liz Hitchcock Lisle, Dave Maier, Susannah Martin, Joanne McBrien, Nick Medina, Trish Mulholland, Judy Phillips, Richard Reinholdt, Katja Rivera, Michelle Talgarow, Jon Tracy, Megan Trout, Matt Stines, Beth Wilmurt, Hanah Zahner-Isenberg.

Number of Plays per Season: One to two.

Casting and Employment Practices: Accepts headshots from AEA members; attends TBA auditions yearly.

Previous Season Offerings: *Twelfth Night, Our Town, Bonnie and Clyde, The Electric Ballroom*.

Recent Season Offerings: *Antigonick, Top Girls, Eurydice*.

Awards, Citations, and a Few Notable Achievements: the Will Glickman Award for *Dog Act* and *Beowulf*. San Francisco Weekly citation for 2011 Best Theater Company.

The Company's Mission: To create bold, relevant, affordable theater that spurs audiences to reexamine.

Speaking on Behalf of Shotgun Players: Patrick Dooley, the company's tenacious, confident leader.

ASIAN AMERICAN THEATER COMPANY/FEROCIOUS LOTUS

San Francisco, California.

Established: AATC, 1973; Ferocious Lotus, 2010. Nonprofits.

Founders: AATC, Frank Chin; Ferocious Lotus, Lily Tung Crystal, Leon Goertzen.

Key Current Personnel: AATC is currently on hiatus, but is expected to perform and advocate again as an organization. Ferocious Lotus was formed from a bounty of the company's associates, including current artistic director Lily Tung Crystal and cofounding artistic director Leon Goertzen.

Distinguished Company Members: AATC—Dennis Dun, David Henry Hwang, Amy Hill, Lydia Tanji. Ferocious Lotus—Rinabeth Aportol, Christopher Chen, Will Dao, May Liang, Mina Morita, Ogie Zulueta.

Number of Plays Produced per Season: Varies.

Casting and Employment Practices: Currently, Ferocious Lotus is working primarily as an in-house collective, but is actively looking for new collaborators through its associates.

Previous Season Offerings: AATC—*Beijing, California, Intake/Outtake II*.

Recent Season Offerings: Ferocious Lotus—*Mutt, Crane*.

Awards, Citations, and a Few Notable Achievements: AATC has been acclaimed for decades as one of the country's most progressive and equality-minded theatrical entities, in terms of giving opportunities to Asian performers, directors, and playwrights. Ferocious Lotus has accomplished the same goals, and wishes to open up its artistic home to artists of all races and genders. Lily Tung Crystal was also the recipient of the 2009 Theatre Bay Area Titan Award.

The Companies' Mission: To share the stories of Asian American artists, and the world as a whole.

Speaking on Behalf of Ferocious Lotus: Lily Tung Crystal, the company's fiercely intelligent leader.

THE BARROW GROUP

New York City.

Established: 1985. Nonprofit.

Founders: Seth Barrish, Lee Brock.

Key Current Personnel: Seth Barrish, Lee Brock, Executive Director Robert Serrell.

Distinguished Company Members: Academy Award winner Anne Hathaway, Academy Award nominee Vera Farmiga, Emmy winner Tony Hale.

Number of Plays Produced per Season: Seventy productions per year, encompassing plays, readings, and workshops.

Casting and Employment Practices: The company operates as an inclusive meritocracy—new members must be approved by the entire company, based on evaluation of their work. More than 2,000 students per year attend TBG's acting classes, many of whom become company associates as they develop into professional performers.

Previous Season Offerings: *When I Wished I Was Here.*

Recent Season Offerings: *Short Stuff 7.*

Awards, Citations, and a Few Notable Achievements: A 1995 Drama Desk Award; a 2013 Lucille Lortel Award.

The Company's Mission: To forward realistic, moving theater, and educate the next generation of top acting talent.

Speaking on Behalf of the Barrow Group: Its vital leadership, Seth Barrish, Lee Brock, and Robert Serrell.

A number of highly accomplished theater professionals have also generously contributed their wisdom to these pages. Sage insight is also offered by:

—COREY FISCHER, cofounder of the former and highly respected company The Jewish Theatre San Francisco/A Traveling Jewish Theatre (TJT). Fischer is a longtime writer and performer known for his work and collaboration with film director Robert Altman, and his stage work with Joseph Chaiken. Also, Aaron Davidman, TJT's former artistic director.

—**SHELDON EPPS**, former artistic director of the Pasadena Playhouse and a Broadway director whose work includes the Roundabout Theatre's staging of *Blue*.

—**LYLA WHITE**, former executive director of the Pasadena Playhouse and a respected fund-raising force.

—**RALPH REMINGTON**, former artistic director of the Living Stage at Arena Stage and an esteemed actor/director.

—**LESLIE B. JACOBSON**, former artistic director of Horizons Theatre and a renowned feminist theater artist/producer.

—**DAVID FULLER**, a well-known director, Broadway and off-Broadway actor, former coproducing artistic director of Theatre Ten, and former artistic director of Jean Cocteau Repertory.

—**DONA LEE KELLY**, former general manager of Jean Cocteau Repertory who has also worked with Dodger Productions, with Robert Cole Productions, and as a faculty member with Stella Adler at New York University's Tisch School of the Arts.

So there's our illustrious list of experts. Whatever reason you have for reading this book—whether you're a theater student, a budding pro looking to found your own company, or a fan who loves reading about backstage blood, sweat, and tears—there's a lot of fascinating stuff to be learned from these individuals' hard-won experience, clear-cut perspectives, and concrete advice. This is how a theater company rises, solidifies, and consistently delivers, to its audiences and on its profit potential.

PART ONE

ROOTS

Precious Little by Madeleine George
directed by Marissa Wolf
Shotgun Players 2012 Season
Pictured: Nancy Carlin, Zehra Berkman, Rami Margron
Photo by Pak Han

Chapter One
How We Came Together

That any theater company comes together at all, ever, is a miracle.

The reasons why one chooses to set out on the path to starting a company are, of course, rife with good intentions. Usually, there is a burning need on the part of a founder to express a dramatic truth very specifically. He or she recognizes that in order to do this with any measure of control, he or she will have to work independently—you don't wait for someone to cast you in your dream project or write it and hand it to you. You need to do it yourself.

An admirable goal, for sure. Once you decide you are indeed going to start your own company, your next logical step would be to look around and try to find other people to participate in your vision. This, frankly, is where stuff can get weird. What if the people you choose are flaky and not dependable? Or have egos the size of Cleveland? Or things start off great, but pretty soon everybody starts fighting over everything from material to who has the most lines in your debut show to who broke into the petty cash box to buy pizza?

Or how about financial hurdles? Ignorance about money is the fastest way a theater company founder can run his or her dream into the ground. You need to think ahead to plan a feasible financial vision if you want to last longer than three seconds.

So those are a few possible pitfalls. Now for the good news! You can beat the odds. How? A big-picture plan toward building longevity is what you want to be focused on. You don't need to be independently wealthy with a huge staff to make your theater company work. You do need information from those who have been there—experience is the world's greatest teacher. If you don't have it yourself, you can still make like a sponge and soak it up from those who have been around the block.

In this chapter, our successful subjects give us an understanding of the origins of each of their companies, covering issues like artistic impetus for starting, how founders and staffers met up and determined their common goal, early business planning (or shockingly, lack thereof—but even mistakes can be lessons), compromises, soldiering through difficulty—you name it, they've been through it.

These companies' roots are diverse, yet they do have one thing in common— they made it. Take heart and inspiration, starting with Berkeley Repertory's resolve to integrate fine literary properties with the San Francisco Bay area's 1960s sensibilities.

COMMITMENT TO WORDS AND COMMUNITY

According to Susan Medak, managing director of Berkeley Repertory: "Michael Leibert started the company in 1968. Michael's group began performing in small storefronts about six blocks away from the campus of the University of California at Berkeley.

> The decision Michael made to settle in Berkeley had to do with what the community stands for. This community loves itself. It loves its words, loves ideas, and prides itself on its tolerance. My sense has always been, a theater company's relationship with its surroundings is the key to its success. A friend of mine who's been very successful in the theater has always put it best: "In this business, geography is destiny." What's marking the companies that have been successful in a mainstream area, like Wichita, Kansas, is that they best know that small-town world. In Berkeley, the audience is and always has been completely driven by a love of the written word. And Michael's original commitment was to literature-based work. So in the beginning, the company was producing Arthur Miller, Alan Ackbourn, very literary shows.
>
> Michael was a very charismatic leader. He was in love with actors, but he was a very troubled human being, incapable of growing personally. This eventually became a problem, because your challenge, as a company, is how to build the structure that sustains what you want to do. It gets uncomfortable when a founding artist—and I think this is true of many founding artists, not just Michael—struggles with building and growing in the long run, like how at that time, the company was not committed to new works.
>
> After starting things up, Michael then worked with a small resident company on six to eight shows. The memory of that moment in time—the late '60s, the relatively new idea of political activism—for the actors, it was indelible.
>
> Berkeley, known for its activism and university sensibility, informed this company. The company moved to a new space on College Avenue, a 150-seat storefront, with a big peace sign on the front.

Mitzi Sales, former managing director at Berkeley Rep, came on the scene then:

> I think the basic impetus, as lore would have it—and I was there three and a half years after it got started—was, you know, Michael was looking for something to do; he'd gotten out of grad school, and he'd been in the theater department. He had some friends who were Equity actors, so I think the most important thing that Michael Leibert did was start the theater as an Equity company. He did this because the actors he knew and wanted to work with were already members of the union, at least a couple of members of his closest coterie.
>
> He had a very successful production of *Woyzeck* at the International House Space in Berkeley, and he thought, "Wow, what a piece of cake! I'll just start a theater." There was this little space on College Avenue, which is not particularly far from the campus—straight down the street. And all of the people that he would be working with were already living in the neighborhood. He thought, "We'll put on *Woyzeck*, it'll be a big hit, we'll sell all these tickets, we'll build the theater, and people will come." Well, of course this was very, very difficult.
>
> But the thing that Michael had that other people didn't have was a wife with money. So he had a patron, and one of the ways to start a theater company is to find a patron.
>
> Michael originally named the group the Theater. When they went for their articles of incorporation, Michael was told, "No, no, no, you have to have some distinguishing name."
>
> And so, the Pomegranate Players was picked. But it was a joke—they were never really advertised as the Pomegranate Players; nobody thought they were the Pomegranate Players.

REBELS EMBRACING RISK

For Steppenwolf, the desire to make an artistic statement was fueled by confidence and fearlessness. The founding members convened in 1974, in Deerfield, Illinois, to put on their first show at a Unitarian church. This original meeting of the minds was facilitated by the fact that each founding member recognized they had in common an intense love of the theatrical art form, a need to express themselves through it, and the smarts and self-assurance to know innately that being true to that, they couldn't fail.

Michael Gennaro, former executive director of Steppenwolf, relates the tale of the company's inception:

> Keep in mind the founders being Jeff Perry, Gary Sinise, and Terry Kinney, they all kind of knew each other—I think Gary and Jeff knew each other the longest, and then Jeff knew Terry. Their first production was *Rosencrantz and Guildenstern*

Are Dead. After they did that, they said, "We gotta keep this going." Kind of their impetus, within that first group of which there were about nine people—some of them are still around, like Al Walter, John Malkovich, Laurie Metcalf—I think if you ask them, their impetus was, "We couldn't get work anywhere else. We can do things with a certain visceral style—that's what we're all about. We're as good as anybody and we can work like that." And I think underlying all of that, all of the time, was to never settle for anything less as far as they could go. I mean, in some ways you could say it's just a striving for excellence, but beyond that it was like, no performance is ever set. It's like, we keep improving upon it every single time we do it.

I think, then, the insularity of the group kind of drove them all the time. What was the financial vision? They didn't have one. How many staff members? This is a group of people who just got together to do everything and the whole point was just to get onstage and work together. The trust that developed over time, and the way of working together as an ensemble, that was the driving force.

The group had people they admired, like John Cassavetes. They would tackle any play, regardless of the age requirements. If someone wasn't right, too bad. If they wanted to do it, then they would do it. They saw themselves as rebels and did what they wanted to do. So, everybody had their day jobs, which included John driving a bus and Gary working in a hat store. But their whole day was made up in getting together and working as a theater. Strangely enough, that's still the driving force of this theater. This theater has never really been driven by—there have been, kind of, plans—but that's not really the way it's worked.

SOCIALLY CONSCIOUS VISION

For Jack Reuler, a desire to keep a social leader's dream alive compelled him to start a theater. Utilizing its status within a community service organization also allowed him a feasible financial vision from the very start. Jack, founder and artistic director of Mixed Blood, says: "I started the organization right out of college. I'd gone to college intending to be a veterinarian, and somehow [Mixed Blood] helped me to take a left turn—a great left turn.

A childhood icon of mine was always Martin Luther King, and seven years after his death was when I decided to start the theater, at a point when the civil rights movement was at its lowest. When I was at school, I had a job with a social service organization called the Center for Community Action [in Minneapolis], which was to seek out needs in the community and set up programs to meet those needs. There was this community theater, Theater in the Round, it's called, which is still the primary community theater in the Twin Cities. They did a production of *The Great White Hope*, and Ernie Hudson (*Ghostbusters*) played the lead. The show was quite successful, but then there was a financial issue. Ernie said, "If I'm going to keep doing the show, and I'm going to keep playing the lead, then I need to be compensated for my efforts." The media took up on it, interpreted it to be a racial issue, and the public actually started sending Ernie money.

In retrospect, I really do think it was about money, but the point that was certainly revealed, to our area, through the media, was that there was an absence of opportunity for the professional theater artist of color to make a living. As I was thinking about who I was politically, and as a twenty-two-year-old, this showed me an impetus. I said, "Here's what we need to do: try to find a home for Martin Luther King's vision onstage, where we can create a world not necessarily as it is, or was, but how we want it to be, as viewed through that lens." That was the impetus for the organization, and why I come to work every day.

I was actually a senior in college when the Ernie Hudson event came up, then sat down and laid out what the theater was going to be. Really, for the first four years, it was a program at the Center for Community Action. From the time I decided to start the theater until we did the first show, it was just me. No staff. By being part of the Center, which was pretty much a fledgling organization, I had what little support there was from there—a typewriter and a bookkeeper, who handled the whole organization including our program.

In terms of finances, it was 1976 and the $30,000 budget that we had came from three primary sources: CETA, a public employment program; Bicentennial money; and the Jerome Foundation. I think those three sources made up 100 percent of the budget. We did six or seven shows, and everybody got paid, right from the beginning. Other than board membership, we've had very little volunteer effort.

That first summer, we had a company of twenty-three, which as I remember was ten African Americans, six Native Americans, seven white. We worked three shifts, nine to twelve, one to five, seven to ten, every day. Working the show, rehearsing the show, working tech.

EXPLORING YOUR IDENTITY THROUGH ARTISTIC EXPERIMENTATION

Corey Fischer's desire to learn more about his own ethnic culture actually begot one of the country's most exciting alternative theater companies, the Jewish Theatre San Francisco. That interest, plus a background in the intriguing world of experimental theater, got a company's juices flowing. Mr. Fischer says of the company's early days:

When we started, for me it was a natural evolution based on a number of experiences I had had in the two or three years prior—experiences with other experimental, or you might say, alternative theater companies. Working in New York with Joe Chaikin, and at the same time, being increasingly curious about and interested in all the aspects of Jewish culture that I had not grown up with—out of that mix came a desire to do some work in theater from a Jewish perspective, not really knowing what that meant. Theater for me has always been a tool to explore and discover rather than a place to simply plug in ready-made assumptions.

Naomi, Albert, and I had known each other for a number of years in various contexts. Naomi and I had done a lot of theater together. Albert at that time was mainly a musician, a singer, and a songwriter. I had seen his work and admired it. So I asked the two of them to join me in creating a piece. I didn't realize we were starting a company.

We were working on a particular piece based on a series of legends that I had found. Albert and I performed, and the three of us cowrote. I also made masks and puppets. We spent about nine months working on that, and opened it in March 1979, at a church in Santa Monica called the Church in Ocean Park. It was very progressive, and somewhere along the way, it became clear there was a whole world that we wanted to continue exploring.

On our first trip to New York later that year, we got an incredible review from the Village. We were performing at Theatre for the New City in their old space, when they used to be on Second Avenue, and had a wonderful response from both audiences and critics alike. That kind of launched us. There was no initial financial vision. If we had thought about that, we probably would never have gotten started.

A VITAL VOICE

Gil Cates accomplished legendary work in virtually every aspect of the entertainment media.

As a film producer and director, he guided the Oscar-nominated films *I Never Sang for My Father* and *Summer Wishes, Winter Dreams*, plus directed and produced numerous award-winning TV projects with esteemed actors such as Faye Dunaway, Christopher Plummer, and Natalie Wood. Adding to his illustrious reputation, Mr. Cates served two terms as president of the Directors Guild of America and produced fourteen Academy Awards shows. This winner of seventeen Emmy Awards was not just astoundingly talented, however—he had a deep desire to give back. A committed thespian dating back to his college days at Syracuse University, Mr. Cates founded the UCLA School of Theater, Film, and Television, serving as its dean from 1990 to 1998; his efforts to expose his students, and the city of Los Angeles as a whole, to top-notch, original performances led him to found the Geffen Playhouse in 1995.

From day one, Mr. Cates recognized that his theatrical voice and sensibilities could truly resonate throughout the community. He first immersed himself in the local theater scene. "I would always be very interested to see what my theater colleagues at companies in LA were choosing to produce during their seasons," recalled Mr. Cates. He continued:

I would see work at the Odyssey or the Mark Taper Forum or the Kirk Douglas, and looking at it, appreciating the taste of these colleagues, I became aware of how much I wanted audiences here to see quality work that was of *my* taste—work that hadn't been done here already. I also wanted theater students in Los Angeles, in particular UCLA students, to have the opportunity to see professional productions they could truly learn from. This in itself is not a readily available option, because LA is a very difficult theater town—theater is not as accessible here as it is in other parts of the country. Here, there is a larger focus on "event programming"—but to me, a true event presentation is Annette Bening in *Female of the Species*, the artistic achievement of this piece of theater being the event.

So this is the kind of work I was initially motivated to do—work that had something to say, work that great artists would feel comfortable doing in our supportive environment.

To me, from the beginning, every play we set out to do should express something we really want to say. I've traveled around the country seeing lots of theater and have encountered the vision statements of many diverse companies. What ends up happening many times is that a company says, "We're gonna do the classics!" but ends up doing Neil Simon. Nothing against Neil Simon—but you need to try to stay true to yourself. Do the good, imaginative work you set out to do. That was our intention at the start, and we've stuck to it.

We decided to do *Cat on a Hot Tin Roof* with John Goodman and Brenda Fricker. It was such a great production and watching it with our very appreciative audience, I remember thinking, "If this theater failed, people would miss it." I think that was the moment I realized we'd made it to our first big milestone; we were doing work that made a meaningful statement, and that work was really reaching people.

GREAT MINDS THAT THINK ALIKE

In the 1970s, Chicago was exploding with the creative energy of improvisational comedy.

There was no lack of enthusiastic performers who wanted to express themselves this way; the trick was finding your comedic kindred spirits.

Founding and Artistic Director Paul Zuckerman has been with Chicago City Limits since those early days:

Chicago City Limits as a company did its first show on Labor Day 1977. These were all actors participating in the workshop program at the Second City in Chicago.

It's probably fairly similar today, although there are probably more opportunities, in terms of improvisational theater, than there were then, but basically, Second City was the carrot for most of the people in those workshops. Chicago had kind of a unique atmosphere—lots of improvisation going on. Each city seems to have its specialty. Chicago—you think of blues and improvisational comedy.

In addition to the Second City workshops, there were lots of bars and clubs around town where groups were encouraged to perform. Out of those workshops in Second City, very similar to our workshop program today, people got together, a couple of people formed a group, the group worked at a club for a little while. They usually had artistic differences, which I think pull groups apart the most. If you notice some basic artistic differences at the top—it's almost like a relationship—they're going to get worse as time goes on.

Chicago City Limits is really an evolution of a bunch of these groups that formed, performed in a club for a week, two weeks, or a month, then something splits them apart, a couple of people at the core move on together to find some others, and this goes on and on. Most groups fall apart at some point; once in a while, though, a snowball gets bigger as it rolls down the hill. Two people from one group find three other people, one of those people turns out to be in sync artistically with the others, and the group evolves.

So by 1977 we had a core of people who shared an artistic vision. At the Second City, they had moved almost entirely away from performing improvisation to mostly a sketch comedy show. There was this real need amongst ourselves to perform what we were doing in workshops. That stuff was fun to do—the audiences were enjoying it, we enjoyed doing it. So Chicago City Limits, out of this evolution, started performing a combination of improvisation and sketch comedy in clubs.

We were five actors and a stage manager. A small group, but doing everything. Performing one or two nights a week, rehearsing six or seven days a week. You can't get enough of it. You talk it, you sleep it, you eat it, you breathe it. I still had a job working at an ad agency at this time. We'd work the clubs, then go to somebody's house, 12:30, 1:00 in the morning, we're workshopping some of the stuff we did. And we're talking about it, we're drinking, and it's late, 2:30, 3:00 in the morning, we're talking about, "Hey, you gotta be real in the scene and you've gotta emotionally connect"—it just becomes your religion.

You've gotta have that fire in your belly, because there's great adversity every step of the way. We didn't have any financial vision—our vision was totally artistic at the time.

COMPROMISE OR ELSE

David Zak started Bailiwick Repertory with six friends. They shared a common artistic vision that was very strong. The problem was, everyone seemed to want to pursue that first and foremost—the administrative nitty-gritty was not quite as appealing to take on.

The great weapon Bailiwick had in its initial arsenal, however, was David Zak. He stuck with the founders' original vision, and carried it through for twenty-six years. And he did it essentially by himself, ultimately becoming the only standing member of that original group. "Bailiwick was founded in 1982 by a group of seven artists and was always envisioned as a directors' company as opposed to an actors' ensemble," David recalls.

Several of those founding members went to Webster in St. Louis; several of us subsequently met doing theater in Chicago.

Developing a common goal was very difficult. Everybody wanted to work on the artistic stuff—the administrative plan was more complex. Over the first twenty-four months, six of the seven original members left for various reasons—some went Equity, etc.

TRADITION WITH A TWIST

Who knew that the birth of some of history's greatest stage musicals occurred in 1876, on the banks of the Connecticut River? William Goodspeed, a shipping and banking magnate, made it all happen when he built the Goodspeed Opera House on the water in East Haddam. A great lover of the arts as well as business, Goodspeed was dedicated to presenting innovative work to his community from the get-go. When the theater officially opened in October 1877, its first (and very successful) productions were *Charles II*, *Box and Cox*, and *Turn Him Out*. Unfortunately, after Goodspeed passed away the property changed hands, ceasing to operate as a theater, functioning instead as a World War I militia base, then a storage facility for the State of Connecticut's highway department. Fast-forward to 1959: Goodspell Musicals, a group dedicated to preserving the theatrical traditions William Goodspeed held so dear, stepped in to restore and renovate the Opera House. By 1963, their work was completed, the Opera House was rededicated, and Goodspeed Musicals' initial production *Oh, Lady! Lady!!* opened to great acclaim.

Michael P. Price, Goodspeed's current executive director, was among the personnel that first season; he was fresh out of college and determined to make his mark on the company. "As a smart-ass kid from Yale who knew all the answers, I lasted six months," Price recalls. "In 1968, I came back again—at that time, I was able to use my background at Yale in architecture and theater, and had better ideas, as I'd gotten a little more mature. I don't think we had a good vision until 1971—we floundered until we hit upon our artistic philosophy, which became rediscovering musicals that are not often produced and also working on new musicals. We really had the field to ourselves at that time and we grew with that notion, as a nonprofit producing quality. Our location was beneficial—Connecticut has a very sophisticated theater audience. We had a very hospitable community in which to build our audience—people who really make the theater their concern. It was a friendly place to grow."

BUILDING A BRIDGE

Founded by playwright Frank Chin in 1973, Asian American Theater Company served as a launching pad for some of the best new works of the past decade, including output by David Henry Hwang, interpreted by some of the world's best actors. The company won a huge following by challenging traditional viewpoints of well-known playwrights' material—for instance, their groundbreaking production of *The Importance of Being Earnest* by Oscar Wilde, reworked to focus on the perspective of Asian characters.

The company also prided itself on being extremely inclusive, welcoming audiences, supporters, and artists of all races into its creative family. One of the main facets of the company's mission, admirably, had to do with connecting people of all races and creeds to the traditions and issues concerning those of Asian and Pacific Islander descent. In fact, much of the company's work evolved as a buffer against anti-Asian sentiment in society; offering up creative dialogue, Chin and his collaborators reasoned, was a highly effective way to combat the ignorance and misconceptions that fuel racism in society.

A QUICK STUDY

Susan Albert Loewenberg didn't set out intentionally to turn the traditional theater paradigm on its head, but she achieved just that in record time. Her company, LA Theatre Works, began life as an arts program for the incarcerated; she's since developed it into an innovative stage and audio publishing business.

I think the thing that's unusual about LA Theatre Works (which has officially been in existence, that is to say, incorporated as a nonprofit since 1974, but which actually started around 1972 in an informal way) is that where we started is very, very different from where we've ended up. In fact, our name was even different—we were called Artists in Prison.

The impulse was that we were a group of young theater artists—actors, writers, directors, designers—coming out of the social action of the '60s, mostly from the East Coast, who found ourselves in Los Angeles at a time when theater was very, very dead. Basically, LA was a place for fourth-rate touring companies. I was born in

New Jersey; I went to Sarah Lawrence and grew up in the New York theater. I was going to New York by myself on the train from the age of twelve to the American Academy of Dramatic Arts—I was a child actor. I was used to a certain standard.

[But] we found ourselves, these transplanted New York theater people, working [in Los Angeles]. I was an actor, I had nothing to do with production. I was working in film and television and doing an occasional theater thing. I'd met up with a number of people working at the Taper in various capacities, and we began meeting and talking. One of them was very interested in doing workshops in prisons. We decided to see if we could go into a county jail and do theater games and improvisational workshops, and we did. We found it fascinating.

I remember observing what was going on in these workshops was a lot more interesting than what was going on in the theater scene in Los Angeles. It was just more authentic and more organic. It was more like what we were used to.

At that time, I didn't even know what a nonprofit organization was. I didn't know what a grant was. I didn't know what matching funds were. I mean, nothing. I was, I think, myself, at a crossroads. I had decided to give up being in the theater, and I had gone to graduate school at UCLA in history. But I was still doing some jobs, involved with this informal group. Somebody said, "Well, if you incorporate as a nonprofit organization, you can actually get some money—you can get what's called grant money." I said, "I'll take it on."

I connected with a young woman, Linda Lichter, a young lawyer. She's still on our board today, and is one of the top entertainment lawyers in Hollywood. She incorporated us as a nonprofit. She's still looking over the contracts!

By that time, we'd begun to branch out in a number of situations where people were incarcerated and it was beginning to get kind of interesting. I remember finding out about grants, and applying for our first grant with the California Arts Commission, which was the predecessor to the current California Arts Council, under Governor Ronald Reagan. It was relatively informal—I remember there was a three-person commission. I put in my application, somebody helped me with it, and I began to understand what a match was and all of that. I pleaded my case and we got our first grant, which I think was $2,400. We were off and running.

As Artists in Prison, we made a reputation, a pretty fast one, between 1974 and 1980.

We actually started doing full productions with inmates that were based on the old theater games acting exercises model. We would bring in a writer, do improv, we'd have a workshop leader, begin to construct a script out of the improv, all of the stuff that kids are still doing today. We began expanding to work with the Federal Bureau of Prisons and the state prisons. We'd actually get people on the federal level furloughed to perform these plays at the Mark Taper Forum lab and at UCLA and USC. We'd also do them inside the prison walls. People would actually come down to the prison, be checked in, and be able to go into the auditorium to watch these things. We got a national reputation in a short period of time.

We got our first funding from the NEA in 1976, under a program which no longer exists called Expansion Arts. Then we began expanding, not just working in prisons but actually creating plays within the community.

We created plays with various segments of the community—I remember liaising with the Women's Building, and doing a fabulous play based on a workshop we did with women ages twenty to eighty. We did work with Japanese men, we did all kinds of interesting stuff and began to get funding from other parts of the Endowment and the Arts Council.

We began getting a little bit of corporate funding. We had a group of seven people, a kind of seven-person co-op with me at the head. A lot of those people ultimately fell away—one of them went on to become a very, very successful radio and television producer, one of them is now one of the top production designers in film, another is now one of the top costume designers in film and theater, another is a major playwright, two of them were directors, one of which became a magazine editor, and one is a theologian. So it's a very diverse group. It was very interesting.

STRIVING FOR SUPER-REALISM

Seth Barrish's goal to achieve raw, unvarnished honesty as an actor ended up spurring a movement. Barrish, along with Lee Brock, cofounded the Barrow Group in 1985, setting forth a mission to help other actors communicate their truth as clearly as possible—the duo's motto is, "Well-told stories energize people to do great things." The Barrow Group's approach and acting style focuses on achieving as realistic a performance as possible—and now, more than 2,000 actors a year seek out instruction in the TBG method. Here, Barrish explains how the company's unique concept came to be:

In the '80s, I was an actor in New York—I was just beginning to work professionally.

I'd previously worked as a musical director and guest lecturer; while I was at UCLA, I'd been exposed, through a student production, to an acting style not seen before in the theater. You couldn't really tell if what you were seeing was scripted; the acting was very real, and because of this, the story really affected me in ways other theater-going experiences hadn't. I was deeply, deeply moved.

This style of acting was, to me, important in the same way great films by directors like Alan J. Pakula and Sidney Lumet were—in those directors' works, you couldn't tell people were really acting in a scene, it always seemed. I was inspired by the thought of achieving this kind of realism in a theatrical context, and decided I needed to figure out how to do it myself. So I sought out people involved in that

UCLA production I'd seen, and we formed a company. That was a start, although I ended up leaving Los Angeles to pursue new opportunities.

So, as I was saying, it was the '80s, and I was an actor in New York—and studying voraciously. I was meeting other actors who had great intensity and passion, the kind of actors I thought might be right to try to work with me on this very real kind of work I wanted to do. In New York, I initially had no intention of starting a company, but I did meet actors who impressed me, and who I hoped might be interested in my idea, in what I thought it could be. We started coming up with a wish list of actors whom we thought, maybe they'll do this—peers I'd studied with, actors I'd taught, actors I'd worked with professionally. I mean, we weren't going to get Brando on board, but as the parameters of what we wanted to do got better defined, we knew we wanted actors with a few important traits. We wanted actors who could act and create in this particular manner, who were spontaneous and real, and also importantly who we thought were nice people to collaborate with. People who were kind, generous, who had a good sense of humor, and a quick and easy access to vulnerability—working with those kinds of actors started the mission.

CREATING OUR PERFECT THEATRICAL WORLD

Susan Kosoff, Jane Staab, and Tony Hancock didn't just dream about making a living in the theater—they made that sometimes illusive fantasy a reality. This trio succeeded by pinpointing exactly how they could make enough money to make having their own theater company viable. Through trial and error, they developed a plan that worked.

Says Susan Kosoff, cofounder of the Wheelock Family Theatre:

Tony Hancock, Jane Staab, and I had been working together at the Harwich Community Theatre on Cape Cod for many years. In 1971, we started our own theater on the Cape, the Harwich Winter Theatre. We got all set up and got approved by the board of directors at the Harwich Community Theatre, who knew us very well, for the use of the facility to start a winter company. The Cape, in the 1970s, was very different than what it is now, in that there was a lot of community theater but nothing professional. So the board graciously gave us the use of their facility and paid for the insurance, which was a big deal. They also gave us all of their lighting equipment, you know, everything that was in the building to use. We had a credit line, things like that. We also were given use of a house from people who were away, so we could live rent-free for our first year. Major!

The first season we did a bunch of plays—I think five. We would job in actors from New York, and we would also use community people. The reason I tell this is because we did this for five years—eventually, we didn't have free rent anymore but we continued to have the use of the theater, so we could build an audience. It gave us the adrenaline to do theater—what we really wanted was to do original work, to write our own and give actors from New York, our friends, opportunities and roles that maybe they weren't going to get a chance to do otherwise. They'd come and for that we'd give them room and board and transportation.

For us, there was that incentive to write, to try things out, and we did it for five years.

But we never made a living. We always had to have part-time jobs in order to support the theater. The three of us stayed for the full five years, while other people came and went as staff members. We tried different things—sometimes we'd have a big staff, sometimes we kept it very small. We'd always pay the bills first and then if there was any money left over we would split it evenly among whoever was there. That was the only way we ever made any money. People often ask me why I never got a doctorate degree. I say, "That was my doctorate."

We learned a lot, not only in terms of theater, about how to run a theater and what it would take, but also about the kind of theater that interested us. I think that many of the things that we learned we then took with us to Wheelock. After five years, we realized that if we sold out every single night, every single performance, we still weren't going to be able to make a living. It dawned on us that we shouldn't go on like this forever.

So we stopped and all kind of went our own ways—Jane went to New York to act, Tony traveled, and I went to Wheelock College, where I had been teaching part-time at the graduate school. They had been after me for a while to come on full-time, so I did that. For about five years we all did different kinds of things, all did some theater, Jane doing the most, as she was making it as an actor. I was there in academia, doing some directing, but I would say that my primary work during that time was not in theater. And I missed it.

We knew that we couldn't do what we'd done before. We had to support ourselves with it. We couldn't work full-time jobs, plus handle how demanding theater can be. But whenever we would get together, we would talk about theater and how we would like it to be if we did it again. As much as I loved doing theater, I loved the idea of creating a theater, because part of what I liked best about the Winter Theatre was the community that we had created, the opportunities to do creative work and to work collaboratively. All those things are so much a part of theater!

While I was teaching at Wheelock College, they had at one time had a very good and active theater department. There was quite a wonderful facility there, but it became underutilized and neglected, falling by the wayside. After talking with Tony and Jane, I went on sabbatical and I wrote a proposal to the administration of Wheelock, in which I outlined a three-year start-up plan. It was also very much a concept paper about the kind of theater we wanted to create. Wheelock is committed to working for children and families, so what we proposed was that we would create a theater that would serve children and families—that would be our target audience. We would use their facility and create a professional company.

There were different kinds of things that we took into consideration. One of the things that we really knew was, not only did we want to make a living, but we also wanted to pay actors. On the Cape, people would come up from New York to work, but they wouldn't use their real names because the theater wasn't Equity. So we wanted to work with Actors' Equity.

Then there was a sense of our former experience that really informed how we thought about the theater. For example, we had really loved working with young people and adults together—we'd gotten a lot of high school and young college kids involved, and also younger kids, on the Cape. What happened when professional actors from New York worked with community people was, it raised the bar for the community people and their acting really came up, which obviously affected the quality of the production. In addition to that, the professional actors liked it because they got to be mentors. So that was something else that we built in.

I think also that it had been a long-standing feeling of mine that theater had increasingly become for just a few. It's become expensive, it's often pretty white, upper middle-class, etc. So from the very beginning of Wheelock, we built in certain kinds of goals—a multicultural, nontraditional casting policy. We also really wanted to think about the broadest audience possible, so we wanted our shows interpreted in American Sign Language, for example. Some things like that have become much more common but at the time were unusual.

This was around 1980. We started officially in 1981. It took a good year—it was lots of meetings to get the staff that I wanted assembled, have conversations with administrators, make everything happen. We didn't have a mission plan. I came up with that three-year start-up so that we started small and slowly, then the idea was to grow so we wouldn't blow out right away. The college administration gave us the go-ahead.

THERE'S NO PLACE LIKE HOME

For businessman Richard Pletcher, a sense of the homespun has always been important.

Proprietor of the Round Barn Theatre in Nappanee, Indiana, Pletcher's producing performing arts company is situated at the heart of Amish Acres, a historic farm, heritage resort, and major tourist attraction for families. The theater space itself was constructed from the remains of a 1911 round barn; in 1984, Pletcher put up his first show, the wholesome musical *Plain and Fancy*, which originally debuted on Broadway in 1955. The production's been such a proven crowd-pleaser, it's still running. Now that his work has found its profitable home sweet home, Pletcher can enjoy the fruits of his labor—but starting up the company was quite an adventure, as he explains:

> Starting in 1971, I dabbled in dinner theater until the old space I worked in burned to the ground in 1977. After that, however, our neighbor Jill Stover, who was running a summer stock theater, asked if we could do anything cooperatively. *Plain and Fancy*, which I'd actually done in 1967, seemed like a good bet to try again, so, like in the old days, we staged the show the same way, literally in a barn with just four actors playing all the parts. You'd play one role with a beard on, then run offstage, take off the beard, put on a hat, and go back on as a different character! All of this happened on a six-inch platform stage, with an upright piano for an orchestra. Still, we ran the show for eight weeks during the summer and it did so well, we decided to do it again the next summer, this time with a big, expanded cast of eight!
>
> A while after that, I became aware of a farm in the area—the owner felt it was no longer functional and wanted to sell. Thinking we might be able to use it as a space, I went to see it. There was a tree literally holding the building up! Still, I saw the potential, went to the bank, borrowed a million dollars, and decided to set up the company right there. We fixed up the space, added onto it, invested in a Steinway baby grand, and soon we were ready to work in our new space.
>
> Around the mid-'90s, as we expanded, we started auditioning actors in New York. One actor we chose worked as a masseuse to pay the bills there, and one of his massage clients, it turns out, was an elderly gentleman named Joe Stein—the author of *Plain and Fancy*! We were coming up on the fortieth anniversary of *Plain and Fancy*'s initial success on Broadway and as we were still doing the show, I asked our actor to invite Mr. Stein out to see our version of the show. Joe sent word back to me to have my producer call him—I didn't know until that moment that I *was* the producer! But anyhow, we worked out arrangements for his visit, he came here, and he fell in love with the place. Joe told me, "You really should be doing more productions than just *Plain and Fancy* in that space." I figured out that what he really meant was that we should be doing more productions of *his* work in that space, but I liked the idea, and he suggested we start working as a repertory company. We put up *Fiddler on the Roof* and people lined up—by now, we'd expanded to a 400-seat theater space.

FILLING A QUALITY VOID

New Repertory Theatre came to be because its founders felt there was a lack of a specific type of quality Boston theater in the 1980s. There was no serious, midsize local company doing works that made its audience think, discuss, and challenge assumptions. Entertainment value, however, would never be neglected for dry, boring substance at New Rep.

Larry Lane served as New Repertory's first artistic director. As a small professional theater, the goal was to select and produce works that were quite challenging artistically and intellectually. Additionally, top acting talent was a key component in Mr. Lane's ultimate and ongoing plan for the company.

New Repertory's first season was packed with intelligent offerings that simply had not been the normal fare available to the Boston audience prior to the Theatre's founding. Nowhere else could you see Chekhov's *The Brute* or Lanford Wilson's *The Mound Builders* at that time. The rest of the season included *Desperate Love: Three One-Act Plays*, *The Loveliest Afternoon of the Year* by John Guare, *Canadian Gothic* by Joanna Glass, and *Misalliance* by G. B. Shaw.

STAYING TRUE TO YOUR ROOTS

It's kind of stunning to think of today's La Jolla Playhouse, with its cutting-edge productions and hip reputation, as the home base for many of the 1940s' and 1950s' more traditionally minded film stars. Traditionally minded? Think again. La Jolla Playhouse's famed founders were quite ahead of their time in mapping out a marriage of multimedia.

La Jolla Playhouse was established in 1947 by the distinguished performers Gregory Peck, Dorothy McGuire, and Mel Ferrer.

The goal for the company, as explained by its three founders in a statement accompanying its first program, was that of bridging the separation between film acting and stage acting. Mr. Peck, Miss McGuire, and Mr. Ferrer believed that once a film star became involved with the moviemaking world, he or she became more inclined to put off a return to the common roots of theater that so many performers shared.

Many film actors who started onstage did so in New York. Once they moved to California to start working in cinema, they found that there were very few theaters there to work in. La Jolla's Southern California location, in close proximity to Hollywood soundstages, was intended to allow such movie actors the geographic ease to split their time going from play to screen project. The reason its founders found this allocation of actors' work time so important was artistic; stardom was valuable, but growth as an actor, through work in challenging and quality stage roles, was also vital to the stature of any performer.

COURAGE IS MY GUIDE

The very definition of "A Little Theater That Could," Shotgun Players was founded on a tiny shoestring budget by Patrick Dooley in 1992. Despite lacking

19

financial resources, Dooley committed himself and the company to the daunting concept of taking on shows no one else dared attempt—shows considered too impractical to produce, too controversial, or too tough to stage well (like a huge production of all three parts of *Coast of Utopia*, and an extremely challenging reimagining of *Antigone* entitled *Antigonick*). Using a grassroots, bare-bones approach to mounting each show, Dooley won a huge and loyal following for the company, despite the fact that limited finances required the company to move an astonishing forty-four times before settling permanently into the Ashby Stage space in 2004. Now turning a consistent and healthy profit, Shotgun Players truly sprung from the audacious ambition of Dooley—and through his maverick bravery. Dooley recounts:

My big, real theater lesson came when I got out of college and ended up cofounding the Shenandoah Shakespeare Experience, now the American Shakespeare Center. I acted, I learned what it was like to be part of a company, got paid a little, and got excited. I thought, "What would a life like this be like?"

I also worked with Theatre Memphis. What I started to struggle with, watching actors who performed with this company, was learning what the life of a working actor was really like. I'd see actors show up with their suitcases, living gig to gig. Maybe they'd make a nice check, but it wasn't the healthiest thing for someone who wanted to maintain a family life. It got to the point where the company was doing *A Christmas Carol* around the holidays, and I just didn't want to do it. It wasn't just, I didn't really want to be an actor—people I was working with just didn't have stable lives, and this resonated with me.

I decided to try something else, and worked for a summer with Carolyn Maloney, my aunt, a congresswoman in New York City. I originally came from small-town Virginia, and in New York, it was like, I can't see the sky! It was always dirty, and too fuckin' hot or cold. So I realized working in politics wasn't going to be for me, either. I tried Seattle next—it was that time of Nirvana's *Nevermind*, and I hooked up with a lot of interesting artists there. But it wasn't until I went to visit my brother in Berkeley, California, [that] I found the place I wanted to live. The food was amazing, the cultural appetite was amazing, and Berkeley felt like both a city and a town—you could go twenty miles one way to San Francisco, or the other way to the woods!

I was checking out the theater there, too. I'd heard about *Portrait of the Artist as a Sexual Being* being performed in this basement space, so I dropped in one day when the play was in rehearsal, and asked if I could just sit and watch. I'm sitting there, and this guy, this actor, just quits the show right in front of me, and storms out—the vibe was very *Waiting for Guffman*. I'd mentioned to some of the people I'd met in this company that I'd done Shakespeare, and I was suddenly asked if I would step into this actor's role! Now, I wanted to do a staged reading myself—so instead of doing the part for free pizza and beer, I worked out a deal where I'd act in their show, and then I'd have a home for my staged reading there. It was a good experience, and started me thinking about collaborating with some of these folks again, and how to build a theater company.

The mission of the company I ended up starting had to do with a rough incident I always remembered from living in rural Virginia. I used to frequent this little grill there—the customers were this weird mix of hippies and poets and hard-core guys who worked in a dog food plant nearby, and came in to cash their paychecks and eat. There was this one factory guy there, Red, who was this kind of sexy reptile, but craggy—he'd be there all the time, eating burgers and drinking the Budweiser. I noticed that a classier older man would often come in with a very chic younger woman, and go over to Red, whispering something in his ear. I finally asked Red one day what the man always said to him; Red told me, "I can't tell you all the details, but let's just say once a month, they ask me to come over to their house and break that woman down like a shotgun." As he told me this, I realized, I know so little of the world. It really got to me—the fact, first of all, that these people were making accommodations like that in their lives. I never would have imagined that, and I just thought, "You think you know somebody, what they would do, but you don't."

Later, away from that experience, when I thought about the metaphor he'd expressed—breaking something down like a shotgun—I took it out of the context of his relationship with that woman. I thought, "It could mean also that when it comes to a play, you want to show an audience something visceral, primal, obscene, fragile—human." To do that, you need to focus on material that peels back the surface of the human experience, and exposes those elements. That's how I wanted to do plays—I wanted to break them down like a shotgun. That's why we called our company Shotgun Players.

I knew establishing the company would take heart and hard work. I decided to look at the task ahead of me like a craftsman. It was going to take will, common sense, and bravery, yes, but I said to myself, I can make a go at this. I will figure out a way to pick this lock. I decided to do anything I needed to—pick up trash after shows if I needed to. You can always tell who the owner of any company is—he's the one picking trash off the ground, and I'm not beneath that!

And there you have it. A more wildly divergent assortment of starts you could hardly imagine. Where they went next is even more interesting.

Antigonick by Anne Carson
codirected by Mark Jackson and Hope Mohr
Shotgun Players 2015 Season
Pictured: Kenny Toll and Rami Margron
Photo by Pak Han

Chapter Two
Claiming Space

Obviously, if you want to start a theater company, you'll need to find a space where your company can present its work.

This might seem to be a very daunting task. There are lots of factors to consider, especially if you don't have much experience with the specifics of theater spaces to begin with. You might worry that you'll have to find a perfectly outfitted space, with a huge stage and pristine, top-of-the-line tech equipment in order to attract an audience. You may not be certain about what space dimensions, elements, or tech requirements will be right for your productions. You may have so little money to work with, it seems totally impossible to be able to afford even the tiniest space, or to buy or rent any equipment whatsoever.

Don't worry! Our experts have encountered all of these space dilemmas and more—and each company figured out a way to make things work. In this chapter, we'll travel back to the first venues used by each of our theater groups, reviewing the challenges that needed to be met in terms of staging those initial shows.

COMEDY ISN'T PRETTY

A house doesn't have to be particularly attractive to the eye in order to be filled every night. The audience in a space doesn't necessarily have to be so gorgeous, either.

When an unconventional audience does in fact applaud what you're doing, it can be incredibly fulfilling and can build your confidence regardless of what space you're in. Says Paul Zuckerman of Chicago City Limits: "Tough bars on Chicago's West Side are good training grounds for anybody. If you can work those clubs, you can work any club. The place where we used to perform in Chicago, Kolbart's Komedy Kove, was owned by a former cop and the bouncer was a 300-pound guy with a shaved head. It had been a strip club converted into a comedy club, and I think most of the patrons were never informed. It was a rough crowd. If they didn't like us, they threw things at us.

In retrospect, it was kind of cool, in a way. Behind the bar they had the stage, where the strippers used to be, where we performed. In that milieu, the artistic goal, if you will, started to form. It became a challenge not to perform least common denominator theater, but to win these audiences that were not traditional theater audiences. You go into that club where the truckers are—last time they drove here from El Paso, it was a strip joint, and now it's a comedy club—and you're doing Shakespearean improvisation and they're enjoying it, you go, "All right!"

There's an old saying in show business: if you buy the premise, you buy the bit. If I invite you to a slaughterhouse and I put down chairs and I do a show, and I don't say, "I'm in a smelly slaughterhouse," if I create a reality and I don't break that reality, you will accept that reality. I think the biggest mistake people make coming out of college and they've worked with state-of-the-art lights and state-of-the-art boards and sound, you come to a city like New York, and you're happy to find a shabby black box. It doesn't matter! If it's good theater, it's good theater. And by the same token, you can't dress up a piece of crap on Broadway.

In a very big way, that was the lesson we learned [at the Komedy Kove]. It was all about the show. It was all about connecting with the other actors onstage and with the audience. It's nicer to be in a nicer space; I've worked some beautiful spaces, but I'm not sure the most beautiful spaces have been the greatest shows, either.

In New York, the first space we moved to was the Jan Hus Playhouse on East 74th Street around the beginning of 1982, and we stayed there through the '90s. We sort of outgrew that space. It was still in a church, even though it was one of the oldest off-Broadway spaces in New York. It's no longer an off-Broadway house, but the space is still there. But there was too much sharing of that space. We needed a space seven days a week.

We had our eyes open for ten years, and I always felt we had one shot to fire in terms of making a move—it's very expensive. We looked at lots of spaces that were sort of OK, and might have been OK, but unless it was perfect . . . we really took our time with it.

Chicago City Limits ultimately moved into a space on First Avenue in the '60s in Manhattan. It proved much more visible.

We felt this one was as perfect as any one we were going to find. The location, on the avenue, we felt was very important; it gave us instant visibility. The size of the theater was good; it held two hundred.

Another element of our business that had grown over time was our corporate entertainment, and at the Jan Hus you'd get your clients all juiced up about your show and they'd come, but they're still in the basement of a church. The new space had more legitimacy, if you will. Know when to hold 'em, and know when to fold 'em.

STREET CREDIBILITY

Paul Zuckerman makes a very key point when he speaks about perceived legitimacy.

As we've discussed, beggars can't be choosers when it comes to securing a space. Chicago City Limits proved to its early audiences that if your work is good, you can do it anywhere and get a positive response. But are there situations where right off the bat, it might really pay off to set up at the "right" address, in, say, an established theater you rent on a per-show basis so you can trade on its name value?

Yes—if your fledgling company is ready for reviewers to come and if you're polished enough in terms of your first production offerings that you feel confident you're going to gain good critical response. Critics, certainly not well-known ones, often will not check out a new company's production, no matter how much you call and fax and email and sweet-talk them. This is snobbery, for sure, but that doesn't change the fact that it happens all the time in major cities. This rude practice is rampant in New York.

However, if you are able to afford renting a weekend's worth of time at a very respected venue, say, an off-Broadway space, even though that venue will no doubt require you to advertise as "The Young Whippersnapper Theater Company at" their space, critics may fixate on the off-Broadway name and not so much on yours. Then they may indeed show up to review you. The fact that an off-Broadway house is willing to take your money may appear to critics, and audiences, as an endorsement. David Zak talks about the early performance venues at Bailiwick Repertory: "Our first shows were in rental spaces around the city. Instead of paying rent, we worked on the spaces. I think it helped that we made our debut in a legitimate theater space—it got the critics in early. I think it also helped that our first show was Wycherly's *The Country Wife*. You would have to be insane to produce that show, and so everybody came to see if we were, indeed, crazy."

David Zak was crazy like a fox; he employed a very good attention-getting strategy. Keep in mind that if you follow his lead, you'll have to deal with a number of practical considerations when you're renting a space, considerations that you must have cash to handle. These considerations include insurance, equipment rental, and additional hidden costs. (See chapter 3 for more in-depth coverage of these and other business and financial points.)

Again, too, you need to make sure the show or shows you intend to present in a noteworthy rental space are as flawless as they can be. Until you can honestly say that this is the case, there is absolutely no shame in putting up your work in a school auditorium, a church basement space, even a vacant lot if you have to! It's far better to build your name in baby steps successfully than it is to blow all of your money on a big-name splashy debut that isn't well received.

TOOLS OF THE TRADE

No matter what space you're working in, you want to make sure you've got a good amount of strength in terms of technical aesthetics. This is not to say you need the best lighting board known to mankind—you'll soon read how dimmers that do the job can be found (and have been) in the unlikeliest shape, in the unlikeliest of places.

What you do need to be able to count on is that whatever equipment you can get works. You don't want spotlights that quit on you mid-performance. When you're evaluating a space to see whether it will work for you, one of the very first things you ought to do is carefully evaluate its equipment to make sure it's functional. Equipment function is much more important than the depth of a stage or the size of a room, because those things can be adjusted and dealt with. A broken sound board is a broken sound board, and you probably don't have the money or inclination to have it fixed at this stage.

It can pay off to try to put aside a bit of money to rent a piece of equipment that you know will be reliable. Make it the one that is most important to your work technically—that's a good investment. Also, cultivate others who can compensate for technical shortcomings with clever design sleight-of-hand. Rick Lombardo, of New Repertory Theatre, says, "One thing I noticed, when I became this company's artistic director in 1996, was that historically the Theatre had focused on plays and actors, not physical production. Good plays need strong visual components as tools, so I began finding the financial resources for getting those tools, and dedicating resources toward getting designers."

HOW TO IMPROVE ANY SPACE

So let's go through the actual process of evaluating a space for your company. Whether you are leaning toward a name space or a more low-key spot, there are several key steps in figuring out what space is right for you, and what you can do to make it even better.

Look through the phone book and local newspaper for any and every possibility in your area, first of all. You should know, of course, how much you can realistically spend on a space before you make an appointment to see it. Perhaps some negotiating on rent might be possible, certainly. But keep within a smart ballpark price range—don't let your eyes get bigger than your stomach wasting your time, not to mention the space owner's time, haggling over a space you're never going to be able to afford. Publications like *Backstage* are good resources for advertised rentals, as are lists your local arts councils may be able to supply.

It might seem elementary but never agree to rent a space you haven't visited in the flesh! Space dimensions recited over the telephone don't tell you everything; they practically don't tell you anything. You want to be able to inspect everything up close and personal, strut around on the stage, get your hands on the equipment, eyeball every square inch of the place.

The space you end up in won't be perfect, almost no theater space is. The good news, though, is that a theater space is just a room. It's a room filled with a stage and curtains and boards and seats, sure, but basically, still a room, and you can do a lot to change and improve upon its dynamics with a little know-how. You can, in fact, make virtually any space work to your particular advantage. Corey Fischer, of the Jewish Theatre San Francisco, relates how the company transformed its initial performance space: "We initially performed at a church in Santa Monica, called the Church in Ocean Park. It was very progressive— you know, Santa Monica's a bit like Soho or the East Village in New York but it's got the ocean! That church was very much a cultural center, and they did a lot of performance.

> It was interesting—a year later when we went back to that space, we put a lot of time and effort into putting some acoustical panels on the ceiling, because it was a very echo-y space. We had learned a bit. Our then-technical director figured out a pretty simple way to cut a lot of the echo by putting these baffles up.
>
> It was just a big, open space. We brought in all of our own lights, and Albert and I, during the first performances, were doing everything, including running the lights from onstage. It was very cumbersome. We only did that, I think, for one performance! Then we recruited Naomi's daughter to run lights for the next couple performances offstage. Then a technical director appeared and stayed with us for the next two or three years.
>
> In terms of choosing a first space, my advice would be this: There are a lot more important earlier questions to ask, meaning that nothing's going to make sense unless one is starting out from a place of very deep commitment. Theater is so

hard to do. There's no reason in the world to take it on unless you are burning with passion and commitment and love for what you're doing, for what you want to say and create. Once you get to that—there's a wonderful quote about commitment; I am paraphrasing, but, "Once one is committed, the universe provides."

In terms of space, the two most important things to look for or to try to create are sight lines and acoustics. You can always bring in lights, you can rig stuff, but there's not much you can do without sight lines and acoustics. You can do what we did, putting panels on the ceiling, but that's almost like starting to build a theater. Things that help with sight lines, of course, are having audiences on risers. For the kind of theater we do, we really try to avoid places where there's a high stage and the audience is flat—in other words, a standard auditorium or multipurpose room. Those things are not good, and if we're faced with a space like that or when we were kind of not able to be so choosy, we would at least try to get the people in question to bring in some risers. Sometimes, we would do things in reverse—have the audience sitting on a high stage, put some rented bleachers on the stage, and play on the flat floor ourselves.

Acoustics . . . again, there's not a whole lot you can do. Sometimes if the space is very echo-y, you can hang drapery, blacks, to absorb some of that. It's always deceptive going into a space without people in it. Every space changes tremendously when you get bodies, which absorb sound. They often soften it.

It's easier to deal with a space that's very live in the sense of being very echo-y, than it is dealing with a space that's dead, that already feels muffled when no one's in there. It's going to be even worse when people are in there, and there's really nothing you can do about that except hope your actors have good vocal training.

DON'T GET TOO COMFORTABLE

Once you've found a space in your community that you can afford, work with, and improve, if necessary, whatever you do, don't fall in love with it.

Wait a minute, you're probably thinking. *We have just found this little treasure—we haven't even had our first rehearsal in it yet!* Ah, but you give yourself away. Visions of permanency are dancing in your head already. You picture your company becoming a mainstay in this, your safe, secure little room, integrated in and popular with your landlord, and your community environment, as long as you want to be. Maybe that will happen, but maybe it shouldn't, for one good reason—permanency may feel all warm and squishy and safe and secure, but it doesn't promote growth for your organization. You always want to keep growing. Growing beyond your initial space should always be viewed as a very positive possibility, even from the day you first inhabit it.

Consider this cautionary tale from Leslie Jacobson, regarding a former space of Horizons Theatre: "We got a parish hall space in Georgetown. That helped us build a more stable audience base and to really present a season, because we weren't constantly kind of moving from space to space.

It was a historic building, so that was kind of nice—it had a wood floor, very high ceilings. As a historic building, which predated the Civil War, we couldn't do anything permanently to it. But we really learned how to use that space. Sometimes we'd do shows in the round, or three-quarter round. We'd set it up differently. We had an extremely good relationship with the minister of the church, and he was enormously supportive of our work. He never asked to see a script. I mean, I used to go and meet with him in the spring of the preceding year and we'd go through dates and when we could be in there and when we couldn't and we'd talk philosophy—it was just a very, very pleasant relationship.

But as we became more and more successful, we just took up more space and became more present. Some of the parishoners—it wasn't that they disliked us, but they disliked the fact that there was this other organization. It seemed like whenever they wanted to use the parish hall, the Theatre was in there. It did create a kind of conflict.

As we continued to grow and develop, it seemed like we were outgrowing our space. And this is a time in the late '80s when there was a lot of real estate development going on. It looked as if we were going to move into a space on 14th Street. We started a capital campaign that was very successful and we were supposed to move into this new space in '91. But in '90, all of a sudden, there was this kind of recession. What happened was, the developers suddenly got cold feet—they were supposed to do certain things to the space, and we were supposed to do certain things, so we were both raising money. They were supposed to make the space up to code, have the sprinklers, and we were raising the money for the seats and the lighting equipment and all that stuff. Well, the city started to demand more stringent sprinkler systems and other things to bring it up to code, and the developers suddenly decided that this was costing them more money than they actually were interested in spending. So basically they said to us, "Instead of the space being ready next year, maybe it will be ready in three years."

For a tiny organization, that's like telling you the restaurant you thought you were going to open next month is really going to open three years from now. So this was really very difficult for us. We had done a really fabulous newsletter and subscription brochure for our new season and our new space and we didn't have a new season and a new space.

We didn't have any space, because the minister that we'd had this fabulous relationship with at the church left. He took another parish in another state. The people who were temporarily running things at the church—it looked like we were

29

going to have a new space, the minister was leaving, so this was an opportunity for them to reclaim their parish hall. That's what they did.

We went through a period in the early '90s where we really were nomadic and weren't sure what was going to happen. But somehow, we kept finding places to produce in. We didn't do three shows a year, but maybe we did one or two, or one show and a series of staged readings.

IT'S NOT SO BAD TO BE A NOMAD

Like Horizons did, you may find that renting one space just isn't practical for your company to do at certain times.

Maybe there aren't a lot of good (or safe, or audience-friendly) venues available in your orbit at the moment. Maybe a particular production you're burning to do won't work, or fit into a space that's available to you. Or most commonly, maybe your fledgling group is pressed for cash to the extent that you can't afford the tiniest space you've looked at.

This is not the end of the world by any means. Many companies start their creative lives in a nomadic fashion, moving between temporarily rented spaces to spaces lent by friends or colleagues, and their personnel actually learn a lot in the process. Dealing with no wing space teaches you economy. Encountering a huge, sight-line-obscuring pole running from floor to ceiling in your house makes you resourceful—you learn you can stage around any obstacle, literally. The more spaces you work in, and the weirder they are, the better in terms of stretching your skill set and imagination. I've seen good work performed in abandoned storefronts, in empty classrooms, in someone's aunt's basement, even—once a quality production really kicks in, surroundings fall away, and the only world you remember is the world of the play itself.

Patrick Dooley is grateful for the fact that Shotgun Players moved an astounding number of times in its early years, because he feels being nomadic taught his company members the meaning of a strong work ethic— and helped him bond with them. Dooley recalls, "From 1999 to 2004, we performed in forty-four different spaces. We just did it. We'd put up some large-ass show, then strike it. I was always there to help, by the way—I'm that kind of director, that kind of company director. I want to show the people I'm paying I appreciate their good work, and that I'm right in there working with them."

Pragmatic Planning

So, you can see that things occasionally do just rise up and hit you in the face out of nowhere, and there's no way you can foresee them.

But let's go back to that concept of growth. It's never too early to start planning how you'll get bigger—and the earlier you start thinking about that very thing, the better. Your initial production could prove so popular, so quickly, perhaps, you'll have to add performances, and eventually bigger capacity.

What is the foolproof way to gauge how fast your company is growing from day one?

Simple. It's the seats. How many are you filling? That number is your best indicator of success. Better than audience surveys, better than media response, better even than how much revenue you're actually taking in per any given performance.

Anybody can count bodies in seats. If you're filling bigger and bigger numbers of chairs in your early days, that's proof you're doing things right. So when that happens, how do you grab the ball and run with it? To paraphrase the Clash, should you stay or should you go now? You should stay. At least in the immediate future. Don't get ahead of yourself. But respect the signs of audience growth, and start pragmatically planning your future space needs well in advance of actually making them.

Steppenwolf grasped this concept of spatial growth planning very, very well from its earliest days. Michael Gennaro says: "The company's first performance space was a church basement, up in Highland Park—Immaculate Conception Church. Someone kind of said to them, 'Hey, you can make use of this space'—I think it was a sixty-seat space. That's why [the original company members] started working there.

> There were basically, literally, tops, three or four rows of seats. So you were on top of them. That was when the buzz started happening down in Chicago about, "You gotta go see these kids up in Highland Park." They were just experimenting and taking everything as far as they could take it.
>
> One of the things that makes this place unique—and I've run a number of nonprofits now—is that the normal structure is, you have an artistic director, an executive director, and a board. That's the structure. In this place, in between those, amongst those three constituencies, is the ensemble. Their influence factors into every single decision that's made in this place, and that's the way it's been for twenty-five years—whether it's buying real estate or whether we're going to change the board structure, they are always consulted. What that does is continually bring you back to the original artistic vision of the company. Some people go, "Well, I think this is the kind of work we're going to do, so let's find a space that works." No! What you're trying to do is say, "This is what our mission is, this is what our work is—any space can fit that, as long as we remain true to that work."

You have to be kind of entrepreneurial, as well as lucky. The space kind of just doesn't really matter at one point. Because every move Steppenwolf's members made thereafter was driven by the fact that you couldn't get into the place [they were performing]. You could not get a seat. Every move worked from that point.

After the church basement, the company went down to the Hull House, which was a little bigger space, in 1980, 134 seats. Basically, you're judging the capacity. That was a moment where everybody kind of looked at each other and said, "Wait a minute—now we're moving down into the Loop. We're not as protected as we were up in Highland Park." Because up there, you know, they could kind of do whatever they wanted—what were people going to say? That was a move that caused some people to leave and then bonded even further the people that were together.

They went down there and obviously the place went crazy. They did all the same things and upped the ante again—brought on new ensemble members. The next move was in '82. The company moved onto Halstead Street, into a place that had 211 seats. So they upped the ante again.

At some point in time, things came to the same crossroads—you can't get into the theater, too many people. So that's when probably the biggest step they had made in some time came. They had a board made up of friends and some business people, with one person in particular, the chair at the time, Bruce Sagan, who is quite a visionary. They said, "You know what? It's time to build our own theater." A lot of the board was like, "You're crazy—that's too big of a step!" They ended up building the space we're in now, which is a 511-seat theater, and took a real gamble in doing that.

The first year—I think they had had 1200 subscribers, something like that; up on Halstead they went up to, I think, 14,000.

ANYTHING IS POSSIBLE, AND HERE'S PROOF

The space you have to work with may not seem ideal to you. Maybe it's tiny, or maybe it smells like someone squished rancid tuna sandwiches under the radiator. Maybe it's freezing cold in the winter and is sure to be boiling hot in the summer. Maybe you don't like it, you feel like you've had to settle for it, either because finding space in your area is nightmarishly hard to do or because it was all you could afford.

Still, anything is possible for you to do within its walls. Adversity can sharpen your thinking and make you see ways to clear up a problem better than you think. Your desire to do great work is the barometer of how well you can suck it up and handle space adversity.

Absolutely nobody was doing more unconventional work in a more unconventional space than Susan Albert Loewenberg in the mid-'70s. No matter what disasters you might think could befall you, she had it worse and made it work. Susan Loewenberg's fine example of doing just that:

> Within the prison, they had an auditorium so you could present things. We would work in classrooms, actually do the workshops. You can't imagine what it was like. In theater, everything is possible—it's an everything-is-possible environment. In prison, nothing is possible. Everything's a problem.
>
> You had to work with lockdowns and people getting into all kinds of trouble and people not showing up. But you were also working with a lot of fabulous, interesting raw talent, bottled-up creativity that just needed to be released. It was a very interesting challenge.

THE VALUE OF INTIMACY

Intimacy is also key within any space setup. No matter how large or small your space is, setting it up so the audience is as physically and emotionally intimate with your actors as possible makes the room, and the work, electric. If you have flexible space, you can try rearranging seating in the round or three-quarter configuration around your stage, if possible. That forges an instant bond, pulls the audience into the action of the play physically, and gives them the illusion that they are part of the show, if they're close enough. Lighting the front rows subtly works even better to foster that sense of inclusion.

If your actors are in literal spitting distance of the audience, it's actually a good thing! Mitzi Sales remembers arriving from Texas in Berkeley and seeing the audience-friendly theater she'd be working in vividly and positively. Mitzi says:

> It was very small—153 seats. It had started, actually, as, I think, an eighty-seat theater in this storefront, and after a couple of years they had managed to break out one of the walls that surrounded it. So it became three-sided; the audience was on three sides of the stage.
>
> It was an old, brown shingled building that was raised. It had originally been a home in Berkeley. The really beautiful neighborhoods around the University of California, as you drive through or walk through the neighborhoods, there are these lovely old, brown shingled homes. It's sort of the quintessential Berkeley look.
>
> What happened on College Avenue was, it became a little neighborhood/commercial site area. There had been this home, and whoever bought the property had raised the brown shingle up and put a building with two storefronts underneath it. So what you had was this odd little building on this

little commercial strip. When I say "little" commercial strip, we are talking two, maybe three blocks long. The theater was in the area of College and Ashby, a neighborhood/commercial district, surrounded by neighborhoods. Which was charming! It was so homey.

You had this very, very interesting, very comfortable, very intimate theater space. You were practically on top of the actors; you could feel their heartbeat. Everything about this was appealing.

THE DEVIL IS IN THE DETAILS

Intimacy is a good thing to pay attention to. In fact, you should be paying attention to absolutely everything. It's remarkable what people don't notice. Shocking, in fact.

I've seen productions performed completely on the wrong set in repertory, because one company was too lazy and careless to strike the other's stuff. Didn't it occur to them how tacky that made their show look? That is a pretty extreme example of poor taste, granted, but ignoring details can be just as telling and just as obnoxious. Don't leave old drops hanging from your space's previous owners just because you don't want to take them down. The audience is, of course, going to notice, be insulted at your lack of sophistication, and hold it against your show. It's arrogant and disrespectful.

Go over your space with a fine-tooth comb, and change whatever's hanging loose, sticking out, peeling, or exposed. If there's the front bumper of an old Dodge in your wing space (I've seen that as well), remove it, won't you, please? Your actors don't need to be stepping around old garbage any more than your audience needs to see it. A clean space makes everybody happy.

Be very vigilant in terms of period details as well, especially if your space has been around for a long time. When Ralph Remington assumed the reins at the former Living Stage in 2001, he made sure the space was brought up to date visually. Mr. Remington says: "The space was kind of a black box, built in a way for audiences to come in—the company wasn't doing a lot of going out. Now, there is more going out [with productions], as opposed to, you know, people coming in [to see shows].

It was painted white. White walls, with photos mounted of images reminiscent of the times—Che Guevara, very '70s images! It had to be updated. The photos that were there had to leave, the posters had to leave. You're doing rehearsals, you're doing performances, you need to be surrounded by modern stuff.

So the space was updated, with a new backdrop, new technical stuff.

A CONVENTIONAL SUCCESS STORY

Susan Kosoff, Jane Staab, and Tony Hancock could be seen as tremendously fortunate in the quality and workability of the space they were blessed with. Here's a good illustration of the pluses of a traditional space setup and how to deal smartly with its few minuses.

Susan Kosoff has this to say about the space provided for the company by Wheelock College:

The house was quite handsome. We were grateful. There were no obstructed views, the seats were good. So the view that the public saw from the very beginning was a good one, in that it was inviting and it was attractive.

The lighting equipment was old, but it was adequate. Over time, of course, we started to make changes and it was completely overhauled. The lighting system needed to be new, all of that, which is a huge expense. The college actually absorbed that.

There was no intercom system. There was a lighting booth and there was a sound booth but you couldn't talk backstage—and there's a big distance there! We would, in the beginning years, rent equipment to do that.

The stage dimensions are strange. It's about twenty-seven feet deep. I think that because the proscenium opening is large, it gives you a sense of expanse, and it's about forty feet wide. There were pipes for hanging things.

All of this we've upgraded over time, slowly. In addition to the lighting pipes, there wasn't much in terms of drops. The actual equipment was minimal, and we really had to build a stock up. There were no tools for building, no power tools.

It's 650 seats. That was one of the reasons we knew we could do this. The theater on Cape Cod had 200 seats, and what we'd realized was that you had to have volume in order to make the kind of money we needed to support a theater. Either that, or charge very high prices, which we weren't interested in doing.

It helps to think about what productions you want to do. The space on the Cape was a twenty-by-twenty-foot platform, essentially, but we made it work. But we knew what we were getting into. The advantage of Wheelock was that we had a big house and a big space, but it also meant that our sets cost three times as much as they had on the Cape. But for us, it was OK because we wanted to do very cool sets, and young people in particular like the visuals. We wanted to be able to have some technicals because I think that's become such a part of the culture now. I'm not so crazy about it, to tell you the truth.

The space was old, and in many ways it was a blessing, and in many ways it was a challenge. We had to work with it. It took us a while to figure out what kinds of sets worked the best, which ones were possible and which were too big for us. The wing space is small. You can fly things.

Tony really got to know the space really well, so he could also work with guest designers and we could make the most of our sets. We really weren't interested in renting sets or anything like that. We really wanted to do it all ourselves, so we did!

AN UNCONVENTIONAL SUCCESS STORY

Jack Reuler made his space work just as well by doing it all himself. In his case, however, his theater space didn't start out as a theater space. It didn't start out as a church basement, or an empty meeting room, or any of the other logical possibilities that come to mind. Instead it had a much more unexpected and historic past life. Here's how Jack Reuler made an unlikely place into a dramatic oasis—for nearly no cost:

In those months between when I decided to do theater and when I started doing theater, I actually went out looking for a space. The offices of the Center for Community Action were upstairs from this 1887 firehouse. After a day or two of running around, looking at spaces, they just said to me, "Well, why don't you just go downstairs?"

That's what I did, and we've been here since the very beginning. It was a war story only in that our building had been a fire station from 1887 to 1963, and our lab, to this day, is where they used to keep the horses and my office was used as a bathroom.

It was literally just a big, open sixty-by-forty-five room. Beautiful wooden floors. It wasn't a theater and I think what I was hoping to go out and find was something that was ready to have plays in it. So where the war story comes is, how do we do that—turn it into a theater?

They were building a bridge across the Mississippi River, about three blocks away. At night, we would run over to the construction site and take the plywood they were throwing away. We had to jump our van every time we tried to start it, so it wasn't a very good getaway van. So we built seating platforms and we built stages.

We found a guy whose store had this really antique lighting system—God brought up light for the first time with these lights. He stored them under the merry-go-round at the state fair, and in the spring of '76, as the snow was melting, we went under the merry-go-round and got probably twenty-eight lights and six dimmers. That was our first lighting system.

I yearn for those days. As a matter of fact, somebody just starting an organization now came by here, looking for things we wanted to get rid of. I was like, "You have hit the bottom of the barrel."

The University of Minnesota was remodeling the student union, and they gave us two hundred folding chairs. The same guy who rented us those lights for almost nothing was an electrician and sort of did the wiring out of our service entrance to give us the juice to run the lights with.

It is a classic black box, in the sense that we probably have six or seven configurations of where seats and stage are. The first year, of the six shows we did I'll bet we had three or four configurations.

I've gone and done shows in many different kinds of spaces. I think I'm completely free to assume the possibility of a space by never having had a conventional space. We've got a garage that we rent that has an entire rig of genie lifts and trusses and lights and curtains and we get hired out all the time to go into a million types of spaces to do those shows. I guess if I had to give a piece of advice, in Minneapolis right now there's a huge number of nomadic, homeless organizations that I used to think had a great benefit. They didn't have the headaches of a facility and whatever it takes to run a facility. But now there's become such a shortage of space for the number of groups; it's not about money, it's just about the space. If I had to make a recommendation, I'd say get a space rather than remain mobile.

I like site-specific stuff, but that is a change of pace from what we do normally.

SLOW AND STEADY HAS ALWAYS WON THE RACE

In terms of vast improvements, like the ones Jack Reuler had to make literally from the ground up, it pays to start moving on changes quickly since they take time. For upgrade work, however, it can be a smarter idea to try to live with the conditions you have for a short while, then upgrade your equipment or cosmetics gradually. This, of course, applies as long as you have adequate, working equipment with which to run your rehearsals and shows, and as long as the premises are safe for actors, staffers, and audience members. That's essential.

Here's a tip to remember, though: don't depress your company members. They may lose morale if they have to stare at peeling paint on the dressing room walls for too long. Paint isn't all that pricey, so buy a bucket and a brush and freshen things up. You'll be surprised how much goodwill a simple act like this will buy you!

The old adage, "If it ain't broke, don't fix it," also applies. Take a good, hard look at your space and identify its structural "minuses"—are they actually pluses? OK, so you have very little backstage space, but you *do* have a raked stage, with gorgeous sight lines.

Yes, there is a huge pole running vertically through the center of your house, but couldn't that lead to all kinds of interesting staging options for your directors? Analyze the bones of your space, in an imaginative sense. You'll probably soon realize that certain upgrades shouldn't be made, as they will ultimately detract from the work you ideally want to do.

Michael Price of the Goodspeed is no stranger to the difficulties his historic house presents, but finds that working with his team to adjust, rather than renovate, pays off:

> Our biggest handicap has indeed always been the limitations of our space. We've got a 398-seat house, no wings or lofts, twenty-two to twenty-four performers in a show at times, about eight to ten musicians in the pit, two SMs on each show, and multiple sets. We're doing an impossible thing, producing in an impossible house, but we keep doing it! Wonderful people from New York come here—directors, choreographers, musical directors—and everyone makes each show work, because everyone respects the history of where we are working. We also have a space issue for artists when it comes to housing. That is a big problem. However, creating an artists' colony is a wonderful solution, so we might do the most within our limitations and be able to support wonderful artists in a spirit of great cooperation.

TIPS TO REMEMBER WHEN CHOOSING AN INITIAL SPACE

Ask Questions

No question is stupid. When you're physically within a space and looking it over, don't be shy about asking the person you're potentially renting from every question that comes to mind about your surroundings, from whether the roof leaks to where the light switches are.

Safety Is Vital

Is your space up to code in terms of public safety requirements, such as fire code?

Has there ever been a major fire in your space or in the building it's located in? If so, is your electrical wiring going to be safe? Such a fact is important knowledge to have. Research your space well before you make a final decision. Go to your local city hall and look up information on the dwelling that's available by public record. Ask around. Arm yourself with any and all bits of knowledge that can have an impact on your decision whether to move in or pass.

Don't Decide Alone

Of course, any cofounder or company members you've already assembled have an important say in where they're going to work. Bring everybody into the space and let them see how they feel within it, if possible. Another bonus: you have new and objective sets of eyes to go over any details you might have missed, plus ask additional questions.

After your group has looked at the space (preferably everybody can get together and field-trip to several spaces, not just one), get together in an objective space and discuss everyone's feelings and opinions. Don't be a dictator and think it's your way or the highway in terms of final decisions. Listen to your people. Making the decision as a democracy will actually strengthen your bond as a creative unit as well—this will be your first decision as a cohesive team but not your last.

You're the Tiebreaker, Though

Democracy is good, but for sure, there are factors your company members may not know as much about as you do, such as financial considerations. If everyone is urging you to take a space you don't think you can swing financially, feel OK about telling them that. They need to understand that sort of thing. Same goes for any other major reasons you alone are aware of that would require you to decline, such as safety considerations or any other important factors.

Beware of Hidden Costs

Will signing on the dotted line for your space require a security deposit? First and last month's rent up front? Insurance paid up front? Maybe questionable little fees could be snuck into your deal, like a stake in electric or water bills. Make sure you fully understand any and all hidden fees before putting any deal for any space in writing. Consulting an attorney is always a good idea; if you think you can't afford one, an organization like Volunteer Lawyers for the Arts might be a helpful resource.

Don't agree to any terms that make you uncomfortable, financially or otherwise.

Mutt
A coproduction between Ferocious Lotus Theatre Company and Impact Theatre in
Berkeley, CA
Photo by Cheshire Isaacs

Chapter Three
Our First Business Plan

One of the toughest lessons any theater professional has to learn is that art and commerce walk hand in hand. Focusing your attention solely on the fun and fascinating creative aspects of your company will mean you don't survive. Period.

I have always felt that one of the biggest problems with most college and university theater arts curriculums is that they rarely even broach the subject of finances. Not simply for those who want to start their own companies, but for aspiring actors, directors, writers, and designers as well. In order to succeed in the business of theater, you have to have a good grasp of the fact that it is a business in the first place. Whether your goal is to make it as a thriving troupe or solo, you are guaranteed to waste tons of time, money, and earning potential learning the hard, cold realities of the business once you've entered it.

If you've already dipped your toe into the professional world, you know how intimidating the theater business can feel. It's all based on first impressions of you and of your work, for the most part. If you make the wrong first impression with someone, you don't get another shot, good-bye, here's the door, see ya later. It's a career in itself just trying to figure out what the "right" impression is, too; it's different to nearly every mover and shaker you meet in the business. This is true for actors, directors, writers, designers, and, yes, budding company heads who are instantly judged on the business and artistic value of their choices, their business acumen, their planning skills, and their understanding and articulate expression of their own mission.

Say you need to present your vision for your theater company to potential funders, or write it up in a grant proposal. Do you really know what it is you want to do now, a year down the line, five years down the line? Money folks aren't going to give up the green to an unfocused pipe dreamer.

Don't feel too bad, though, if you feel you're at a disadvantage in terms of business know-how and experience. The most established theater companies, like those we're consulting, have been in that exact same position. They've overcome their initial shortcomings in this area and done just terrific, due to life experiences. You, too, can learn what you need to know and do just fine.

In this chapter, our subjects will speak their minds on a variety of issues regarding business matters, reflecting upon their initial plans (or lack thereof) and related points. We'll give you food for financial thought and key business facts you should know.

Let's start off with a basic reality check.

Says Paul Zuckerman of Chicago City Limits: "In the beginning, we didn't have any kind of a financial vision. Our vision was totally artistic at the time.

Talk about clichés about show business and business, but it's a harsh reality you have to face. It becomes more and more of the evil twin as times goes on, and as you do reach success. All of a sudden, you go from a band of people working together to the need to pay rent, to the need to pay auxiliary people, the need to generate income because you can't do this for free your whole life. So all those financial needs start to spring up, and you start to develop—I'm not sure it's a business like you would develop if you went to Wharton—but it's a good idea to start thinking how you're going to do it. How are you going to get the money? What are you going to do with the money? How can you sustain it?

A lot of it is trial and error, but a lot of it is learning, and not making the same mistakes twice. For instance, advertising is expensive. You need to do it, but you've also got to learn who's drawing the audience for you and who's not. Even though something might be a great deal, maybe something four times as expensive really gives you the income. Whereas something else, it's nice for you to read your name in the paper, but that's all you've got.

In New York we started to try to find a space. We wanted to be able to flourish as a theater company. We found a space on West 42nd Street, for what we felt was expensive but affordable rent for at least short-term. One of the first things we did was hire a public relations company. Talk about money well spent! My ABC in the *New York Times* this weekend will cost hundreds. For about the same price as that each week, you could hire a public relations firm. If I get the lead article in a Friday *New York Times* theater section, I've bought myself what, $20,000 worth of publicity? I couldn't pay for it if I wanted to pay for it. So we immediately threw everything into rent and public relations.

We're a theater company—no show is all that important compared to the ensemble within the show. But let's say I've written a play, and I've gotten it up in Duluth and somewhere else, and now it's kind of gaining momentum. I want to hit the big city, let's say go off-Broadway. Well, you get your backers and stuff, there's a budget, you do a kind of traditional theater model. Ninety-nine-point-nine percent of the time, you lose money. Once in a while, you have a hit.

You can't look at any one show, you can't look at any one defeat or victory as the be-all and end-all.

That's good, basic strategic thinking, and a pretty thorough summation of the variety of financial challenges you face as your company both starts and matures. Before we go any further, let's go over some financial basics you need to be aware of from the word go.

BUDGET AND INITIAL EXPENSES

You can never have enough money to spend on operating your company. Never. But you probably don't have much at all at this point, right? A proper budget plan will maximize what you do have and allow you to generate more income. Consider the following: low overhead is the best guarantee of success and survival. Think before you spend as much as a single dime. If you can put off an expense in your early days, put it off. Also, don't employ more people to work with you than you absolutely need in the beginning.

Here are the initial steps you can take to get your financial strategy off the ground:

1. Add up all of the absolute expenses you must pay out per week. You must pay monthly rent on your space—break that figure down to a per-week figure (it can be easier to really see your expenditures clearly if you look at them in a smaller time increment). You should pay your actors something (and you may have to if you're using Equity people—more on that later). So figure that amount in. You should pay your crew (a must, if you have a pro stage manager who belongs to Equity). You should have money, even just a little, to do some form of advertising, best case scenario—add that to your total. You must factor in rental fees, faxes, phone calls, insurance (we're getting to that), everything else you can think of. That's step one of making a workable budget.

2. Now add up all of the capital you have to work with, including any income your company has already generated—say, if your first show has already gone up (but you really should make up a budget before that ever occurs). Hopefully, you've got enough to cover your initial expenses. If not, call your dad and beg tearfully. Just this one time.

3. Dad may be able to provide one get-out-of-jail-free card, but next time, it's going to be all up to you. Determine how much money you're going to need to stay solvent and make a profit, by calculating the number of seats you're going to have to fill per performance to cover your expenses (plus make a little cash over, hopefully). Are you intending to sell concession items? You can project that potential profit into the mix if so. But please, be brutally realistic about what you can make.

4. No matter how little money you have, plan for the unexpected catastrophe expense. Even a little money can help cushion emergency financial blows. Try to put a little cash aside from your profits each week, just in case. Try, at least.

5. It's never too early to start projecting into the future, budget-wise. Surround yourself with other people who can take some of the load off your shoulders by keeping a clear head where planning is concerned.

Rick Lombardo (New Repertory Theatre) has this to say about business planning: "Keep three things in mind short-term. First, mission—why do we do what we do? Next, work out a realistic budget document. Then, manage on a day-to-day basis.

> A long-range plan means you ask where is the institution now, then ask what you see yourself becoming? To get there, you need a constant dialogue with your staff. Plus, you've got to keep your eyes open in terms of survivability—you must know the answer to, "Why does it matter?"
>
> I like a three-year planning process, from soup to nuts in terms of budget to production.

INSURANCE CONSIDERATIONS

Most rental spaces, not to mention unions, will require you to arrange for insurance. It's hard to paint an exact picture of what you'll need to take care of here, since every space will be different. Every production, depending on the number of personnel you're using per show, may have different insurance requirements as well.

It's a safe bet, though, to plan for adequate coverage in the event of a tornado inside the building during showtime. You definitely need to ask Actors' Equity about workers' compensation requirements as well. They vary according to the number of actors you're employing, and workers' comp is not a gray zone— if you need to provide it, you need to provide it, or Equity can penalize you financially and/or shut you down totally.

Even if you're not working with Equity, it's a good idea to take a look at insurance for your actors' welfare. How can you get the best deal on sufficient coverage? Pull out the phone book and call around to every insurance company listed—some actually specialize in theatrical insurance, especially in large cities. Be totally honest about your situation so you can get adequate coverage for a good price, sure. But don't scrimp and pass on buying enough insurance— especially if you find you need specific coverage for audience members. The last thing you need is a patron falling down your stairs, suing you, and ruining your company's reputation and finances before you've barely gotten started.

If you're lucky enough to be covered by an overseer—such as your landlord making it his or her policy to take care of insurance needs, you're lucky. It does happen—if you have educational sponsorship like our trio did at Wheelock Family Theatre, for instance. Their main concern was just working out a standard budget, with no complex extras. Susan Kosoff says: "My initial budgets for Wheelock Family Theatre were based on previous experience mounting shows. All insurance concerns were addressed by Wheelock College."

If that's not the fortunate position you find yourself in, what's a ballpark picture of how you go about covering your insurance needs sufficiently and economically? Here's how it's been done in the past. During the Mixed Blood Theatre's earliest days, says Jack Reuler, "We got liability insurance for ten cents per patron. We paid workers' comp with payroll taxes. There was no health insurance at the very beginning, but we hooked up with Equity after about fifteen years. Quite honestly, not all that much has changed since then, except for health insurance for staff."

A good point: unless you are paying full-time staffers full-time salaries, it's very probable you will not be held responsible for health-insurance coverage. Again, Equity requires health insurance for its members for some productions— check this out if you think such a situation could possibly pertain to you.

UNIONS AND UNION COSTS

Actors' Equity Association, as we've covered, is the professional actors' and stage managers' union, based in New York City but governing nationwide and with related union presence abroad. Equity exerts a great deal of control over the productions it sanctions for its members to appear in. The organization is very protective of its members' interests, but will certainly be fair to a company acting in good faith as well.

Although every case is different, depending on the kind of agreement a producer or theater company reaches with Equity, the production entity may post a bond with the union. This bond ensures coverage for the cast in case a show runs into trouble. The amount of the bond is evaluated and set by the union.

45

There is also a large assortment of contract categories Equity negotiates with different types of theater companies. Here's a primer:

—BAT (BAY AREA THEATRES)—This contract is specific to San Francisco area theaters with a seating capacity of 399 seats or fewer. A company's box office revenue determines a minimum salary guarantee for Equity members. Performances are limited. This contract is used primarily for specific productions, rather than long-term for everything a theater company might do.

—CAT (CHICAGO AREA THEATRES)—Similar to BAT. This contract has a tier system for salary minimums based on the employers' operating budgets.

—DT (DINNER THEATRE)—This contract is dependent upon the size of a venue's seating in term of salary amounts.

—FNPTC (FUNDED NONPROFIT THEATRE CODE)—An arrangement for small New York–based companies that takes a piece of the company's income pie, about 15 to 20 percent of profits.

—GAA (GUEST ARTIST AGREEMENT)—This contract allows for a company or school to employ one Equity member temporarily.

—HAT (HOLLYWOOD AREA AGREEMENT)—Similar to BAT and CAT arrangements.

—LOA (LETTER OF AGREEMENT)—Very helpful to a beginning company. This arrangement can allow a company to use Equity talent without paying steep salary fees, as long as the company demonstrates the intention to move toward a more profitable Equity deal in the future.

—LORT (LEAGUE OF RESIDENT THEATRES)—The regional theaters' contract.

—NINETY-NINE SEAT CONTRACT—Allows certain companies to pay Equity members on a per-show basis, in a small (ninety-nine seats or fewer) house.

—SHOWCASE CODE—Allows for Equity members' salaries to be waived for a short-term production. Minimum compensation may be required. A show has to close up permanently following its run under this agreement.

—SPT (SMALL PROFESSIONAL THEATRES)—Individually tailored arrangements for companies with house capacities of 349 seats.

—STOCK CONTRACTS—For summer stock companies, mainly.

—TYA (THEATRE FOR YOUNG AUDIENCES)—Arrangements for companies producing children's theater.

—U/RTA (UNIVERSITY/RESIDENT THEATRE ASSOCIATION)—For educational venues.

You don't have to work with union actors, especially in the very beginning. Yet eventually, most good professional companies do so. Jack Reuler, of Mixed Blood, continues: "I approached Equity when I was twenty-four, because I had no idea how to manage a staff and loved the idea of a set of common rules by which we all had to abide. That naïveté proved to be a great move. Chicago had the COLT contract, and we just mimicked it, years before LORT." The combination of working with Equity and using COLT as a business model paid off for Jack.

If you should choose to approach Equity, it can be helpful for one member of your organization to build a relationship with the union, which can lead to fruitful negotiation for years to come. Your company negotiator should show himself or herself to be a trustworthy individual who plays fair and respects actors' rights (always important; more to come on that shortly in this chapter). Susan Kosoff says: "The only union we've worked with is Actors' Equity. We have a point person on staff who has worked with them since the beginning and negotiates with them on a regular basis. In the beginning years, we did a lot of our negotiating with AEA in person—it seemed more persuasive. But as time went on, we've done more via electronic communication."

Society of Stage Directors and Choreographers (SSDC)

The professional directors' and choreographers' union. SSDC acts for its members in contract disputes, sets salary minimums, and monitors relations between members and producers.

The Dramatists Guild of America

The national playwrights' union, which governs contracts for the production of its members' original work.

United Scenic Artists Union; International Alliance of Theatrical Stage Employees

The recognized unions for behind-the-scenes theatrical personnel.

A KEY POINT IN SALARY PLANNING

An actor's life is tough, filled with rejection, disappointment, and under-appreciation. Actors work very, very hard for little pay.

47

So even though you may be struggling financially yourself, show love for your actors by paying them what you can. Even if Equity doesn't require it, a stipend, no matter how small, expresses appreciation for an actor's value. So, budget accordingly. When she headed up Horizons Theatre, Leslie Jacobsen recalls, "The one thing we did start with was the commitment to pay artists. Artists very often will do whatever it is we all do for nothing, because our passion is so great. We felt that just as women don't get paid what they're worth in the workforce, artists, whether male or female, don't get paid. So actually, we started paying our artists before some of the other theaters more financially solvent than we are did.

> We were one of the first small professional companies in the city to pay its actors on a regular basis. It was a profit-sharing model. I would say that historically, although we had some very good managers, the organization's focus and energy has gone more into the artistic product than into the nurturing of the organization itself—and that that's a problem.
>
> I don't think that's because we made a conscious decision to do that, or that we voted on it. I think the kind of people who over the twenty-five years have collected around us have tended to be more the artistic type than the business type.

Your theater will get a reputation among actors as a good place to work. That, in turn, will attract wonderful performers to you, and raise the bar in terms of your artistic output. Jack Reuler advises: "Get good talent and pay them—it'll come back. When talent is compromised for budgetary reasons, the mission and quality of programming are compromised."

CONNECT WITH YOUR COMMUNITY

From the get-go, it's very important for your company's financial health for you to fully integrate with and cultivate the goodwill of your community at large. But of course, you can't do this cynically. Nothing is sleazier than apple-polishing. You have to genuinely like the people in your town in order to win their patronage and big-picture support.

Michael Gennaro addresses the Steppenwolf organization's genuine love for its roots and community, and how that informs its business sense. Says Gennaro, "The thing that's passed on down [here], through the administrative side—this ensemble approach, and approach to teamwork, flows through everything that goes on here. I think it's one of the things somebody said early on about this place: the idea is to go as far out on the limb as you can, and the worst that can happen is you fall off.

That's kind of the thinking that goes on, whether it's marketing or development or whatever, which is: Don't look at the old models. Create new ones.

We're fortunate that we're financially viable enough that we can take risk. But at the same time, it rarely doesn't pay off. You look at these things where boards say, "Don't try this—nobody else is doing it." But I've rarely found a time when it doesn't work.

You see [our people] on the stage, all they're trying to do is be better than they were the night before, and it influences the staff. They look at it and say, "I gotta do a better job."

Any of those books you read about core missions of companies, you know, Hewlett-Packard, Apple, whatever—they're all the same.

All of these people (the company members) would say, "This could not have happened, perhaps, in any other city except Chicago." It's clearly their roots and their commitment to Chicago. I think it's because, A, we've got a mayor who believes in the arts and the theater. B, it was kind of a working-class, we're-gonna-do-this-no-matter-what [attitude]. If you look at the Chicago Cubs, this city supports homegrown. They're loyal to the death to their people. You watch Gary Sinise go on *The Tonight Show*, every third word out of his mouth is either "Steppenwolf" or "Chicago." They're true to their word. When they come back here, they go to the Cubs games or the Bulls games or they work with the mayor. It's not just lip service.

I think that is a key that every company trying to get going has to remember. They can't let go of their community.

So how exactly do you go about maximizing and utilizing the support of your community? There are easy and effective ways to do it.

Fund-Raising

Capital campaigns may seem like a pretty faraway option when you're first starting your theater company. After all, who's going to pledge money to your company when they have no idea who you are and when you've yet to establish a track record?

That seems like a logical assumption, but it's actually a misconception. You can successfully solicit capital right out of the box. So how? One tried-and-true method is to hold a fund-raiser to establish your company in people's minds as early as possible.

David Zak says:

The only really effective business decision that was made was to hold a fund-raiser at a downtown hotel prior to our first performance. That venue—a downtown hotel—was donated and also gave the event some prestige.

Real planning only came later, when we had a permanent home and, therefore, ongoing rent payments to make.

Talk about making lemonade out of lemons. Bailiwick Rep had yet to so much as move into a space but still found a way to assert itself in its community and raise capital without any performances under its belt to trade on. If Bailiwick did it, you can do it.

If you know of any business or organization that has a beautiful space, by all means, ask to borrow it. It's great if you're friendly with someone in a position to do the lending, of course, but if you're not, it's worth trading a season's worth of comp tickets to secure the privilege.

Use your local media—newspapers, TV, the web, whatever sources you can find—to give you names and contact information for wealthy arts patrons in your community at large. Contact businesses and large corporations in your area by phone and ask who at their organization is the proper representative to invite to a community fund-raising event. Expand your search outside of your town, too, especially if you live in a small place without a lot of viable contacts—try combing through a large city nearby.

Print up a simple, classy invitation to your event, one that's very professional, yet very warm. Include, of course, all pertinent info such as date, time, etc. Send out any promotional material about your company you have ready, such as a season brochure, with your invitations. Don't forget to invite your local media to cover the event—TV coverage is terrific and, at least, some newspaper photos are needed to help herald your arrival and spread the word about your company even further. Offer yourself up for interviews, too—this is not the time to be a blushing wallflower.

The event itself doesn't have to be elaborate—serve good wine and cheese, cocktail party–style. Plan a performance to showcase your company's talent. Mingle and talk to as many folks as you can—deploy other company members to do this as well. Needless to say, when you're chatting up the fourth cousin twice removed from Howard Hughes, don't ask directly when he's writing you a check. Just be very accommodating about answering questions, find something you truly like about each person you're talking to, and focus on that to make your interaction with that person the most pleasant. Do that and money will come your way.

After you've established relations with a donor and that donor has, indeed, given you funds, whatever you do, don't take that donor for granted. Maintain goodwill by keeping each of your donors abreast of the work your company is doing and work to create a personal, one-on-one bond. Gil Cates of the Geffen

Playhouse is a great believer in connecting on a genuine basis with his funding base. "The recession has presented us with hardship, as it has most companies. I keep talking to our donors, however, and there is a great sense of support for our work—they kept giving throughout our times of hardship. So of course we've stayed committed to producing strong new work, even throughout these tough financial times—we commissioned a new play from Donald Margulies that also played in New York, and we took Carrie Fisher's *Wishful Drinking* to Broadway as well, even though it initially wasn't going to go."

Board Relations

It's never too early to start thinking about a board of directors. You first need to put up a great production or two to get people excited about being involved with your organization. Still, your pre-performance fund-raiser will help you get to know which people might be most enthusiastic about serving on your board early on.

It's good, indeed, to put together a board as soon as you can. The reason for this is roots, community cohesion. A board that is tightly meshed within the community fabric will work hard on your behalf to bring new folks into your company's fold. Berkeley Repertory's leaders realized this early on. "Michael hired Mitzi [Sales] as business manager and managing director and the two of them together were a strong team," says Susan Medak. "Because of the kind of growth the company needed, it needed to not only be artistic, but also institutional. You can't not have a sense of what you're building business-wise. A board of directors came together, as a base of support to build community support. You can't do without fund-raising. But also, so important was that the community was saying, this is an organization that is going to be held in trust by the community.

> Helen Barber was our first board president. She was very strongly responsible for helping and keeping this institution viable. The board was deeply devoted to the theater, and the artists and board members grew tighter all the time. Caring for and feeding actors was a priority.
>
> In terms of a business plan, in terms of finding how to effectively start the growth of the organization, Michael and Mitzi found that help by the two of them building that board.

GRANTS

If you have a crystal-clear vision of where you see your company going, both artistically and commercially, and you can express this well on paper, then there very well might be grant money out there waiting for you.

Grants can come from a variety of sources—the government, private institutions, public institutions, foundations, and more. Locating grant sources is easier than you think—you can search them out on the Internet or in your public library. You can make a call to your local government and see what opportunities might be available. You can network within your civic community to find out what local grant money you might qualify for. The Foundation Center, headquartered in New York City, is a wonderful overall resource for nonprofit grant seekers. (See appendix B for more specifics).

Almost all grants require that the applicant parties be incorporated as nonprofit organizations, so you will probably have to go through the process of incorporation before you begin sending in those proposals. To apply for a grant, you will have to go through an application process, prove financial need, and write a proposal clearly outlining your company's goals and philosophy, as stated above. You will in all probability be competing with other arts organizations for each grant you apply for. This is why it's so important to know your mission and be able to express it clearly, to convince the powers that be of its worth.

The National Endowment for the Arts is a very well-known and generous source of funding, which, in the past, has provided much-needed support for small theatres. Susan Albert Loewenberg recalls her early experiences with the Endowment.

> We'd started getting money from the theater program of the National Endowment for the Arts; we then applied for the first institutional advancement grant. That was the first round of grants that the Endowment did to take small organizations and raise them to another level.
>
> It was a big deal. Fifteen organizations were selected across the United States. They weren't just theater, they were a mix of visual and performing arts organizations.
>
> We developed a business plan—changed our name to LA Theatre Works. By that time, we had begun to get out of the prison business because a lot of the funding had dried up. The Endowment was no longer funding work in adult prisons.

Of course, It should be noted, however, that government funding for the arts has suffered in recent years, and at this time, the NEA is not a source upon which a small, start-up company should depend.

EXPECT TO MAKE FINANCIAL MISTAKES

Whether you get grants for your company or not, no matter how much you plan and fund-raise and know, you're bound to make financial mistakes in the beginning. This is nothing to be ashamed of. It's to be expected, as a matter of fact.

The thing to remember is to see your financial mistakes as learning experiences, so you won't repeat them. If you feel naive about money matters, weirdly, at times, that can actually work in your favor. You might unknowingly make bolder moves that actually pay off, moves you wouldn't make if you knew more, and you were acting too cautiously. (Although that is not an endorsement of making crazy financial moves in any way, shape, or form).

Remember, too, that even if you're green and stumble around a bit at the beginning, determination to succeed can carry you past all that—if you're willing to persevere past financial hardships. Mitzi Sales tells us what happened to Berkeley Rep when a personal falling-out had financial repercussions. "By the time I came, Michael and his wife were divorced—there was no patron. As a matter of fact we had a loan of a somewhat modest size that we were repaying [to his wife]. It was very much hand-to-mouth. I do not think there was much of a long-range plan.

> Had I been a more experienced manager, I probably would have run in the other direction as quickly as I could, because I would have been able to look at the books and see—"Oh, my gosh, we can't meet payroll! We can't pay rent!" Although it was practically nothing—we couldn't pay payroll taxes, even more important. But somehow, by that time, there was at least a core audience, and there was a small, small subscription base.
>
> There was really no fund-raising to speak of—very, very, very little. So we sort of learned as we went, that first couple of years. Michael and I didn't take a salary for a couple of years. I was married, and my wonderful husband just supported me during that time.
>
> Michael lived upstairs, off the dressing room, in a little sleeping porch. The house that was raised up that became the offices and dressing rooms had a kitchen, had a couple of bathrooms, you know. So he managed in that way.
>
> We just clung on.

SPECIALIZED TRAINING CAN PAY OFF, TOO

In today's professional theater, though, sometimes you need something more, like specialized training. We know that everyone working in the field doesn't have a degree from Harvard Business School. One of the beautiful things about drama, as an art form and as a business, is that talent, enthusiasm, hard work, and dedication of one's time can indeed get your foot in the door. It is essential for certain positions, however, that you have a firm grasp of what your work will entail before you start doing it.

Naturally attending a solid, respected college program is highly recommended background. Theater management programs are growing by leaps and bounds—if you really want to produce your own company, such business training might serve you better than an MFA in directing. If you don't happen to have that background, even while you're starting to work on your company, squeezing a business-oriented night school course into what minuscule free time you have can help a lot. You could also gain work experience, say, if you still need to keep a day job, by taking a position in the administrative offices of an established theater company. This can be invaluable in helping you totally understand the workings of an administrative office setup, one, and two, specifically how finances flow correctly in a professional setting. Three, it's always great to learn from a supportive mentor.

Lyla White, formerly of the Pasadena Playhouse, suggests,

I think definitely [there's a strong need] for business training. If you have an executive director who does not understand fund-raising, who does not understand board development, who does not want to mentor a young staff . . . you need to mentor a young staff. I say a young staff because what people are paid to do in the administrative part of a theater is not the same as they would make somewhere else.

It all comes together when that curtain goes up. When that curtain goes up, we all feel a part of what happens. That is the exciting moment for us—it happens here 302 times a year and six openings. We get a chance to just say, "We did that and we did it together."

Just as on the stage [the actors] are all playing different roles, we all play different roles in the administration. I hope my staff, and believe my staff, all feel as though they play an important part in getting that play on the stage.

Director Sheldon Epps seconds that opinion.

I think it's a huge problem, in the American regional theater, that there is no learning curve. You can graduate from the best graduate school as a directing student, and come out having no idea how to be an artistic director. It's an entirely different skill.

Before I became an artistic director, I was very, very fortunate that a grant that I got from Theatre Communications Group provided me with a residency at the Old Globe Theatre. For four years, under that grant, I had my real master's program training in what it means to work in, and to run, a large-scale institutional theater. I would have been completely lost about what the job actually is if I had not had that experience.

I would encourage anyone who has an aspiration, and I hope there are people out there who have aspirations to do it, to try to find a way to have that kind of education. You don't get it in school. You only get it by going to work at a theater company, and finding out how to keep that balance, how you keep your head, when you're thinking about not only the play on the stage, but the marketing of the play, the selling of subscriptions, the care and feeding of the board. Learn to be a good ambassador to the community, who you are depending on to provide a large part of the resources for producing that play that you want to do.

Ralph Remington, formerly of the Living Stage, began his theatrical business education training with a most novel enterprise that novices could be well served to try out themselves. Ralph advises, "Look at the business angle of theater as a means to an end. I had to learn to do that well to get where I wanted to be artistically. But doing that, then you're more marketable, which actually helps your career. It's a good thing!

I went to college in Berkeley. One of the good things that they did was offer a production seminar, a year-long thing where you, the student, had to create a theater from scratch on paper. You put a theater anywhere in the United States in an actual community, on an actual street, get a space, name the theater, create logos for the theater, create everything from the ground up. Budget every production, every play, everything had to be drawn up and written out, your personnel, everything.

It was great. For me, once the idea was on paper, I knew I could do it in life. I'm surprised colleges don't do more of that—it would help students a lot.

KEEP YOUR MARKETING FOCUS: THE BEST BASIC STRATEGY

At this early stage, you probably don't have a lot of money available for marketing. You may, in fact, be relying on free public service announcements on TV and radio, free ads in free newspapers, circulars, and a grassroots poster-hanging campaign in your community. Believe it or not, that's OK. (More on the details of marketing in chapter 7.)

Your most important marketing lesson, one which will serve you throughout your company's lifespan, you need to learn before you take on any marketing ploys that are more complex: keep focused on the main purpose of your company.

If you keep track of that main purpose, you can communicate it to your potential audience clearly and continuously, and people will come to see your work. It's important not to get too distracted by other details, like newfangled programming schemes and sticking your finger into a multitude of other pies. Concentrate on your company's main reason for existing in the first place.

Dona Lee Kelly, former managing director of Jean Cocteau Repertory, elaborates.

> You have a lot of specific priorities. When I came into Jean Cocteau Repertory, they were doing so many different things that really moved the focus of this administration away from the core activity. The core activity is producing great theater. That's what it is. Getting people into the seats—that's another thing. I wanted form. It had to be focused. I had to tell funders, "These are the reasons we are doing this." It's really getting back to articulating the artistic growth, changes, and initiatives.

Michael P. Price believes in stressing his company's main purpose directly to the Goodspeed's loyal, longtime patrons. He explains,

> After forty-two years, I really think of myself as the proprietor of a general store. I always make a point of talking with our audiences personally and warmly, and our staff is so warm and friendly; this attitude has really helped us add to our subscription base. We've been able to build because we have such wonderful "fans in the stands," to use a baseball analogy! Our marketing also focuses on consumer comfort levels— our personal relationship with our audience is the greatest part of what we do and our staff really respects our audience.

FIRST SEASON FINANCIAL GOALS

Of course, your main goal is to make it to a second season. But what are some of the other steps you should take financially for your first season?

To Turn a Profit

This is pretty obvious, yet it doesn't always happen so easily. Sometimes, it takes a while for a theater company to make a little money, perhaps beyond season one.

If that seems to be what you're facing, don't freak out. Try not to rack up too much debt. To avoid debt, a little extra capital raised however you can raise it sometimes makes that small difference you need. Susan Kosoff (Wheelock Family Theatre) says,

> The first few years, we did all right. We were in the black, and the college continued to support us; they have remained very loyal to us. They give us a stipend; it's not

huge, but it certainly has helped. Many times, it's made the difference between what we've been able to make and what we've needed.

We were lucky. We got a couple of grants early on. That was kind of good, in the beginning.

To Be Able to Pay for Marketing

It's a great sign if you can find the cash to upgrade your quality of marketing. Cash well spent on a judiciously selected newspaper ad that will reach a lot of people really does bring in patrons.

To Be Able to Pay Yourself a Salary of Some Kind

During your first season, maintenance is your goal. This means that even though you may be making a little money, you need to put it back into the company. Pay your expenses, pay your actors, and pay your crew. Then pay yourself last. If at all.

You will make more money eventually if you stick to your focus and make your art the best that you can make it, so be patient. It will be tempting to treat yourself to a little of those box office profits—but keep your hand out of the cookie jar.

So set yourself a goal of a $1 salary by season's end. This money you can take without guilt and with a great feeling of accomplishment. One dollar is literally the sign that your hard work is paying off! Just don't spend it all in one place.

Maybe you'll find you can pay yourself a salary of more than $1. Wouldn't that be great? It just might happen.

To Be Able to Make Sense of Your Taxes

I have just one thing to say—save your receipts.

Oh, sure, you need to find a good tax preparer or accountant to help you out in the end, but before that occurs save every scrap of paper that comes with everything you buy. Put it in a clearly marked file folder or box and don't lose that file folder or box.

Also, save all your payroll and expenditure information. Save all paperwork pertaining to fees you pay a union, if applicable.

Save receipts for major purchases. Save the receipt you got when you bought that lightbulb during your first tech weekend. You would be amazed at how many theater folks tend to flake out when it comes to the drudgery of organizing financial information. Just do it as you go along throughout the year and you'll be amazed at how much time and tax money it could save you in the future. Use your computer, loaded with financial record-keeping software, to help you keep track of income and expenses and project budgets and to organize your numbers for tax time.

FUTURE SHOCK

It may seem rather ridiculous now, at this time of your humble beginnings, to dream about where you'll be financially in five years. It's especially mind-numbing to consider when thoughts of future achievement immediately make you think about the work you've yet to do in order to get to a place of security. Go there, though. You need an idea of where you're going in order to get there.

When it comes to future hopes within a five-year scope, Terrence Dwyer (La Jolla Playhouse) believes in the power of certain key artistic responsibilities: "Integrity. Unpredictability. More visibility sometimes broadens your scope and your cash flow."

La Jolla Playhouse takes the impression it's making on its audiences very seriously. It aims to grow, but very smartly pays attention to what its patrons expect and enjoy as well. This brings up another important point in long-term financial planning—proper product evaluation, which you must always keep in mind.

What's your product? The shows you offer the public. Your artistic output is what you're selling, plain and simple. So to make money, to some extent, pay attention to feedback and give the people what they want.

Some foolish theater folks dismiss audience reaction as the impressions of lowbrows who don't really understand the intellectual genius that's been so generously parked in front of them. Theater is for everybody, so don't be an elitist. The audience is smarter than many artists give them credit for and if the audience gets wind of the fact that you think they're a pack of morons, they'll stop coming to your theater, and you won't make any money.

Ask a few experienced theater personnel, maybe a director, actor, or writer you respect, to come see your company's work and give you an unvarnished opinion. Invite as many of these people as you can, in fact. Better yet, from a financial point of view, ask a producer with a good track record or an administrator from a successful theater company to attend and to give you an honest evaluation of your show's commercial potential.

If you hear negative comments, push past emotion and think of them as an opportunity for information. This doesn't mean you should take nasty, jealous or empty, mean-spirited "advice" seriously—blow off comments you know are just catty.

But do ask questions of those people you trust and respect, if they know what they're talking about. You don't have to use every suggestion. Still, any kind of feedback will help you determine whether you should jettison something you're doing that in the end will cost you money. If tons of people tell you the same comment over and over, by the way, it's a safe move to believe them and make an objective change.

PROCEED WITH CAUTION

Go slowly when it comes to money matters in your first season. Jack Reuler (Mixed Blood) suggests not overplaying your hand, either in terms of planning or trying to do too much too soon. "Don't overproject box office. Remember, the more you do, the more you lose—that's nonprofit producing."

Work on making your first production the best it can be. This will help get your name out there, which will bring in an audience, which will, over the long haul, help your company to become a financially viable organization.

Where Were You When They Killed Victor Jara? by Deborah Rogin
directed by Stanley Spencer
Shotgun Players 1995 Season
Pictured: Patrick Dooley and Lance Brady
Photo by Richard Reinholdt

Chapter Four
Funding and Financing

Coming to grips with the basic realities of your theater company's first business plan, as we discussed in the previous chapter, will provide you with a powerful, and weirdly unexpected, sense of relief. Monetarily, you know you've got your work cut out for you, and now you've precisely identified what kind of steps you need to take to get your group on its financial feet. It's daunting, yes, but also freeing to look at these kinds of specifics and say, "OK, I'm ready to take action."

So in a financially challenging market, and climate as a cultural whole, how precisely do you start raising initial capital? You get creative immediately. Understand this: even though you'll hear from all kinds of naysayers, "Nobody's starting a theater company right now! You can't turn a profit!" if you want to do so badly enough, you find a way—and you don't necessarily do the conventional things your fledgling competitors may be doing to amass cash. Getting a loan, for instance—you can do this, but it's important to look at the weight this very traditional strategy may plop on your shoulders. How much interest will you be paying? How high will your overall payments be? What happens if times get a little lean, and you default? Not to mention the fact that since you're probably at the start of your production career in terms of earning power, finding a lender willing to take a risk on your prospects may be a little tricky or, sadly, downright impossible. It's important to carefully consider these points before you attempt to borrow *any* money.

So, back to thinking creatively. You want to brainstorm ways to gain sufficient financing to carry you through two seasons, initially. This is highly doable, and won't lead you to make financial leaps that are too ambitious, or be so cautious in your approach to making money that you won't have enough cash to stage shows as generously as you should (audiences notice when your work looks too bargain basement). Out-of-the-box funding opportunities *are* out there today—in fact, they can be surprisingly plentiful, if you're willing to turn over a lot of rocks and stick your neck out a little.

For many new companies, though, that's the crippling fear: embarrassment. First-time producers often don't want to broadcast that they're seeking funding, and so logically, they don't get any. Know this: there is absolutely no shame in going after the money you need, and letting people know you need it! You're pursuing a pure, noble endeavor in terms of sharing your art with the world— and good art changes lives. If you tell virtually everyone you know about the work you want to do, and do so with a gutsy, go-for-it attitude, you'll attract admirers—and cash will follow.

So how do you start? Here are a few unconventional funding strategies to get you thinking about what might work best for your company.

USING A SHAREHOLDER MODEL

It might not occur to most theater professionals, but shareholding, as a capital resource, has been in place since Shakespeare's times. And you don't need to have assembled your board yet to do it, either.

Shareholding can work extremely well for companies comprised of members heavily involved in the same commitment—in other words, your actors fervently share your vision, and you feel very sure you can trust them to stick with the company for the forseeable future.

Here's the basic concept: you have, say, twenty actors and playwrights/ directors/designers/crew members willing to purchase shares in your company. You can set how much each share would cost—say, $500 to $1,000—and once that amount is paid in, your participants will gain a percentage apiece of the cash your company generates when it starts to become profitable. You use the total amount of money paid in by your shareholders to purchase set and costume materials, pay for performance rights, and run the company in general (economically, of course).

The pros to a company member shareholder approach: your group is invested—literally and figuratively.

You're more likely to work happily in tandem when it comes to doing great work that gains patrons, because everyone obviously benefits. Also, shareholders are more likely to be proactive in terms of generating more money on an individual basis—like designers reselling old set pieces to put cash back into the company, or actors taking the initiative to do a sing-along community fund-raiser on a free weekend. Transparency is another plus; everyone knows what's on the books, and everyone's equal.

Unless it's not. You, as the producer, need to be very careful not to personally make significantly more profit than any of your shareholders will see—this will defeat the purpose of the financial togetherness you're cultivating. Also, you need to know what you'll do if a company member decides to bolt—a written shareholder agreement should essentially and clearly spell out how profits will be taken out in the event that a shareholder wishes to terminate his or her participation.

Also, shareholders have voting power—and those whose lives are intricately involved in your company's financial outcome will probably not be shy about using it. Make sure that shareholders can't, and don't, band together to try to push forth ideas in your company that are fringe, or go against your principles and ideas.

Maintain your presence of control.

You always want to be careful about bringing outside parties in as initial shareholders, unless you know these folks like the back of your hand. Too many cooks can *really* spoil the broth in a situation like this. Say an actor's wealthy grandma is willing to scoop up multiple shares—it sounds great, until Grandma decides her investment gives her a say into how every show will be staged, and wants her granddaughter cast as a lead until infinity. It's better to avoid this kind of issue altogether by staying very inclusive at the beginning of any shareholding effort—keep it just among your company members. If it works, you can expand out later.

WEB FUNDING

If you're a little naive or a little desperate, money-raising scams on the Internet may pique your interest.

Watch out—if it sounds too good to be true, or pops up on Craigslist, it's a mistake to follow through with any capital offerings.

There are, of course, legitimate ways to raise cash on the web. The two most popular sites for creative projects:

* **GoFundMe.** This donation site allows you to raise cash for whatever reason you cite—as much as you can attract from friends, family, and complete strangers. You set the goal amount, and describe in depth the project (your company as a whole, or a specific production) you're seeking financial contributions for. Donors will then contribute toward your goal, and often will leave you feedback as they do—obviously, good intentions are most often posted. You can withdraw any money you've raised while still raising more, and you'll pay a 5 percent fee for each donation to GoFundMe, plus a deduction of approximately 3 percent from the amount you raise.

- **Kickstarter.** This project-based site has helped over nine million creative artists raise about $2 billion since its inception; successful actors/directors like Zach Braff have even taken advantage of Kickstarter (Braff funded his 2014 film *Wish You Were Here* from its backers). It's crucial you know your goals for any work you're soliciting Kickstarter funds for; backers are very clear about the information they'll seek from you, such as what the work will accomplish, how you intend to work, your credentials and the credentials of your collaborators, and how long it will take to bring your work to fruition. Backers will also want to know how their money will be utilized in as much detail as possible. You'll answer these questions by putting together a clear, concise, info-packed "project page," so backers know how their participation will matter. You'll also be expected to offer backers "rewards"—swag like T-shirts, fun perks like walk-on roles, or a chance to read original work as it's being staged.

GoFundMe and Kickstarter can really be a boon to your fund-raising coffers if you're very, very open and honest with your supporters—if they have a good experience with your company and feel their efforts and support are appreciated, you've probably made a true and permanent ally. What you want to watch out for is a backer who's a little too much in love with the idea of "feedback"— you need to set boundaries, and clear ones, in terms of letting backers know that their suggestions are welcome, but that you have the final say on artistic direction.

Always remember: it's great when someone respects what you're doing enough to offer you money, but you don't have to take them up on that offer if your gut's telling you they might not be the right fit.

GETTING THAT GRANT

Nabbing a generous grant might seem to be your very best bet for funding— you'll be awarded based on your company's merit, which can give you an early sense of esteem and accomplishment. The problem is, as you probably already know, there just aren't enough grants to compensate the large number of companies applying for them.

Unless you target meticulously, that is. You can land a grant that seems elusive at first glance if you know your company's strengths meet its criteria, and you aren't shy about saying so. Research any grant you're interested in from top to bottom—the web is a great resource, as is the Foundation Center (www.foundationcenter.org). Make sure your company fulfills what the grantmaker seeks to find—be it specialized material, company member experience, or artistic/technical proficiency. Really sell yourself in your application—give the grantmaker all required info and more, outlining every reason your company should be chosen. Then don't waste your time applying for every other grant on earth; just focus on the grant(s) that you know in your soul you deserve.

Ferocious Lotus's Lily Tung Crystal started her company by winning a grant—and she won it the right way.

Crystal showed her work off to best advantage, and when she didn't obtain the grant she wanted the first time, she didn't hesitate to seek it again. Crystal explains how that grant helped her start building her company immediately:

I got a grant from Theatre Bay Area—I'd been involved in a series of workshops there, where you get feedback on the business side of acting. It's about teaching you to do a career map, for example. So the second time I applied for it, I won this grant alongside TBA's Titan Award, which was great!

As an actor, I knew that for Asian American actors, the issue was that there are just not that many roles. So part of my plan was to found an Asian American actors group. Around this same time, I was writing an article for *American Theatre* that focused on three generations of Asian American actors. Interviewing these very interesting people led me to meet Leon Goetzen, co-artistic director of the Asian American Theater Company—the night we met, we decided to form a theater company! We just clicked. I also got encouragement from people like Naomi Yzuka from Berkeley Rep.

Right after we decided to work together, it turned out that AATC had one weekend available in their space, so we decided to put a production together. The company had gone into hiatus at that time, so we were very lucky to be able to not only use their space, but garner their support for our work from this early connection. We hired five writers, three directors, and twenty actors to do a series of five comedic one-acts. This was in 2010, and I had my son around the same time. If you had ever told me that I was going to give birth to a baby and a theater company at the same time, I'd have thought you were crazy! But I did both. I made everything work.

And our show was very well received.

Next, working with director Desdemona Chang, we put up a very simple, traveling one-woman play. In 2014, we produced the play *Mutt* and in 2015, J. C. Lee's *Crane*. From the beginning, the challenge was getting the word out that we existed, and that we do good work. Our association with AATC was an honor and a big help, but getting people to know our work, kind of our solo stuff, has been an important thing to do. People loved *Crane*—they thought it looked gorgeous and loved the play. We sold lots of tickets, and I was so grateful to the community here for supporting us. We were embraced as we tried to get new work off the ground. The show was magical, and it was heartening in the way it helped our company to band together.

DON'T BE SCARED TO START SMALL

It's also important to remember that while a big pile of cash is nice to have from the get-go, most companies simply won't enjoy that luxury. You may have to take fund-raising baby steps—and that's OK. Again, it comes down to how good your work is—if you get people excited about the first project you put up especially, they'll contribute to your second. Let them do this in reasonable increments, and you'll build goodwill *and* capital on a consistent basis.

Patrick Dooley of Shotgun Players followed this template, and his patience paid off.

Our first play was *Edmund*—we put it up around the time of the Rodney King riots, and the material had deep class and race undertones. It inspired a lot of conversation. We rehearsed it, did it, got good responses from audience members and critics, and so we said, "Let's do another one." We had no season, no subscriptions at first, but still, our attitude was, "Let's do this." We decided to rally around each other and just go forward.

We decided to sell subscriptions for a lot of plays. Then, in 1997, we received nonprofit status—this allowed us to double our budget. We were getting popular! We'd be performing in a forty-nine-seat space, but we'd fit 100 people in, thanks to bench space. Every row of seats would be filled. In 1997, we were able to use this space in back of a print shop—we were squeezing 120 patrons in there. People were everywhere! The fire department showed up and shut us down—but once they left, we did the show anyway. No one came back to stop us, because there was a huge fire elsewhere in the city!

We had a few shows that were breakout hits. We did shows at places like Berkeley Rep and Aurora, got attention, and then the donors and grants started to come. Being a nonprofit did mean doing more work that I wasn't that excited to do, but we were experiencing growth, and making money. I was able to hire a managing director, a bookkeeper, and a development director—maybe they were only working fifteen to twenty hours a week at the start, but we were getting somewhere. I could give people health benefits.

Then we could say we were in the black. I feel what really helped us get there was the idea I had that I'd never spend more than I knew I could make. So eventually, I could really pay performers. Sure, we had some hiccups—a few shows that tanked. But we kept going, and it was working.

INDIVIDUAL IMPACT

Lots of companies think the trick to early funding is sweet-talking seed money out of folks they know—obligating their families and friends to lend capital that, chances are, they'll never get back. This is problematic for two major reasons. First, your nearest and dearest don't get anything back for their investment—free tickets to a show, maybe, but except for personal affection toward you, what's their upside? And second, money and loved ones just don't mix. Once you accept that check, your relationship will shift—you may feel guilty if you can't return their money, and they may feel resentful if you're not as appreciative as they feel you should be. The dynamic spells trouble either way.

It's so much better to raise money from individuals you don't know personally—but to whom you can offer a service for their contribution. Interested in teaching acting, and contributing to a budding performer's evolution?

Charging for your services is the perfect way to give back. Seth Barrish of the Barrow Group wanted to share his knowledge in just this way—and was able to boost his company's finances at the same time. Barrish recalls,

> I'd been teaching privately, and around 1990 or so, we decided to form a school. All of a sudden, there was a place of this group of interested artists who were not company members, but who we wanted to see succeed. We wanted to see these people fully utilize their talents and skills. So this helped us build an abundant Barrow Group community! We want to work with the most outstanding talents, to teach and pass on our style and approach; now thousands of actors have learned our approach.

Barrish's founding partner Lee Brock enthusiastically agreed with this idea, and jumped in, with the company's executive director Robert Serrell, to make it happen.

> Our original mission was to do plays that would deeply touch people. We knew we had something special; we knew we could inspire and enlighten. We put so much energy into this; creatively, we have been very consistent. Business-wise, as every company does, we've faced financial challenges. First this was because we were nomadic in terms of the work we were doing, but then, we shifted our focus to the school, and that truly helped us to evolve. Money was still a challenge, but Robert

then came in and changed things. He reframed things, and people could recognize, and register, these positive changes.

Barrish also stresses the importance, as a company leader, of regularly reminding yourself *why* people should want to financially contribute to your vision.

I think any producing entity's initial goal, and ongoing goal, is of course to produce plays that don't lose money. Then, of course, you want to continue to develop your work, and *make* some money. Robert has come up with a business plan that allows the company to be solvent—an enormous challenge for a business model in these times, in which the theater is changing so rapidly. Robert's attention to this allows us to evolve, both creatively and business-wise.

Apart from this kind of wise planning, I think the most important way to stay financially successful, for any company, is to ask yourself, "Why am I doing this again? Why is my company unique?" We do it because our work feels real to us, and our audiences—that makes our work compelling and different. If you want to keep your core clientele and expand your company as well, you need to remind yourself of your mission, and make sure you continue to be committed to it.

That says it all. Stay clear, honest, and determined, and the money will follow.

SUCCESS STORY: THE LABYRINTH THEATER COMPANY, NEW YORK, NY

The LAByrinth serves as the perfect example of a company that built a sterling reputation on its road to financial success. Originally led by the late, legendary Philip Seymour Hoffman and gifted thespian John Ortiz, the LAByrinth Theater Company began life in 1992 with a core company of thirteen actors who shared a need to exercise their creative muscles in every theatrical aspect possible.

This meant each company member would get a chance not only to perform works they dreamed of tackling, and to originate exciting new roles, but also would write, direct, produce, hang lights, paint sets—in short, participate in a true, and rare, theatrical democracy. The company's hallmark of peerless quality, especially in the area of new works, was quickly cemented, and as the company grew, it gained more esteemed members, including Ellen Burstyn, Ethan Hawke, Bobby Cannavale, Chris Rock, and Michael Shannon, and also great playwrights as associates, including John Patrick Shanley, Eric Bogosian, and Cusi Cram.

LABrynth draws sellout audiences to all of its shows, and additionally to its financial benefit, operates incorporating wise corporate relationships—the company struck a lucrative deal with Time Warner to sponsor new play development, for example. Currently led by artistic director and respected director/costume designer Mimi O'Donnell (who was Mr. Hoffman's partner), the LAByrinth is a constantly growing, fiscally stable, artistically lauded company that's sure to inspire theater professionals for years to come.

The Farm by Jon Tracy
directed by Jon Tracy
Shotgun Players 2009 Season
Pictured: Stephanie Prentice, Sarah Mitchell, Kristoffer Barrera, Sergio Gonzales
Photo by Benjamin Privitt

Chapter Five
Finding Our Core Acting Troupe

A truth accepted by many theater people is, casting is everything; once you assemble the appropriate people for the appropriate roles, much of your work is already done. I think it is true that an actor's persona can bring a lot to the table, yet I also believe you must carefully evaluate a performer's talent, technical abilities, and team player tendencies before making a final casting decision.

When you are putting together an acting company, it's vital you consider your overall priorities first, whether they be fitting players to specific shows or roles, qualities you prize in a person you'd like to work with, or whatever else matters crucially. Then you should take care to be sure actors mesh well with you, your director, his/her fellow cast members, and your ultimate goals and vision for the work. Even if you intend to job actors in, you still must use the same evaluative method.

The only time you really have to do this is during the audition process. A well-planned tryout schedule is the ideal way to screen. There are tricks that never fail to reveal the best and worst of your potential cast members. They are fully covered within this chapter.

Every company profiled is surprisingly different in relation to how it handled the task of casting and what its casting philosophy has evolved into. Your company, too, will develop its own unique casting techniques. Casting can be done by a certain practical theory to some extent, but it also happens by feel, as when you know someone is right—or wrong.

To be good at casting, and to do the best by your company, approach it like a psychologist might approach a patient. Evaluate technique but use your intuition and your people-reading skills as well.

Most importantly, trust your instincts. You already know inside what it is you really want, and your gut feelings are the way you repeat that knowledge to yourself.

GOOD VIBRATIONS

First off, go into auditions with the best intentions. Don't expect trouble. Don't get off on the power trip of having people reveal themselves to you through their work just so you can blow them off. Actors are a vulnerable lot. Their art comes from a deep, emotional place. They suffer almost constant rejection from idiots who do not understand the finer points of the acting craft, who only understand they need to cast someone taller, thinner, shorter, or fatter. Make it your business to understand where actors are coming from. Run your auditions humanely from the start, and you'll give actors hope regarding the quality of the production you might all end up working on.

If you're not an actor yourself, it would be a wonderful thing if you'd pick up a good book on acting method before you even start the audition ball rolling. Of course you're busy, but try to make the time to do even a little bit of reading on the complexities of what your actors do on a daily basis. I guarantee you'll be impressed with the effort that goes into a good performance. A classic primer to check out would be *Respect for Acting* by the legendary Uta Hagen.

The beauty of an actor's dedication is very well illustrated in the following reminiscence by Paul Zuckerman, who talks about the communal determination of the Chicago City Limits acting company. "I would say laziness wasn't there. This was a group, when we moved to New York—seven of us stayed in two hotel rooms for a year. We had no money, really, so all of our time was spent rehearsing, talking. The religion is loud and clear here—our series of adversities and successes really binds people together strongly. You become a family.

I think there was a stubbornness we had in common, an up-against-the-wall mentality. Maybe it was that we were children of the '60s and had that glimmers-of-the-revolution sort of orientation. The adversity, in some sense, forged strength, and the difficulties became challenges, and small victories became major victories. And you know what? We didn't come out of a sort of traditional theater background, so I feel that we might not have taken chances if we knew more. It was a riskier theater. I remember a reviewer early on saying the thing he liked about us the most was that we weren't so stage-smart.

You had to learn how to do things that maybe you would have been taught somewhere else—like how do you end a scene? Well, you had to figure out how to end a scene—does it come full circle, yeah, that works sometimes, or do you resolve a conflict, yeah, that works sometimes, or does the relationship evolve, yeah, that works sometimes—but you don't know that till you've done a bunch of those things, unless people teach you that someplace.

GIVING NOTICE

Whether you're placing your casting notice in the newspaper or posting it on a call-board, you want to make sure it's specific. If the roles you're casting call for precise physical requirements, say so. If it's musical talent you seek and you need singers who act or actors who move well, say so. If age requirements come into play, do tell. If you must require that your cast give up large amounts of their time to rehearsal, be up front about this.

You also have to come clean about money. If you intend to pay your company a stipend only, say so. If the positions you're casting for are salaried, make sure this is clear. If participating in your production is sanctioned to earn performers points toward membership in Equity, state this fact. If you can only use union actors, or can only use nonunion actors, explain this in your casting notice. Don't be concerned that such honesty will limit the number of actors who will be auditioning for you. You can always hold more extensive auditions beyond your initial tryout date. You can't, however, lie to people about what your production can offer them and not expect them to bail on you once they discover the truth. At the same time, be flexible regarding your casting needs. Don't write out role descriptions so rigidly that you aren't open to that happy accident—a great actor showing up who maybe doesn't look exactly as you visualized, but who can certainly slap on a fake mustache.

Also, it is really recommended that you try to budget for some form of payment for your performers. If you are working with Equity, as you know, varied forms of compensation will be required. If not, even a small financial token of appreciation is the fair way to go. It will also foster good feelings, as will paying each of your actors exactly the same amount. You want camaraderie, not hierarchy. The only exception to this rule is, again, Equity specifications you are required to fulfill.

Jack Reuler (Mixed Blood) was completely honest with his initial company members at the time he hired them, especially about the upstart nature of his enterprise. He remembers back to the circumstances of his early hires:

It was really a company. We were offering ten weeks of employment at I think $110 a week. We were looking for people who could work those kinds of shifts.

I'd picked the plays, so I sort of had this little grid. The first season we did *Status Quo Vidas*, a play called *Brother Champ*, an original play, then a play, perhaps the

73

first and only production, where all the Native characters in the play were played by Native actors. Then we did a tour of *Dutchman*—Lou Bellamy, who was the artistic director of Penumbra, directed that. Then another play called *Black Cycle*—sort of a forgettable piece. That was our first season; we did ten weeks, five shows. They ran from two to three weeks each.

I've always valued human chemistry over talent. If I had to make a trade, it was, who could sacrifice a summer to be in a hundred-year-old fire station with twenty other people? I was still so thankful people wanted to participate, it was really, "Are you sure you know what you're getting into?" Because I certainly didn't know.

A lot of those people from that first company stayed for a long time. Don Cheadle did his first show, I think he was twenty-two, an original play called *Liquid Skin*, in which he played a man going through a sex change. It was really more about the people around him and their reactions, a really interesting piece of art. He was young and new and he was great then and he knew he was going to be a star. He stayed and did three or four shows between '88 and about '93, and then he directed a couple of shows.

I think the greatest of the people who have worked here are the ones that have stayed working here. A lot of people come back. I think in the earlier years, Mixed Blood was a stepping-stone to get somewhere else and now it's a place to aspire to.

MATERIAL CONCERNS

Prior to the first day of your auditions, you need to sit down with your director and musical director (if you're working with one) and decide as a team what, if any, specifics you're looking for in terms of casting. Make a general casting blueprint that you can refer back to when you need it. Susan Kosoff, of Wheelock Family Theatre, says:

We started *Alice's Adventures in Wonderland*, and that's a show that is so dependent on Alice. We knew who we wanted for that when we chose the play. We wanted to do the play because we knew it was enough of a children's classic to be appealing, but we also knew who we wanted to play that role, and we got her.

We cast some other people that we had worked with in the past and we had open auditions. We talked to everybody we knew. Over time, we've gotten better and better people at auditions. Our first show was a musical so we needed people who could sing. For example, the woman that we got to play Alice had gone back to school at Emerson College, so she had a couple of friends who we used in the show. We sort of called on past people that we knew.

We just did a variety of things. We had an open call, people came, and we tried to put together the best cast we could put together. We now have people who have been in eighteen, twenty shows with us.

We did [in 2001] *Rebecca of Sunnybrook Farm*, and there's a woman in Boston, an African American woman considered one of the best in Boston [who was in it]. She's said to me, "I will be in any show you ask me to do once a year, because I believe in what you do." Then there are other people who want to work, like the quality of our work, and audition for us. As we're choosing the plays, we think, frankly, in terms of, this person could play this, or this person could play that.

We do try always to have a mix in our casts. Our casts are large; that's another thing that's different about us from other theaters. We don't limit cast size. Because we also want to get a lot of young people involved, one of the things we've had to do in recent years, because we've had so many student matinees, is that some of the smaller parts for younger people will have two, maybe three cast. We always try to have a mix in our casts of people we've worked with before and new people. We want to bring on new professionals, and we also want to bring on new young people to develop their talent.

THAT OBSCURE OBJECT OF DESIRE

If you're putting together a permanent company, in addition to being concerned with fitting material needs, you're going to want to work with people you like. Also, you're human, so you're going to be attracted to those individuals who satisfy your desire for certain tangible, or intangible, personal qualities.

The qualities that are supremely coveted in actors are as far-ranging as the companies these performers may be judged by. Still, here are a few things a good leadership might keep an eye out for. Says David Zak (Bailiwick Repertory): "Many people in Chicago are great at a very naturalistic style. We were looking for people with excellent classical training, especially vocally. And, of course, if you look hard enough, you can find them!"

From Rick Lombardo, formerly of New Repertory Theatre:

I look for people whose first goal, overall, is to commit to the artistic product to their fullest extent. The people I know at New Rep, I think, share the same human and artistic values. For example, the quality of last season was extraordinary. So the question becomes, can we do really challenging work this year, artistically developing from last year? I lean on artists really hard and want them to have team values.

Working with friends can be very tempting—and of course, most companies are woven with a web of personal relationships throughout their history. This is a fantastic boon to your work when everyone gets along, shares similar artistic goals and values—and are uniformly serious about the work at hand, above all else. It's great to have fun doing theater—it's absolutely essential, in fact—but having fun, and wasting precious time on less-than-productive social activities are two different things. Patrick Dooley explains the difference from his own experience:

My core group of collaborators and I had a lot of fun working together from the beginning, six to eight of us. We were doing a lot of really good work, and getting better. The group had always hung out together, too, with people we were meeting and collaborating with. But I got sober in 1998, and things had changed a bit then—it was not a party anymore, so much. I didn't surround myself with lots of dysfunctional people from that point on; the focus was to make quality work. I was becoming more professional, and all of us, now in our thirties and forties, were, too. We committed ourselves to doing a lot of really good work, and getting better at that work consistently from that point on.

Veteran director David Fuller opines:

Everybody must have kindness. When I went to drama school as an actor in the '70s, Alec Guinness came and talked to us. He had just finished shooting *Star Wars*, and he was starting to become so famous worldwide.

We were talking about method versus a technical way of acting, which all young actors have trouble with: Which is the best, if you have to choose? I don't believe there's a choice, I believe it's a compilation of all of it, but anyway, someone said to Alec Guinness, "What do you think about the actor who lives their part between takes, sustains their character, takes their character home with them?"

He said, "I should think they're insane, wouldn't you?" I thought, "That's true." He went on to say that his biggest advice to give a young actor was, "It's most important to be a good human being."

That's kind of how to run an organization. We may become an internationally famous repertory theater, or we may not, but at least we're going to be good people as we run it. I naturally gravitate away from "show business people," which is probably why I'm in nonprofit theater. There is a type that I see often that I just want to take to the side and say, "Could you just stop it?" I don't want to get too existential, but take a look at the sky, take a deep breath.

It comes with age, probably, but you have to assemble people with whom you like to work, first of all. People with whom you can laugh—that's very important. People who have innate kindness. You just have to be nice—otherwise, what's the point? We're in a service organization, anyway, and if you're caught—what the heck are you doing?

BE READY FOR ANYTHING

Right before your tryout date, go through one of the scripts you'll be doing and pull out two meaty monologues—one for men, and one for women. Or, if you'd prefer, choose a classic piece or any other piece you feel will be challenging and evocative of the work you intend actors to do within your company.

Actors will probably be bringing in a prepared monologue of their own. Even if you want them to do that, a cold reading of your choice can be a great indicator of how well a performer can think on his or her feet. Don't be cruel, though—there's nothing clever or cool about throwing a completely foreign bunch of sides at a performer and saying, "Wow me."

Be considerate—give a little information to your auditioners, even though they'll be reading cold. Once you've chosen your material, don't just rip a page out of the script and photocopy it—retype it onto a clean sheet and add a little general paragraph at the top of the page regarding who the character is, an overview of the scene, and a brief description of the play's plot. This is a really great courtesy to the actors.

The audition can also consist of a dialogue scene between two characters. Your stage manager customarily reads the scene with the actor, so you, the producer, and the director can concentrate on watching the actor's work. You also want to put together a brief bio sheet for your auditioners to fill out. Here's how to gather names, phone numbers, union affiliations, if any, even notations of any special skills a performer might want to mention (sword swallowing can really perk up an intermission). Have your auditioners note their availability so you can be aware of potential schedule conflicts.

Seriously, though, leave room for those happy surprises. Oftentimes, a performer's unexpected skills can be a real boon to your company. Here's how producer Leslie Jacobson approached her first spate of tryouts—with a completely open mind.

> We were looking for people who were talented performers but also had an interest in creating material for themselves and for others. Who were able to write as well.
>
> You know, not everybody's interested in that, and that's totally fine. But there are people who are, and we got some extremely talented people who had very interesting skills that we wove into shows. One person was a professional puppeteer as well as an actress and a writer. Some people were singers or dancers as well. The shows used a lot of highly theatrical devices to keep them interesting and entertaining, as well as thought-provoking.

THE AUDITION PROCESS

Plant your stage manager or assistant manager in this waiting area to meet and greet, man a sign-in sheet, and escort each auditioner into your inner sanctum.

Each actor should have filled in his or her bio sheet and been given the opportunity to study sides before you see them. When an actor is ushered in to read for you, take a moment to read over the resume and pull out an interesting fact and use it as an icebreaker. Understand how nervous this person must be. Treat an auditioner as you would wish to be treated if you were in their shoes.

As an actor is reading for you, keep a poker face. Never sneer or laugh or look bored. Don't let your eyes glaze over, even if you're bored out of your mind. It's nice to smile after a performer has finished reading, whether you like their work or not. If you don't think you're going to be able to use them, thank them graciously for their time and tell them you'll be in touch. This is very important. Actors tend to check their messages obsessively—it stinks when you're waiting to hear about a job, and you never get any form of reply.

Even if you don't cast an actor, call and say thanks anyway. Keep it brief, thank them for their time and talent, and simply state you'll be going in another direction. Don't criticize, get personal, or be rude. But definitely say something. If you do like an actor's work and can see he or she would be perfect in the lead, play it cool; you don't want to get an actor's hopes up, then end up casting someone who shows up later and seems even more perfect.

Is it acceptable to take the recommendation of collaborators and friends during the casting process? Of course—the opinion of an artist you really respect can lead you to finding really amazing people. Steppenwolf, needless to say, only works with artists of the highest caliber. Yet a lot of the company's inclusions have been as a direct result of a good word being put in. Says Steppenwolf's Michael Gennaro:

> There is no formal rhyme or reason as to why people are brought in or not.
>
> Over the years, it had kind of been, they would work with someone and go, "Yeah, this person works like us. They have the same sensibility." The artistic directors were always members of the company. Gary was for a while, Jeff was. And the managing executive directors were always people who had been, not so much ensemble members, but kind of people surrounding or had been in productions and kind of had a business sense to them.
>
> In '95, the company and the board decided to make a change, because they had to step up, I think, the business end of the company. That's when Martha Lavey came on as artistic director, who was in the company, and still is, and me, who's the first person from the outside, who's run other companies. Over the past couple of years, I

think there's been maybe a little more strategic thinking involved in inviting people into the company. But it's still kind of a very informal process, one that probably will never be formalized, nor should it ever be formalized.

Some have left over the years. Some have left and come back. Glenne Headley left, but then came back when we won the Medal of Arts. We invited her and she came and everybody started crying and she said, "I'm back." It's kind of like the Supreme Court—once you're in, you're in. It's a lifer thing.

What's key now is, we're also at a point in time at which these people have all matured to an age and a point in their lives where we have to start looking toward the future and youth. Not only youth—I think the two important things are youth and diversity. They gotta be organic to what the place is about or it's not worth doing.

PUTTING TOGETHER A COMPANY THAT WILL GO THE DISTANCE

Personality is a crucial aspect in the casting process. Actors go into auditions with their best faces forward, and who can blame them? They want to get the job they're up for. Unfortunately, if an actor's true personality is less than accommodating and you cast him, this could be big trouble. An actor with a monster ego is an evil snowball that rolls downhill, picking up speed, until it finally smashes your production into smithereens. Other actors often get infected with swelled-head syndrome and soon you've got mutiny on your hands. If you truly strive to put together a company that will last, you need to detect these issues before you settle on your actors (after which it will be a total hassle to make changes).

How to detect trouble before it rears its head? Listen carefully to the way an actor relates to you. Do you feel it's fake or genuine? Does he or she sound like a real team player who wants to work for the good of the show, who understands that if the show works, it benefits everyone? Does the actor frown even slightly regarding issues of money or billing, if you so happen to drop these topics into the chatter? (A closer look here: why not state flatly that your cast will be billed in alphabetical order? An ego-stoked actor will almost always register some level of dismay about that). Most importantly, what is your gut telling you about this actor? Do you like this individual? Do you like this individual's work? If so, cast away, my friend. If not, keep looking. It's your call.

Mitzi Sales (Berkeley Rep) is of the opinion that an actor's willingness to play parts of any size is a good indication he or she will benefit a company. "We had a small core, and those actors did every role. That was very good for the theater," says Ms. Sales.

I think that the only thing they had in common was the desire to perhaps work in a company together. So there was a certain willingness to play small roles, to not always be in a featured or leading role. They recognized the importance of supporting each other.

They're actors, so there was a certain amount of ego and all of that. But I do think there was a remarkable amount of loyalty from a great many individuals.

Eventually, people drift off to Los Angeles or come to New York, of course. But a great many people stayed for a rather long time. Fortunately, the San Francisco Bay area is a very appealing place and it does attract artists. We were fortunate to be in a place where there were a certain number of people. ACT was graduating people and so on.

BE PROFESSIONAL

If you want to attract good people to your company, present yourself in a professional light. Actors want to work for good leadership, just as you want to work with good actors.

Keep your demeanor smooth. You will catch more flies with honey than you will with vinegar, so said the wise man. Show your auditioning actors right away that you're a cool, organized, fair, reasonable boss. State flatly that you intend to handle conflict or problems in this company with negotiation, honesty, and common sense. Make sure you stress communication above all—tell your potential cast members that you'll be up front with them at all times and that all you ask in return is that they will be similarly clear with you.

Gil Cates of the Geffen Playhouse stressed the importance, too, of expecting optimum professional commitment from your actors. "In terms of personnel, how do you get the highest-quality artists to want to work at your place?" he asked rhetorically.

In LA, actors, for the most part, don't want to deal with theater when they can make movies—sometimes they'll actually try to duck out of a performance for a film job! I don't think that's respectful once you've signed on to do a stage role, so you can't let them out. They need to recognize that you're serious in terms of the theatrical work you do, so it's important to show them the point of view of, they can create art onstage with you.

WINDING THINGS UP

Huddle with your director and musical director, if you've got one, post-audition to choose actors for callbacks. Decide which actors might fit which roles, and call them back in to read more material for you, especially if you are torn between two or more actors for one role, or one space to be filled within the company. Callbacks are also a great chance to test how quickly actors can learn music or pick up dance steps.

At callbacks, feel free to bring in pairs of actors to read together, in varying combinations, to help you decide final casting. Some actors are so competitive they don't even want to sit in the same room during callbacks. Petty behavior? Sure, and possibly an indicator that this person might be difficult to work with. Keep in mind that callbacks exist for you to exhaust all casting possibilities. A really professional actor will always understand your true purpose and won't be sensitive.

A quick aside: don't discount amateurs completely, either. Sound weird? It's not. I've had good experiences directing actors with very little previous experience, who just kind of show up at auditions and blow you away with their raw talent. I wouldn't recommend you use such a person for a permanent resident position, but for a job-in, a greener performer can be very malleable in the right role. Use the callback process to determine how directable such a person might be.

Once you've seen all the auditioning actors and held callbacks, it's the moment of truth: selecting your final cast. Don't stress out. Go with your instincts, mellowed with your intelligence. Your director is the production team member with the most valuable insight here. Who does he or she feel will be easiest to work with, give the best performance, have the right quality for the right role, have the most talent and versatility in order to handle a demanding company spot? Let your director be free to make the primary choices. As producer you can suggest or veto, but this is properly the director's turf.

You've just fool-proofed your casting process as best you possibly can.

FINDING YOUR ARTISTIC SOUL MATES

Some companies are formed strictly out of ideology rather than out of formal auditions. This fits certain specific company needs, say, those where its founders' mission includes performing original work as well as writing, directing, and producing it. Essentially, this means that once you've found your artistic soul mates, your obvious predilection is to cast yourselves.

The Jewish Theatre San Francisco is a great example. TJT's three original members were, of course, drawn together by their collective need to explore the same cultural and ethnic issues onstage. The addition of Helen Stolzus, a fourth ensemble member, in 1987, was the perfect addition, in that she came into the company interested in the same forms of exploratory expression.

Finding people who feel the same passion for the same type of work you do is essential if you want casting arranging to work out as well as TJT's did.

Chemistry, both personal and creative, is another crucial divining rod some companies elect to use. The Barrow Group's specific performance method and style is so precise and of such high quality that new company members must really step up to the plate in order to join. According to Seth Barrish, it's a matter of both shared sensibilty and compatible philosophy. "When it comes to choosing new company members, we developed a system for vetting people early on, which we still use today," he explains. "We really test people to see if they're compatible with us, with our shared ideas, by consensus. It's a true democracy—everyone in the company has to approve a new member. In many ways this has served us well, but in other ways, of course, it's been incredibly challenging—some truly extraordinary and talented people have not been accepted, because not everyone in the company warmed to them."

A CASTING COUP

This is the tale of how a small, but highly regarded, experimental company became graced with fabulous star power in very little time. This infusion of talent took the company in a new and lucrative direction as well. "We became one of the major, important, smaller experimental theater companies in the United States. We had quite a reputation," says Susan Albert Loewenberg of LA Theatre Works.

Around 1985, someone brought an idea to me that I resisted at first. I had certainly never worked with any name actors—it didn't interest me. I wasn't interested in conventional theater at all. Neil Simon and Wendy Wasserstein were the last things on my mind! However, the idea was that there was a significant resource in Los Angeles—famous actors. They were theater-trained, but they were famous because of film and television. They had no way to ply their craft in any significant way.

One of the things that I had felt keenly for a long time was that I could never figure out why most theater was so terrible. I realized it was because we didn't have great, world-class directors working on things. We didn't have the great international directors coming to Los Angeles—the Peter Halls, we didn't have these people for a variety of reasons. Probably because the centers of power weren't really interested. The Taper never invited these people, it just didn't happen.

So slowly I became convinced that we should do something. We formed a group of thirty-four very famous actors, including Stacy Keach, Richard Dreyfuss, Julie Harris, Helen Hunt, Marsha Mason, Ted Danson, Ed Asner. I mean, it was a pretty historic group. We told everybody they had to kick in $6,000 each, because I didn't want it to be something they were doing as a part-time hobby. They had to make a commitment.

The group was very energetic. We were going to do plays as a LORT theater, six-week runs, bring in world-class directors. We called ourselves A Project of LA Theatre Works. It was a very exciting and interesting time.

We did our first benefit. Oddly enough, we had this idea to do a radio show. We got KCRW involved, our local public radio station. We recorded a play, which they aired live in performance as it was being recorded, onstage. Grant Tinker was running the Culver Studios at the time, and gave us a huge soundstage.

We had eight hundred people there; we charged $250 a ticket. We sold, I think, six hundred tickets at that price, and $50 tickets for the other two hundred. We had Steven Spielberg there, we had Barry Diller there, we had Mo Ostin there, we had everybody there. It was fabulous! We did *Once in a Lifetime* starring John Lithgow, who's part of our group, and Marsha Mason. I think of the thirty-four actors, twenty-five were in it. Helen [Hunt] was in it. Of course, she wasn't famous then, she was a young actress. She was getting there, but she certainly wasn't where she is today.

It was a fabulous performance, but it was a lousy recording! I don't even know how it was broadcast, it was so bad. It's a shame, because it's not salable. Nobody knew what they were doing. People loved the radio show, they weren't that critical, but when I look at it today, I couldn't even use it. But the live show was great!

Here's to all of the casting triumphs in the future.

PART TWO

INTO THE FIRE

This World in a Woman's Hands by Marcus Gardley
directed by Aaron Davidman
Shotgun Players 2009 Season
Pictured: Dena Martinez and Margo Hall
Photo by Benjamin Privitt

Chapter Six
Mounting That First Production

Preparation, production, and rehearsal is not rocket science, but it's certainly key to whether your show—and your company as a whole—develops a decent reputation in your community. Your first show sets the tone. Your goal is to do a fantastic job, yes, but also not to raise the bar so colossally high that you can't get over it.

Should you need to make changes, jump in with enthusiasm and without fear. Even the best theater organizations have needed to regroup at certain points. It helps, too, to remember that the best time to implement changes is when you're first starting out. No intelligent person—be it a funder, an audience member, or even a critic—could possibly think less of a company attempting to enact positive adjustments at the beginning of its lifespan. It's when you don't make the changes you really ought to make that people tend to look at you funny.

THE BENEFIT OF DOING WELL-KNOWN MATERIAL

Giving your audience something familiar right off the bat can be very beneficial in terms of helping your theater gain acceptance. This doesn't mean, however, you can't stretch within a familiar text framework.

Reinterpretation of a famous play through visual, aural, or performance-style means is one option you can explore. Another option is to work with a familiar character or characters in a new format. This can work particularly well, both at establishing some amount of audience identification and also at allowing you creative freedom to try new things.

Wheelock Family Theatre used a familiar character in a new show as a way of demonstrating its very unique place in the theatrical universe. As Susan Kosoff recalls,

We opened in March 1981. "Family Theatre" was sort of a name we just sort of gave to it—there wasn't, to our knowledge, anything like that around. We decided we would define it ourselves.

We wanted to show the range that we thought was possible in family theater. That first year, we did *Alice's Adventures in Wonderland*, which was an original adaptation. We followed it up with *Watcher in the Rhine*.

Out of those shows also came some of our casting decisions. We always try to do shows that have at least two generations in them, the idea being that we really believe if people see themselves onstage, they're more likely to identify with the play.

THERE'S STRENGTH IN STRENGTH

Whatever you do, don't choose wimpy material your first time out. You can't go wrong letting your true flag fly—people will quickly tell you one way or another whether they agree with your hypothesis, which you can only control so much, so be very definite in the material you choose. Take care that it makes your mission statement clear.

Here are fifteen important questions to ask yourself when evaluating a play for production to ensure the material is true to your values as an organization:

1. Do I believe in the message of this play?
2. If I don't agree with the play's hypothesis, is the message still valid and important to share?
3. What does this play say about our company?
4. Am I OK with controversy if this play is received poorly or ignites a political or cultural discourse in my community?
5. Is the play well written?
6. Will my actors find the characters I'm asking them to play dimensional and worthwhile?
7. Does this material push the trajectory of our company forward in a significant artistic way?
8. Am I considering doing this play just to score a financial hit? (Bad idea, obviously.)
9. Do any of the key members of my creative or technical teams have a major objection, for whatever reason, to the material?
10. If so, have I considered their point of view?
11. Could I potentially have access to the playwright, and if so, would I like to collaborate with this person throughout the production?
12. Does the director of this potential production think the play is a good fit for our company's purposes?

13. If the play is a critical or commercial failure, will I regret having taken it on?

14. Does the play truly excite me?

15. What is my overall gut instinct telling me after I've answered these questions: yay or nay?

GET YOUR HOUSE IN ORDER

Now that you've selected your company's first place, it's time to get organized, ASAP.

Not to waste your time or insult your intelligence with elementary stuff you already know, but scheduling rules, my friend. When you're running a company, you've got to be scrupulous about keeping track of audition dates, leaving adequate time for a rehearsal period, and locking in showtimes. Don't leave everything to your director and SM; stay on top of things, and double-check their work, by putting together your own planning system. Here are a few useful tips to get you organized.

How much time will you need for a fully scheduled production period? Give yourself, ideally, one month for pre-production (which includes making a budget, choosing a venue, interviewing directors, and preparing auditions). Then, six weeks, from auditions to opening night, could serve as your production period (although you could do it in four weeks if you had to). If you are developing original material or a new play, you will probably need a longer rehearsal period.

WHAT YOU DON'T KNOW ABOUT REHEARSALS CAN HURT YOU

Your director bears the direct responsibility for a production's rehearsal period, it's true.

It behooves you, needless to say, to stay very involved and informed in what specifically goes on during rehearsals.

Keep abreast of how things are progressing. Drop into rehearsal often and be a positive presence. Ask questions in a friendly way. Stay in the loop.

This doesn't give you license to be an annoying pest or a ruler with an iron fist, horning in on the director's turf. Give him/her the space and peace of mind to make the production great. If there's a problem, assert yourself and help fix it. Don't offer too much advice if it's not really necessary or bend the director's ear with insignificant chitchat or discussion about the state of theater in today's postmodern world. There isn't tons of time to waste, especially for the rehearsal time of a first show.

Susan Kosoff discovered the time crunch factor firsthand. She made it work, though.

The planning time had been great, as you might imagine, for the two productions that first season. But the actual rehearsal time was dictated by our contract with Equity—three weeks, five days. Actually, sometimes we've done a week more, especially with musicals. But pretty much we stick to about a month for rehearsal. I will say I wish there are times when we had more, but almost always, it's OK.

WHEN YOU WANT TO MAKE IT BETTER

The more you watch your show, the more you'll want to improve it.

You can't help wanting to. This is not to say that you were tremendously dissatisfied with the staging, writing, or casting; you wouldn't have put the show up in the first place if you felt it had major flaws. It's simply that the audience, any audience, no matter how large or how small it may be, starts to shift your perspective. The audience becomes a teacher, and if you're smart, you'll become its student. If you are "only" producing the show, not directing it, you will probably want to feed any suggestions you have for improvement back to the director. He is at the helm of the creative end of the production, after all.

Go to your next performance armed with a pad and paper. Note the audience's reactions. Note your own responses to what does and doesn't work. Nobody else has to see what you're writing, so let it rip uncensored. You'll quickly see, when you read over the notes you've made post-performance, which points matter, and you can then take action to correct problems.

Let's look at a few typical rework scenarios you might have to deal with.

RESTAGING A SCENE OR TWO

The easiest fix to achieve.

As soon as you recognize a staging problem within performance, you should alert your director, cast, and crew. Call a rehearsal to make your adjustments as soon as possible. Your director should tell your actors prior to this rehearsal that a change will be enforced, so that no one is thrown off adversely. Actors are habitual creatures. Their sense of security comes from routine and the aspects of a production they feel they can count on, and therefore have some sense of control within. To redo a scene, an actor may have to adjust his or her character motivation slightly and, for sure, will have to adapt visually and spatially, often very quickly before doing an actual performance and making the audience think what's new feels natural.

So, expect at least one cast member to protest or have a mini nervous breakdown at news of a staging change. Reassure this sensitive soul. More importantly, make sure the director takes care to make this actor comfortable with the adjustment. Allow extra rehearsal time when you're restaging. The director should reblock clearly and then drill, drill, drill. Changes must be repeated ad nauseam so cast members can get them into their bones. This not only will result in better staging during performances but also will improve actors' confidence in carrying them out.

If you've only got one pickup rehearsal scheduled per week and there's absolutely no other time to thoroughly cover your restaging, then it's OK to use all of that pickup time—just this once—to get the adjustment down cold. It's ideal to hold one restaging rehearsal, though, then hold a second maintenance run-through rehearsal incorporating the restaging, so actors and crew can get a complete sense of fusion before they embark on a full-fledged performance.

RESTAGING A LARGE PORTION OF THE PRODUCTION

A bigger fish to fry, obviously. First of all, you're going to have to suspend your performance schedule; hopefully it'll be just briefly. This may seem like the end of the world, but it's actually the start of a bright tomorrow. The truth is, if large sections of your production really need to be restaged, your show will never make it if you don't make the changes.

Work out a rehearsal schedule with your director that accomplishes all of your restaging goals in as timely a fashion as possible. Be real when it comes to the amount of time you'll need to allot for this. Next, hammer out an arrangement with your venue. You may be required to pay for stage space even though your show will be dark. That's actually not a bad deal because you can probably use the space to rehearse during what would have been performance times, and your cast will feel somewhat reassured that things will be back to normal soon.

Now, here's a more difficult situation: Your venue wants you to give back your performance reservations so it can make money on another show that's ready to go up. Initially, the venue may promise you can reserve more time when you're ready to perform again, but in reality, unless you can reserve the time that very second and put that reservation in writing, it probably won't work out. If another show is, indeed, put into your performance slot and it turns out to be a moneymaker long-term, the venue isn't going to pull it so you can remount when you're ready. This is just common sense in terms of business.

If you can't get a firm commitment from your venue, I say find a new venue and start fresh. You need to present your show in a place that's got positive energy. You want a supportive, welcoming environment. It's out there—just find it.

REPLACING KEY PERSONNEL

Sadly, if you discover your director isn't capable of staging—or restaging—the production to your satisfaction, he or she is going to have to be replaced.

If your director isn't getting the job done, first sit down and try to talk through the problems. Give your director a chance to explain. If your experience with this person tells you to believe it when your director tells you he or she knows what's up and outlines step-by-step to you how he or she plans to fix the production, takes your comments and feelings into consideration, and displays a willingness to collaborate with you until the show is shipshape, then maybe you can give your director another chance.

If you know that your director is incapable of doing the job, though, you've got to make a change. Tell your director that you do admire his or her initial creative vision, but that in practice, it's not feasible. Don't insult this person. Be supportive, in terms of explaining your issues with your director's performance, because the director probably will ask you quite directly what your specific criticisms are. Be kind, but don't waver. Most directors will be professional enough not to overreact—this is probably not an unexpected turn of events. A halfway-competent director will already know inside that he/she is not delivering the goods.

REPLACING AN ACTOR

Of course, you need to do this in the same calm, kind, rational manner as you would replacing your director. Once again, be supportive of this person's general talent and never be abusive. State your case and let the actor know it's just not working out and you wish them the best. (When you think about it, replacing an actor sounds a lot like breaking up with a boyfriend or girlfriend, doesn't it? You've got to get free, but you've got to be humane, too).

There's one important factor besides feelings, however, that you must consider whenever you replace an actor. That factor would be: mutiny.

I once directed a show featuring an actress so outrageous, so in love with her own talent and fab reviews, that she started stealing scenes and verbally trashing her fellow actors—*onstage*. In front of the audience. It was outrageous. I fired this insubordinate individual—and guess what happened?

All three of the other actors whom she'd been treating so terribly quit in solidarity.

This would appear irrational. It was, indeed, irrational. But I wasn't looking at the situation through my cast member's perspectives. Those perspectives were perhaps a little skewed, but they were skewed through inner vulnerability. I later found out that the actors who quit felt I would never fire anyone. I'd built up a strong sense of family and common support within our company, and they all counted on that. What no one had counted on was a diva exploding among us. So when I did what I had to do, what was best for the show and was in everyone's best interest, the actors I was in fact defending were shocked, felt threatened, and attempted to reject me before I could reject them.

You can't control the actions of other people, but you can avoid unexpected mutiny by calling a cast meeting immediately after you fire an actor. Do this before you bring in a replacement. Tell your group the reasons you did it, clearly outlining the fired party's transgressions as they affected the rest of the cast. People listen to you when their own welfare is involved, when they understand you're playing on their team. Express your support of your remaining cast members. Ask them to share their feelings about what has happened. Get any misconceptions or complaints out in the open before the entire group. Clear up problems together.

REWRITING TEXT

Hopefully, if you're working with the writer of an original show, he or she will have a gung-ho, collaborative attitude. If not, though, you have to expect a fight (maybe just a little squabble, maybe World War III) when you call for rewrites. Always remember this: Without the writer, you wouldn't have a show. Convey your respect. Also, don't think you know how to rewrite yourself. Feel free to express your opinions in a nice, intelligent way, but give the writer lots of credit and slack. The writer is your primary source. A good relationship with your writer is your best guarantee of production success.

YOU CAN'T ALWAYS CALL AUDIENCE REACTION

When thinking about your first performances, in advance of actually doing your first show, you probably figure that there will be a certain demographic who's going to love the production. Say you're doing *The Leonard Nimoy Story* for a room full of Trekkies—it'll be a smash, right? Talk about a no-brainer.

Not so fast. A room full of Trekkies might just be your harshest critics because they are going to have the highest expectations of any audience your company could possibly host. If a specialized audience's reaction is tepid, it doesn't necessarily mean you need to change the show, though. Sometimes, such a group will be focused on minutia that a mainstream crowd will simply not give a hoot about.

Corey Fischer (The Jewish Theatre San Francisco) found that his group's unconventional approach worked wonderfully with audiences who appreciated a fresh sensibility. Even though in a more conventional setting audience reaction wasn't as initially fabulous, it was just a matter of finding an audience niche. "The very first couple of performances [we did] in Santa Monica—immediately it was pretty clear we had something people wanted to see," Mr. Fischer recalls.

> After that initial euphoria, we had some less-satisfying engagements where we were in a more conventional setting, like a Jewish community center. Then we did this tour, where we went to Baltimore for a theater festival.
>
> It was very validating, because there we were in with our peers and colleagues, as well as general audience members. So that was very encouraging. From there, we went to Vancouver, British Columbia, and Santa Cruz, California. Those stops were very exciting to us—all three of those engagements were not specifically for Jewish audiences. We were getting a really mixed audience and people were responding very generously and enthusiastically. That was great confirmation.
>
> We then went back to Los Angeles and ran a production in a tiny theater in the West Hollywood area, a four-week run, and got a lot of reviews from the LA papers that were almost all positive. It was maybe a fifty-seat theater, and we ended up turning a lot of people away. We had a very good run.

GIVE THE PEOPLE WHAT THEY WANT?

Pleasing a crowd is not as hard as it seems. Here's a novel idea: please yourself first.

People respond strongly to a genuine passion displayed onstage. There will always be an element of viewership that clearly does not dig your point of view. But it's really the same in any aspect of life, isn't it? Not everybody wants to be your friend or wants to buy your old car. So what? You might not want to be their friend or buy their old car, either.

I guarantee you that there will be more people responding to your work than not responding to it, as long as you're true to what you want to say theatrically and you say it boldly. Even if they don't like what you're doing 100 percent, they'll appreciate your audacity.

Worst-case scenario: you put something up and people absolutely revolt and throw psychic tomatoes at your actors. Well, you can always change gears. It's wise to measure reaction very carefully, however, before you do anything. Leslie Jacobson, formerly of Horizons, learned this in her early experiences putting on shows for large houses. "Definitely we knew we were giving people things they hadn't seen onstage before. People were very excited—we were doing a lot of plays dealing with mother-daughter relationships in the late '70s. In fact, the book *My Mother, Myself* came out around that time. We were doing our first plays about mothers and daughters before it came out, and then it came out and that obviously was something people were interested in. And we were interested in it—we didn't pick a topic because it was trendy, we picked a topic because it was on our minds.

There didn't seem to be any good plays out there at that time dealing with the mother-daughter relationship, so we actually did several plays on that. They generated incredible discussion, because people felt they were getting to look at something that they weren't able to look at—there weren't any plays being written on that. Sometimes they would make interesting comments that we would think about incorporating into the productions. Again, since we were the playwrights the early performances we could use like previews and make adjustments. Sometimes we waited to do that.

I'll never forget—we performed at a facility around that time for about 800 people. We did a show that ran ninety minutes without an intermission. We felt that was important because we didn't want to break the flow of the evening, but somebody brought up that they wished there had been an intermission so they could have thought about some of the things [in the play] during the break and then come back.

I looked out at the audience and said, "How many of you would have preferred an intermission?" A sea of hands went up, a huge number of hands. So I'm thinking, "Hmm, maybe we should put an intermission in this."

But then I said, "OK, how many of you preferred it without an intermission?" Another sea of hands went up. Probably four hundred people wanted the intermission, but the other four hundred didn't! So that actually taught me something important, which is, it's extremely valuable to get feedback from an audience, but you have to wait a while before you respond to it. Let it sift through before you respond immediately to it. If you responded immediately to everything this person and that person said, when it's all over you might realize you changed this, but if half the people really liked it, why did you change it?

I do think that we really liked working in this way. We did actually about nine shows in this way. We also had workshops on how to develop material using improvisation as a tool, not as an end in itself. It was very fulfilling. It's also exhausting and time-consuming.

HOW TO HANDLE YOUR FIRST REVIEWS
First reviews may seem monumental, but they're really not.

Sure, they make you beam when they're good and they make you hurt when they're bad. Or they do neither, because you've decided you're not going to read them at all, ever.

Not reading reviews displays your immaturity. You ain't foolin' nobody, baby. If you knew for certain those reviews were amazing, you'd have them memorized in two seconds flat. By declaring you are above reviews, you reveal just how much they matter to you.

Also, refusing to read reviews doesn't do your company any good. You need to learn what the consensus is about your company in order to use that information to make changes you agree are necessary, or to be in touch with your community. Reviews also display perception of your company, at least according to the critics who author them. Any and all information and opinion, both good and bad, that you can gather benefits your company's forward propulsion in one way or another.

Most companies' initial openings don't attract Ben Brantley or John Simon, by the way. So if a hugely respected and powerful critic isn't sitting front-row center, his or her dissenting opinion can't really affect your opening night. Small press or TV reviewers can't destroy you, no matter how much you worry about this. The power balance just isn't the same. Your show is also not so huge a positive or negative force yet that it's begging to be knocked down a peg by a reviewer, something that definitely can happen in a heavily promoted commercial situation, like Broadway.

If you get a bad review, take it with a grain of salt. Very few companies don't get at least one right off the bat. Don't feel like you have to take the reviewer's suggestions about your production if you don't agree with them. Don't feel this person hates you on a personal level. Just take it in and file it away.

Many first shows get mixed reviews—in fact, that tends to be the norm. If it happens to you, once again, see what you can learn from it, then move on.

Is there ever a case where a first production gets a phenomenal review from a major respected source and it makes a big impact on a new company? Sure, it happens from time to time. David Zak recalls how his company made a big splash their first time out: "The first show was very intense and very gratifying. Lots of politics going on as the 'pecking order' was established. The *Chicago Tribune* review was excellent, so audiences really came in and things went well." Fabulous! If something similar happens to you, savor it. If not—don't worry. There's always next time.

LET EVERYONE HAVE A SAY

Needless to say, you must also pay attention to audience feedback and, when and if you get one, your board's opinions, which are often a spot-on indicator of community reaction. Michael Gennaro (Steppenwolf) explains:

One element that's been crucial to this place, and is the downfall of many places, is the integration and the embrace of the board. There's been evolution of the board over the various stages of this company. There've been very key decisions as to who the chairperson is, and what they bring to the table at the moment in the time that the company needs. Whether it's a visionary, whether it's a fund-raiser, whether it's a strategic person, whatever it is, there've been very clear choices made along those lines. That is something you have to stay in touch with.

[Our board members] are constantly being called upon for their expertise, and their advice. That just makes things so much easier when you're going out and raising money.

Let me tell you, the day after an opening, you hear from a lot of people about what they thought of the play. It's very satisfying when they call you and say, "I've got some criticism of the play, but acting—first rate. Production values—first rate. Now here's my problem with the play." That's OK.

And/or the amount of people who call passionately upset about a play—that's OK, too. I can't stress enough for anybody starting out how as you're building a company you've got to really pay attention to your board. They're an equal partner. Really important is the chair. You've got to have a leader. There are leaders in the ensemble, people who bring up important issues when they're important, there are people who sit back. There are people who constantly drive the company, Gary Sinise being a perfect example. You're not always going to agree with those people, but you've got to have them.

THE MOMENT OF MAKING IT

Chicago City Limits had this epiphany not simply within its circle of friends, but during its early performances. It became clear the group was on to something major. Paul Zuckerman recalls,

> Success creates challenges. In this milieu of the clubs, all of a sudden we were getting a little bit of an audience. People were coming to see us on a Thursday night. There's a magical time for any theater company where you break from your friends and people you know coming to the general public hearing about you and coming.
>
> If you think of all of these groups, as Chicago City Limits did, which split, then form, then split, then form, there will become a kind of critical mass of people who know, "Oh, they're getting together with these people, and it should be an interesting show." That's how our audience started to happen. We had a couple of regular nights, did some late-night radio, things just to get on the radar. And there was an audience! On Thursday night, you go into the club and you're looking

around and you say, "Gee, I don't know these people—it's cool that they came!" It sort of surprises you.

That, to me, is a real leap, and that's the real obstacle that most theater companies run into. How do you get there? I was reading two interesting biographies, one on Elvis and one on Bob Dylan. Both of them had skyrocketing transitions. Elvis basically went from knowing two songs and performing one of them in public to, six months later, being the biggest star in the country—unbelievable. I guess that fuse ignites faster and spreads wilder and quicker in some instances.

Our theater didn't explode quite like that, but it was a pretty good firecracker. It's a funny thing. There's an old phrase I've heard, "If you're green, you're growing—if you're ripe, you rot." They talk about that in terms of sports teams, too—the hungry team wins. I think there's something to that. In our period of acceleration, when people really started to come to see us, it was also a period of great artistic explosion for us. Here we are now, feeling pretty good about ourselves, feeling artistically very competent, able to really work a crowd. There is no substitute for stage time. Certainly in comedy, but I suspect in every form of live theater, the show you do after 2,000 shows is better than the show you do after a hundred shows.

SEEK A FEW MORE HELPING HANDS

A point of success is also the best time to build up your human resources from the outside. An audience base, of course, is key to start working on in earnest. Assembling a board can be very shrewd as well. Plus, don't discount this as the ideal opportunity to attract some new and interesting talent with your newly minted reputation.

Mitzi Sales gives insight as to how Berkeley Rep mined similar resources once its first flush of success was evident.

It was like, "You know something? We think we can really make this go." So what does that mean? What that means is, finding a board of trustees that is going to help us become a community institution, help us make money, help us make plans. I find it interesting that I stayed for eighteen years, and I often tell people that one of the reasons that it was possible to do that was, every four years, the theater went through a very big transition.

From 1972, really, to 1976, we were scrambling. The company was building. The artistic output was becoming more and more consistent. We attracted some really good actors, a wonderful associate director. People who came through, who were teaching at the university but who also would direct a play at Berkeley Rep, who would act in a play, who would design a set, really gifted directors, designers, and actors. There was an interesting little talent pool that perhaps other theaters wouldn't have had at a critical point.

We were certainly not paying competitive salaries at that point so were relying on that talent pool to help us grow, help us stabilize.

USE THESE KEY INDICATORS TO PLOT YOUR SUCCESS

When all is said and done, there are three specific components that separate the men from the boys in terms of meeting your goals. If you can ace each of these requirements by claiming them as your own, you're doing great. We owe these components, by definition, to Sheldon Epps, who has achieved all of them throughout his distinguished career. Epps says:

> Three things. One is box office success. Crass as that may be, you've got to pay attention to that. When Pasadena Playhouse did very, very difficult, very challenging plays like *The Real Thing* and *Side Man*, they were tremendously successful at the box office.
>
> Two: critical success. Not only writers saying, "This is the kind of play that can make this theater exciting again," but also, "They're doing this kind of play extremely well."
>
> Three: recognition within the artistic community. That there are people—writers, agents, directors, actors—who come to say, "I've heard about what you're doing. It sounds very exciting. I'd like to come and do a play at your theater," or "I'd like my client's play to be done at your theater"—it's a clear indicator that you're once again considered at the top of the heap.
>
> What the effect of that is, because of that respect and recognition, we get the opportunity to produce plays here that we might not have gotten the rights to several years ago.

As can you—if you strive to keep building upon your success.

Mutt
A coproduction between Ferocious Lotus Theatre Company and Impact Theatre in Berkeley, CA
Photo by Cheshire Isaacs

Chapter Seven
Building Word of Mouth

Once your company has established itself, spreading the message about the great work you're presenting becomes one of your next objectives. It's an objective you've got to take pretty seriously, too, for a couple of reasons.

One that's pretty obvious is for the sake of expansion. The more people who know about you, the more people might come to see your show. Thus, your work will be viewed and appreciated by a larger audience base, you'll build a subscription base, and soon you'll be rivaling the Super Bowl for attendance and media coverage. OK, maybe that's stretching things a bit.

Second: for the sake of maintenance. If you start building effective word of mouth within the immediate vicinity of your community, you lend your company an air of stability, whether your company is completely stable yet or not. People tend to respect by osmosis. If your company is mentioned constantly in the local paper, on the radio, or on television, or postered all over town, your friends, neighbors, and local residents you don't know will start to see your group as a new bedrock of the community. They'll sanction your integration by attending your productions, and perhaps one day donating money and populating your board.

In this chapter, our experts will help us make sense of how to best get the word out.

We'll cover the topic from a variety of angles. For example, how did esteemed companies gain momentum in terms of not simply audience attendance, but also critical responses and interest in collaboration from new theater artists? How did marketing strategies change once a company felt the first flush of success? How has networking played a role in that success?

SPREAD THE JOY

The best advertising is really just spreading excitement.

Not a novel concept. But in the case of a fairly new theater company, an organization that doesn't have a lot of cash to blow on marketing itself does have a very valuable tool to use that costs absolutely nothing: enthusiasm.

If you really want to share the thrill of your company's work with others, say so! It's that simple. How do you do this without appearing insufferable and obnoxious? Smile—and remember what it was like to be ten years old, and starring in your fifth-grade play. You were excited and everybody thought you were adorable. I'm not saying you should regress to a childlike state of drooling wonder—believe me, that's not an effective marketing strategy any day of the week. Just recapture the purity of your excitement. When you are truly thrilled about something and express that honestly, your attitude is totally contagious. People want to check out what you're so whipped up about, because if it makes you happy, it could very possibly make them happy, too.

Always promote what you genuinely believe in. Don't try to pull the wool over anybody's eyes—you really can't. If you can successfully fake enthusiasm for a production that stinks and you do, indeed, trick folks into coming to see it, they won't like what you dragged them into. Then they'll either resent being suckered or they'll doubt your artistic aptitude in the future. Neither of these scenarios would do your company much good.

If your enthusiasm for a project isn't genuine, better to keep your trap shut.

MAKE YOUR OWN PUBLICITY

So you're awash in genuine enthusiasm about what your company has to offer and ready to shout this from the rooftops.

Well, shouting from the rooftops is pretty cheap publicity, but then again, using your phone, fax, and email is more effective and doesn't have to be all that expensive, either. So, get organized and make a master list of critics, media sources, and free advertising resources. Free stuff first, before you pay for any expensive advertising. Sometimes a quality reviewer can make your name at this stage better than a giant billboard overlooking Times Square ever could. Paul Zuckerman says, "In Manhattan, Chicago City Limits built primarily on word of mouth. There were some struggles in the early days, but we'd get reviews—the credibility of a positive review in the *New York Times* or the *Daily News* greatly outweighs an ad. Your audience enjoying your show is the best form of advertising."

ACE YOUR IMAGE

Before you start sending out the word about your company, though, you need to determine one highly important criterion—exactly what image is your company projecting to potential patrons? The easiest way to divine this isn't to go back over your mission statement or fondly recall all the plays, playwrights, and performers that influenced your artistic sensibility. Instead, take a good, hard look at the material that makes up your first season. The pieces you choose convey the ultimate clear message about your company to your audience.

Introducing controversial works into a community that is perhaps comfortable with a more conservative artistic menu is arguably the biggest risk of doing well-known work for a brand-new theater company. This is not to say you should censor yourself, ever. It's simply vital to recognize that a hot-button show may incur a hot-button reaction, which could be costly to your box office and long-term prospects for success.

As you'll recall that we discussed earlier, it's crucial to introduce yourself into the fabric of your community in order to build support for your company as early as you can. Another important reason to do this, naturally, is to check out the community demographic. If you've lived in one town your entire life, no doubt you understand this demographic already. You've probably already determined whether a production replete with nude scenes could fly with the locals. (Helpful hint: your gut instinct, in that case, is the right instinct, so put the hippies on hold if you live in a town with a large senior citizen population.)

Setting out to shock for the sake of shock value is a pretty misguided notion. You won't make any money, people will freak out, and your company will get a bad rep before it gets out of the blocks. So don't be perverse. However, there is absolutely nothing wrong with trying to expand the creative horizons of the folks you dwell amongst.

Although the Pasadena Playhouse was an established company for decades, Sheldon Epps faced a debut company's dilemma when he assumed the Playhouse's leadership. He wanted to rejuvenate the theater on a number of levels, opening it up to new audiences. Using well-known works and a diverse sensibility were two strong components in his initial plan of action. Epps recalls,

> I think there were a couple of things to accomplish. As there had been no artistic director, one was true quality control. I made it my job just to really focus on the quality of the art on the stage. That's a job, frankly, that's not terribly difficult. Primarily, what it meant was taking advantage of what I feel is a terribly rich artistic community. The migration of actors, directors, designers, people who have come out here to work in television and film, whose passion and roots are still in the

103

theater, is just enormous. So I just wanted to make the plays attractive both to people I've worked with and people whose work I've admired, who now live out here and I know to be top of the line, and to choose projects that will attract those people, and make them feel, if not well compensated, at least cherished as artists.

The other important thing to me was more diversity in programming. Obviously, because I am African American, that meant doing projects that would appeal to audiences of color. It also meant focusing a little bit more on material that was going to attract young audiences.

The very first play I did here as artistic director was Tom Stoppard's *The Real Thing*. Not only was that material that's a little bit more challenging, in terms of the dramaturgy itself and Stoppard's intellectualism and dazzling wit, it's also a play that's about contemporary relationships. I wanted to do that play because I wanted to attract younger audiences to the theater.

Following that, in the very same season, was the play *The Old Settler*; I believe that was the first play written by an African American writer that this theater had produced in something like twenty-five or thirty years. The following season, doing my show *Play On*, obviously those two shows were specifically targeted to African American audiences with the knowledge that they were also going to be tremendously appealing to the existing subscription audience. Both of those things turned out to be true.

Despite the fact that there was some rumor in the theater's history that the audiences were going to abandon the theater if there was too much work by artists of color, both of those proved to be among the most successful productions that the theater's done. I think it was important to not be afraid to make that statement early in my tenure here and, fortunately, to have success with those productions was enormously encouraging.

THE POWER OF A STRONG REVIEW

In the previous chapter, we went over initial reviews and how they probably will not make or break you, even if they're truly heinous.

As your company progresses, though, the impact of reviews begins to weigh far more heavily. A negative review at the very beginning of your company's visibility is not the end of the world, but if you keep racking up piles of stinking notices, they will start to define you in terms of public opinion. People will ignore you at best and will ridicule you openly at worst. You don't need that.

Still, you do need to get reviewed to earn credibility within your community and also artistically. It all goes back to putting your best foot forward, creatively. At this stage in your company's development, if you read a number of reviews that point out an identical fault, it might be a good idea to take a look at this sticking point in your work, and fix it. This is not going back on your resolve to do what you feel is right creatively, above all other opinion. It's simply smart business practice to fix any product you are offering the public that you find might be defective.

The power of a strong review by a major reviewer is, of course, worth its weight in gold. How do you get a noted reviewer to check out your show? Be persistent. Now, persistence does not translate in any way, shape, or form into stalking, so no night-vision goggles or boiled bunnies, please. Persistence in this case refers to polite follow-up.

Send written correspondence to a reviewer first, briefly introducing your company and describing the production that you're inviting this person to in a fax or email. Send that off, then wait a reasonable amount of time for a response. If you don't receive one after a week or so, a courteous follow-up by telephone is acceptable.

If you get a mixed review from a well-known critic, don't despair. You've still hit the jackpot, promotionally. If you're savvy, you'll choose the best, most complimentary sections of the review—usually it's best to pull out the strongest sentence or two—and put it on your poster and in the body of any and all ad copy you're running. Plaster it into your program. Send it out in all future promotional brochures and literature.

If you happen to get a glowing review from a famous critic, your life is about to change, and how! This is exactly what put Steppenwolf on the map. Michael Gennaro says: "I think the thing that kind of set them off was Richard Christiansen, who's the main reviewer for the *Chicago Tribune* here, went up to see them. He said he was never so exhilarated and frightened at the same time in his life by a performance. They were literally just experimenting, and taking everything as far as they could take it."

BUILD YOUR BASE

Start compiling a permanent mailing list. Such a demographic tool is invaluable. You can send folks promotional material as frequently as you'd like and hopefully spark their interest in your future productions. When your company is ready to start selling season subscriptions, you have a ready-made resource of people who might like to buy.

How do you compile the rudiments of such a base? At the performances of your very first production, insert a contact form in your program asking for names, addresses, phone numbers, and email addresses. In addition to the names you collect directly, round up all of the contact info for anyone you've had positive contact with thus far—this ranges from all of those community movers and shakers you may have invited to an initial fund-raiser, your favorite local radio deejay who gave you a free plug on his top-forty broadcast, the merchants you buy supplies from in your neighborhood, your family and friends. Everyone you can think of.

All of this information ends up in a master mailing list. Alphabetize it and forward a copy to everyone within your organization. Let everyone know that you'd like them to add as many names to the list as they possibly can. Update the list again. Do this as many times as necessary to keep the number of names on your list as high as possible and, in addition, current.

Good-quality presentations are a wonderful way, indeed, to build your mailing list. So is good, quality face time. If people like you personally, they're more likely to want to become involved in your theatrical enterprises. David Zak (Bailiwick) explains: "Our mailing list started with all of our school chums, teachers, people we worked for. For a while I was delivering plants and put everyone I delivered to on the mailing list. In fact, our donor base—probably at least a third of it—consists of people I met either at school or through that first job. Sometimes people have never attended a show here but liked me and keep making donations."

THE FUNDER FACTOR

It's also a good idea, once you've got a few solid shows under your belt, some reviews to trumpet, and an emerging audience base, to up your efforts at attracting funders.

Separate from applying for grants, you might want to consider organizing another fund-raiser, if you've already held one prior to your first opening. If not, throw your first. Invite corporate representatives and local philanthropists to an evening at your space, complete with a full performance. (See chapter 3 for more on fund-raiser specifics.)

No funder gets into the financial end of the business solely to champion great art. This doesn't mean a great many don't care to back good work— lots genuinely wish to associate themselves with quality, thank God. From a funder's perspective, though, quality needs to be commercial. Put yourself in the funder's shoes. What's the upside to pouring dollars into a show that six people are going to want to see? Funders are interested in material that smacks of wide appeal.

They also have a frequent aversion to controversy. After all, a local funder isn't going to want to risk his neck by getting behind a show that contains material sure to raise the ire of the community that supports his company. This is why funders often pass on the spice and embrace the vanilla.

Figuring out your potential funders' sensibilities, then, can be a helpful step in building relationships with them, which in turn might build your company. Listening to funders' feedback is the smartest forward move that you could make. You don't have to agree and implement these changes, but if they make sense to you, why not give them a whirl? It also wouldn't hurt, if you do think the advice some big cheese is handing you might have merit, to ask this cheese whether he or she would be willing to come back and see the show again, once you've tried his suggestions.

You owe a funder your best creative efforts, at all times. You owe a funder courtesy—take this person's calls. You also never want to waste a funder's time or the money this person is donating to your cause. You want always to respect the reputation of any business or corporation who puts their resources behind you.

THE NEXT LEVEL

Hard work and good planning pay off.

Once you recognize the telltale signs that your organization is expanding, you need to start thinking in terms of your next step. What are your goals, longer term? How will you best achieve them? What resources are available to help you get what you want to further help your company?

Mitzi Sales (Berkeley Rep) knew how to take stock of her company at just the right time and take it toward the next level.

The first four years I was there, it was scramble, scramble, scramble. Then, in 1976, we realized, "Now we get it. We've managed to build up an audience, we're attracting some donors and in order to keep going, we really need a larger space." Financially, it doesn't work, 153 seats doesn't work, we needed a larger space, we needed a larger audience, which is potentially more subscribers who become donors. You build people up.

In order to get a new space, we needed a board of trustees. We needed people who were committed to this particular theater to help us build this community institution. Until that time, the board of directors on the nonprofit organization papers were Michael, me, and Doug Johnson, and I think an attorney friend of Michael's was also on the articles of incorporation. It wasn't the traditional board of trustees of a nonprofit organization.

So we looked around at our community, at our supporters, at our donors. When we started, of course, all of our board of trustees were in the neighborhood. Then it actually grew fairly rapidly after that, because you talk to people and then they know somebody else—"I know an attorney, I know a banker," whatever.

So we put together our board of trustees and rewrote our articles of incorporation and our bylaws. The period between 1976 and 1980 was the institutionalization. When we thought we needed a new theater space, all we really wanted to do was stay where we were and just figure out how to expand that space. Really stupid—it was not going to work strategically. That was an organic process of thinking, "OK, what do we do?"

Fortunately for us, the neighborhood association was alarmed at the idea that we would be expanding because it's a neighborhood—the parking situation! The traffic situation! They were not thrilled.

So we started having to think beyond this cozy, charming, comfortable neighborhood. We found a site in downtown Berkeley, near public transportation and a parking garage. We bought that space, raised the money to build a theater, and that was 1980.

NETWORKING KNOW-HOW

Every form of industry utilizes networking as a useful business strategy, and theater is no different. Theater, actually, is one of those professions that's partially built on hot air. If you've worked onstage or backstage in any capacity, you know all about the dominant role juicy gossip plays in keeping life interesting.

Beyond scurrilous talk, conversation that builds relationships has big value. Getting to know your community, for example, can lead to unanticipated good fortune on a regular basis. Susan Kosoff demonstrates how reaching out to all segments of your audience and supporters can build great word of mouth.

We did a lot of networking in the early years; we put a lot of stock into it, and still do. It's very time-consuming if it's done right, but it pays off in both the short-term and the long-term. It's especially beneficial for theaters like us, with a targeted audience and a limited advertising budget.

We certainly did reach out to the Wheelock College community, but it's a small school. One of the things that we did—we realized immediately that people didn't know where we were, so we decided to reach out to the alumni, because they had an allegiance to the college.

Because we had done theater for years together, we did have an audience that we could reach out to. We started building our mailing list very early on. We also hooked up with Arts Boston (a resource group) right away to get the word out. We reached out to the schools where Wheelock had student teachers and other kinds of placement, hospitals, social service agencies, that kind of thing. We used that whole network as well.

That was really our strategy in the beginning. It's something we have maintained, but we're not as dependent on it anymore. We were lucky—a man came from *The Christian Science Monitor* with his kids. He gave us a fabulous plug for our first show. We also got a nice piece in the *Boston Globe*. So those two PR things were extremely helpful in the very beginning.

Right after that, we got a very bad review in the *Boston Phoenix*. It really was devastating. This was incredibly cynical and sarcastic—the fact of the matter was they were totally wrong. I don't even mean about the show, I mean about their assumptions about who we were and what we were trying to do, like we were some kind of "Christian coalition"! But I don't think bad reviews hurt us. I think the fact that we were reviewed gave us legitimacy.

We weren't able to pay for much advertising, so we did things like posters, which we still do because that's how we reach the people we want to reach. We did mailings, hung posters in lots of different neighborhoods, relied on public service announcements and calendar announcements. We tried to take full advantage of all the free things.

By the second year, we just knew we had to advertise in the *Boston Globe* as well. We wanted to advertise in more neighborhoods. Maybe where other theaters wouldn't. At one point, there was a TV reviewer in Boston who loved us. When we were doing *The Miracle Worker* [the TV station] followed the girl who was playing Helen Keller at school and at rehearsal. We got a lot of different kinds of breaks like that, and we continually try to seek those people.

If you've lived in the environment yourself for any length of time, it's very important for you to weave your company into the fabric of this community you know so well. If you happen to be new to the community in which your company is located, enlist the natives to help your cause. It's probable that you have a number of people who've spent their whole lives in the community. Great! Instruct them to talk the theater up to as many locals as possible. Civic familiarity and pride can also really help your organization declare itself.

If you happen to live in a big city, though, you can effectively use a network of friends and business contacts to get your company known. Civic pride is a fact of life in big cities just as well as small towns, too, by the way. Just consider the groundswell of unity that New York City experienced post-9/11. It doesn't always take tragedy to make this phenomenon occur either—something good (like your work!) can bond and inspire as well.

Lyla White, formerly of the Pasadena Playhouse, shows us how it's done:

I'm a Pasadena person. This sounds like I'm bragging, but I know almost everybody in town. I know the members of the city council and the city staffs, and I know the

109

donors because I've worked in this town a long time. I've lived in this town. My children grew up here.

That combination worked well for us, particularly in what I did. I tried to raise the donated dollars, manage the ticket sales, and manage the ticket revenue. It worked really well.

UNUSUAL MARKETING MOVES

Thinking in an innovative way about your marketing concerns can benefit your company tremendously. Especially if you don't have a lot of cash to make mistakes with.

This might seem to be a bit of an oxymoron. After all, don't you need lots of cash to throw at your marketing strategies in order to be productive? It might seem impossible, but it can be done if you put your mind to it. Let Jack Reuler (Mixed Blood), who's proven himself to always be ahead of the curve, show you the way:

> One of the things we wanted to do, in our initial list of objectives and still today, is to attract a nontraditional audience. Part of what I've hoped to do throughout the years, with varying levels of success, is dilute the notion that live theater is an elitist, white art form. I continue to believe that [it's not].
>
> The first year, before there were child care laws, we took a piece of what used to be the hayloft in our space and provided child care to the people who came to the shows. We had the van that the Center for Community Action used. In the evening, we would go to centrally located low-income neighborhoods and offer transportation to the theater. I wish we still did it. It was a great idea.
>
> Our top ticket price was $2.50 and if you were on public assistance, it was $1. The people not only got free transportation to and from the theater, they paid a buck when they got there. I think we had a total marketing and publicity budget for that five-show or six-show summer season of $300. We made it work.
>
> The press has been very good to us. If they needed a sound bite about the arts community, I was always good for a quote. It was at a fairly young age, when I was the longest-standing artistic director in town at about thirty. A lot of people had left. Somehow, I was catapulted to be spokesperson for the theater community. I think that my ability to interact with the media was great for the organization.
>
> I would say that there should be a point person of an organization with whom the press, public, and audience members identify the institution. A visible, vocal leader. Some really good artists and artistic leaders just aren't media-savvy. Just be a representative and the one that people buy into.

GIVE YOURSELF CREDIT

If you don't sing your company's praises to the universe at large, who will? It's neither boastful nor offensive to let people know about your achievements and the fine entertainment you have to offer.

Major players in the theater game know the value of strong self-promotion and freely tout their company value. Here's Sheldon Epps, speaking about the value of self-promotion during his successful days at the Pasadena Playhouse:

> There was a lot of excitement just on the basis of the kind of programming we were announcing and the reception to that programming. But that doesn't do you a whole lot of good unless you blow your own horn, unless you get the word out there.
>
> So one of the things we concentrated on was to trumpet our success, certainly here in Los Angeles, but also on a national level. To go after stories in *Variety* and *American Theatre* magazine. Beyond just publicizing the plays, we really publicized the institution, saying, "This is not the place you thought it was. It's not the place it was six years ago. Attention must be paid!"
>
> I was very vocal about saying to the staff, "Let's not be shy about how good we're doing. Let's be aggressive about blowing our own horn, about displaying our pride in the work that we've done."

OFFER SOMETHING DIFFERENT

Now that you're feeling all bold and sassy, why not use your forthright promotional attitude to plug a few unique programming ideas? Special programs can be a great way to get the word out big about your company. Used imaginatively, offers, discounts, and special events often will prove to serve as a strong catalyst to build interest.

Do the unexpected—midnight shows, Sunday morning matinees, playwrights' forums, get-to-know-our-actors nights. Don't get cheesy, though. Serving beer, for instance, in a desperate attempt to attract local sports fans looking for something different is a highly misguided notion. Gimmicks appear gimmicky, for the most part. Hosting costume contests for which the audience members dress up as their favorite Shakespearean character borders on Dungeons & Dragons-esque. Even dance parties à la *Grease* on Broadway are tough to pull off on a smaller scale.

Try something classy, intellectually enriching, and respectful of your audience's needs and interests. Director/playwright Q&As, poetry readings that pertain to the theme of a production you're doing, a weekly cabaret, post-show discussion groups—anything that engages your audience's creative intellect and imagination will be received enthusiastically.

THE VALIDATION OF OTHER ARTISTS AND A DOSE OF REALITY

The Jewish Theatre San Francisco was paid the highest compliment a company can be paid: other theater artists wanted to collaborate with its members. This portends very well for the artistic effervesence of any company, in terms of infusing it with fresh talent.

Word of mouth is definitely working in your favor when your talent speaks so loudly that your peers validate it. Many actors, after all, are quite competitive with each other. In a case when all competition is overridden by admiration, you know you're doing something right.

Even when great future work with new colleagues is in the offing, though, things are never perfect. Even a respected reputation doesn't change certain realities of the business. Corey Fischer enjoyed the lauded position his company is in, but remained aware of day-to-day challenges. Says Fischer,

> We went to New York and there we really got the idea for our second piece. Soon after coming back from New York, at the end of that year, we began work on our second piece.
>
> We toured it, began touring larger venues, went back to New York, had a tremendous response there, and so it went. People have to understand, there we were, years later, by all accounts a successful experimental theater company. And yet, we still were constantly struggling.
>
> It's not an easy life. There's no job security. In a sense, we went year by year. Every year we again faced having to figure out how we're going to make the budget.

A STRONG REPUTATION CAN SUSTAIN YOU

Even though things can be difficult at times, it's amazing how long you can trade on a solid reputation. In order to maintain your edge, after you've gotten your theater's name around, remember: pay attention.

Stay objective. Take your community pulse as often as possible to make sure that your audience is being continually satisfied by the artistic output you are offering them. Even if you employ someone to do your marketing, stay on top of things yourself.

If you sense that your reputation for quality is starting to erode or that your patrons are unhappy with something, like a higher ticket price or seats that aren't comfy enough, take care of the problem. Susan Albert Loewenberg (LA Theatre Works) says,

> No matter how bad it is, you can never let yourself panic and be discouraged.

Figure out a solution. I'm a good crisis manager. I can figure a way. Sometimes there's no way out, but I think as you get older, you put things in perspective.

Every experience, either good or bad, teaches you and makes you stronger. Use your experience to keep striving and building your name even further. Keep soliciting audiences and critics. Seek out new funders. Present work of only the highest quality.

Don't rest on your laurels. Your reputation is your currency. Work hard to get the image you want, work hard to preserve it, and work even harder to further it.

God's Ear by Jenny Schwartz
directed by Erika Chong Shuch
Shotgun Players 2010 Season
Pictured: Keith Pinto, Beth Wilmurt (background) Melinda Meeng (foreground)
Photo by Pak Han

Chapter Eight
How Social Media Helped Us Succeed

The advent of social media arguably changed every business's potential for the better—theater companies included. By using web outlets properly as a tool, it suddenly became possible to get your organization's name, mission, and work out to millions. If done right, social media can help your company earn capital, sell tickets, and work as the perfect performance platform.

There are pitfalls, too, of course. Social media usage can really backfire on a company if you don't show yourself in the best light. Maybe you're networking with the wrong people. Maybe the work you and your associates are presenting looks less than professional. Maybe you aren't correctly targeting the outlets that could benefit you best, creatively and financially.

Really, it all comes down to knowing your company and its strengths like a book. Identifying what you do best, then showing everyone on the Internet how well you do it, is all it takes to succeed. Let's take an overview of the resources social media offers, then pare down the important points to keep in mind when establishing, cultivating, and maintaining the ideal web presence.

PICKING THE PERFECT PLATFORM

You're no doubt familiar with, and most likely an avid user of, a number of ubiquitous social media outlets that are excellent for sending out virtually any kind of message or media possible. Here's a basic primer of the web's most used sites for these purposes:

- **Facebook.** A Facebook page packed with your company's vital info, positive reviews, and up-to-the-minute breaking news can be an incredible boon to your company's promotional capacities.

- **Twitter.** The best way to speak to your community about the ideas and issues your company cares about—and a fast and easy way to promote a show.
- **YouTube.** The tried-and-true place to post promo clips, full performances, theatrical symposiums, and advertising material.
- **Instagram.** Creating beautiful visual images, either still or video, is easy here. You can get instant feedback on your work from your followers on the material you post.
- **Skype.** Chatting face-to-face with your companies' connections not only helps you spread the word about your work, it's a go-to for business meetings with collaborators and potential investors to boot.
- **Vine.** Used imaginatively, Vine is a great tool for capturing the attention of out-of-the-box audience members—say, tweens, teens, and twentysomethings. Create an intriguing clip from a play this sought-after demographic would be attracted to, send it out, and you're speaking a (potentially profitable) new language.
- **Periscope.** A live video stream that's perfect for broadcasting red carpets, studio performances, fund-raising events—the sky's the limit.
- **Snapchat.** More than a billion "snaps"—brief messages or screen images that self-destruct after usage—have gone out since Snapchat's inception. A great way to promote discounts—you send users a coupon code as they arrive at your box office that they can redeem immediately, for instance.

Whatever platform you think works best for your company, follow this golden rule: when using it, don't be cheesy. I think we're all familiar with "reality show–style" web posts—material in which the participants are a little too pleased with themselves, and way too phony. Talking "confessional style" directly to the camera is extremely grating to watch and cheapens the quality work you're trying so hard to get noticed. The best policy is just to be yourself and to communicate your enthusiasm for what your company is about in an authentic way. Don't try to be cute or clever. Don't post cloying backstage or rehearsal footage when you could be posting a moving monologue that would *really* impress people. Bells and whistles will never translate as well as the essence of your art.

EFFECTIVE PUBLICITY STRATEGIES

The strongest PR weapon any theater company can wield is a meticulously maintained website. Period. The end. So many companies start strong in this regard—their graphics, photos, and history pages look flawless. But then, after that initial rush of, "Oh, we look so cool!" fades, the reality of having to continually update the info on a company page starts to grind. How many times have you visited the site of a company you really like, only to find their new season offerings haven't even been posted? Once is really too often.

Think of your website as a twenty-four-hour-a-day business card. Anyone in the world—literally anyone—can look at it at any time (something I think most people forget about *everything* they post on the Internet). Imagine the theater artist you most admire—a great actor, say, a legend like Sir Ian McKellen, whom you'd kill to work alongside—checking out your website through a Google search. (Something like this could conceivably happen—top theater folks are a curious bunch, and smart enough to stay informed about all aspects of the business). Would you be proud of the content your idol would see? If not, time to do an inventory and clean things up. Update all your info, sweep out the photos, videos, and posts that paint you in a sloppy light, edit your company blog so it looks less like a rantfest and more like intelligent opinion. Make a professional impression—there's no excuse not to.

A professional approach also applies when you're advertising work through a press release, or on Facebook and Twitter. You want to keep your information clear, concise, and punchy. Don't include every great review your show has racked up—just pull the best line or two from your most prestigious or most glowing notice. Linking to a press photo? Make it a good one. It's remarkable how many blurry, badly shot images are put out as promotion, or how many production stills featuring wooden-looking actors make their way into theater PR. Always shoot for your best shot image-wise.

INTERACTIONS AND REACTIONS

The immediacy of being able to network with potential business partners, and/or communicate with your audience via social media, can be an incredible boon to your organization. It's important to strike the right balance, however. Here are some wise points to keep in mind whenever you engage a new contact online.

- **Research beforehand.** Prospective partners, either creative or financial, should be checked out before you reply to that direct message. Most people are very trusting; of course, you're flattered if you get contacted out of the blue by a stranger about how much they'd like to work with you. Keep your head, though, and Google this contact thoroughly. You must objectively evaluate whether communicating with them would be helpful or a waste of your time.
- **Say less, listen more.** Ask any prospective work contact to tell you in detail about their experience, accomplishments, and ideas before you share your own. In a live conversation, letting the other guy talk without interjecting is a very wise and powerful evaluation method—it works just as effectively in the virtual world.
- **Don't agree to business points in an email unless you know your collaborator.** Keep your tone indefinite—what you put in writing could commit you if you're not careful.

117

Your audience can be a wonderful barometer for how well your company is doing, via comments on your pages, too. How seriously should you take their opinions? Well, that's up to you. Obviously, you can't be thin-skinned if a troll slams you just because it's fun. Constructive criticism, though, should always be evaluated, if you see it's well intended. You don't under any circumstances have to agree with it or implement it—your artistic choices are yours, period—but don't dismiss a solid point that you *do* think could help your work improve. And of course, it goes without saying that complaints about your company's service should be dealt with immediately—the customer, from a patronage perspective, is always right, so don't hesitate to respond to any business question or concern.

And then there are your actors and other company members—no doubt a good number of them have their own personal social media networks. Let everyone know you expect them to only interact positively with patrons, and ask them to spread positive word about the work your company is doing.

SOCIAL MEDIA AS MATERIAL

A new and exciting trend among many companies is incorporating social media into an actual production.

Maybe you can start a description of a character on Twitter, and ask followers to add another aspect to that description in 140 characters or less. Maybe you can ask audience members to view a portion of your new play, and vote on how the scene should end. The possibilities and ideas are endless.

Your set designers can also use social media as part of a stage tableau—screens filled with live feeds, audience participation via their phones incorporated on a backdrop, Instagram images blown up as movable pieces. Read the Success Story at the end of this chapter as a primer on how to do this right, then start coming up with your own concepts.

CREATING MORE CAPITAL

When it comes to raising money, gaining investors, and attracting sponsors, social media can be very useful indeed. The key is, of course, to make sure you're dealing with reputable sources as you navigate the financial waters. Here are three web entities that have produced success for nonprofits:

- **Chip In.** A donation-seeking site that operates similarly to GoFundMe. You access crowdsourcing dollars by presenting your company/project in detail to potential benefactors.
- **Social Vibe.** Corporate sponsors evaluate your proposed work/company. If they like what they see, sponsors will then donate capital to you, in exchange for receiving ad space on your social networks.

- **Convio.** This site offers nonprofits the chance to utilize integrated marketing programs to improve their fund-raising profiles, and connect to more funders through their web presence.

In addition, PayPal access can be a very useful financial tool, when it comes to processing payments and ticket sales and making other transactions. Robert Serrell, the financially savvy executive director of the Barrow Group, saw the possibilities connected to PayPal and maximized them. Serrell explains,

> The company had experienced some financial difficulty around 2010; I felt that since the art Seth and Lee were inspiring and producing was so beautiful, we needed to be getting all of that programming up on the website, so people everywhere could know about it.
>
> Through a consistent process, we were able to work out a payment system for the website through PayPal, which then allowed us to get more databases. People lined up to sign up for this information.
>
> I think, too, growth financially stems from diversifying our programming. We identify diverse revenue streams, from core programming and beyond.

That's always crucial: identifying any opportunities, be it through social media or elsewhere, that allow your company to grow and your message to expand. Be a forward-thinker; take the good points social media offers you today, and keep up with technical innovation, so your company keeps its all-important cutting-edge.

SUCCESS STORY—NEW PARADISE LABORATORIES, PHILADELPHIA, PA

The true definition of a cutting-edge, multimedia company, New Paradise Laboratories was founded in 1996 by Whit MacLaughlin, who wanted to create a movement-based performance troupe with a difference. NPL incorporates social media directly into the production of its experimental works by using Facebook, Skype, YouTube, SoundCloud, Flickr, and other Internet outlet resources in innovative ways. For example, audiences can use social media to "meet" characters in upcoming shows, and often can actually interact with NPL playmakers to influence the development of these characters, and new works themselves, through social media posts and chats. Furthermore, NPL performers work through every social media platform imaginable to create shows and choreography 24/7, making their work as immediate and time-efficient as possible. The company's approach is widely praised, and its work has been enthusiastically received at festivals such as Humana; I think NPL is an incredible business and creative model that will be extremely influential to readers who want to utilize social media effectively and imaginatively.

119

Hamlet by William Shakespeare
directed by Mark Jackson
Produced by Shotgun Players 2016
Pictured: Cathleen Riddley, El Beh
Photo by Pak Han

Chapter Nine
The Biggest Problem We Ever Faced

Usually, once a theater company achieves some measure of progress, a gigantic, disturbing, hulking crisis will rear its ugly head at the worst possible moment.

Sometimes, in retrospect, such a crisis doesn't turn out to be so terrible after all. I directed a musical in Boston many years ago. One Friday night performance, the house was packed, the cast was hot, the show was playing the best it ever had—and then the power went out. No lights. No juice to power equipment. Nothing.

I must admit that I freaked out in those first, dark moments (dark meant in both its literal and figurative definitions), but cooler heads quickly prevailed. The audience was digging the show so much, they volunteered to go out to their cars and get flashlights. Our stage manager ran to a nearby deli and bought batteries. A friend of mine in the audience happened to have a battery-operated keyboard in the trunk of his car that the show's music could be played on. Mind-bendingly, the audience trained their flashlights on the cast in unison, and the show indeed went on.

Needless to say, that was one of the greatest nights of theater I've ever been privileged to be a part of—and it started out looking like a complete and total disaster. Lots of theaters have weathered similar crises that appear large-looming at first, but thankfully can be taken care of effectively.

Other times, problems are more complicated. If you don't handle them the right way, they can spell the end for your company, worst-case scenario. To a less severe degree, they can cost you time, money, and energy, three important things you can't have enough of when you're maintaining a theater company.

In this chapter, our experts will discuss the biggest problems their companies have faced and how they coped. Their big issues span a very wide gamut, but the common lesson we can learn from the experiences they relate is this: every problem ultimately has a solution. Sometimes the solution is one you're delighted with; sometimes it's not the end result you want at all; and sometimes you end up with mixed results. But everything does indeed pass. If you throw your smarts and strengths—both as a businessperson and as a human being—at a hairy problem full tilt, it can pass a lot faster.

Some of the problems our experts have faced were quite concrete while others presented themselves in a more abstract form, but all were tough. I'd also like to give our subjects extra thanks for their honesty in sharing these problems in the first place. It's easy to talk about good times, but not a lot of laughs to go back over the bad stuff.

TALENT IN TRANSITION

No company can stay together in its entirety forever. Theater is a transitory business in general and there are always opportunities for talented people popping up.

Actors, as a general rule, relish the chance to play as many different parts as they can—that's one of the big reasons most choose their profession in the first place. Sometimes, actors will become very successful in one role, or break out from a company in terms of reviews, and the heavens will rain offers down upon them.

Other times, personal issues—such as the desire to change one's life in some major way—lead to a job departure. Hopefully, one company member at a time elects to leave, but there are scenarios in which you can lose two or more company or cast members at once. This can throw your organization into unexpected turmoil.

Beyond the obvious recasting hassle, keeping your creative purity can be tricky, as new blood can change its dynamic. It can also be painful when friends and coworkers you've loved working with leave. You may develop some serious nostalgia for the way your company was—until the day your new people deliver you some magic. Paul Zuckerman reflects back on the ramifications of personnel problems Chicago City Limits has had to deal with.

> One of the biggest was, there was a point at which the original cast left. It started when one actress decided to have a child, another got an opportunity in California, so from 1985 to 1988, the cast turned over. I think the biggest challenge was going from individuals—because in some sense, the five of us were Chicago City Limits—to making it an organization.
>
> You have fundamentally different orientations among the participants. The first group was the fundamentalists, the religious zealots, the crazy ones ready

to die for the cause. The second group consisted of people who are in love with improvisation—and that's always been the bottom line. If they don't love it, I don't want 'em because they're not going to want to be here. But they also don't have the emotional commitment and connection that the original people did. That was the challenge, to develop a company out of that.

It's not an all-or-nothing thing. To this day, it continues to be a constant battle as people evolve, as society evolves. Yes, when you have that new cast and that new work, all you can think about is how good it used to be and how do you get them there. Then one day you're sitting there saying, "This is a great show." That's where it is. I don't know if it's a one-day thing, or if you just kind of reflect on it at some point.

THE ISSUE OF DEBT

Very few theater companies operate without some level of debt. It's quite hard not to fall into that trap. If you've got a good managing director making sensible decisions, plus you yourself stay on top of your company's finances, your debt load will probably be on the lighter side.

It can be very rough, however, if you've inherited the problem of debt from somebody else. Say your managing director suddenly leaves the company and you check out the books and find a mountain of unpaid bills you thought had been taken care of.

Terrence Dwyer walked into a debt problem at La Jolla Playhouse but pulled the company out in better shape than ever, thanks to some crafty planning.

In 1992, I got a call from the search committee. Des had put my name in for the job. I walked in knowing the theater's great artistic reputation, and that the organization had the finest artistic director in the country.

Once I got to work here, I discovered that basically the organization had accumulated a debt of about $1.8 million by the end of the 1992 season. It was a very, very difficult circumstance. There were huge cash flow problems.

The debt was eliminated in 1997. The easiest challenge in doing that was budget-watching. But to come out on the other end in strong shape, we needed to fix long-range planning problems so we'd reach that outcome of no accumulated debt. So we began a capital campaign.

When you have solved debt, as we did through this campaign, your credibility improves. This affects how well you do with fund-raising and your marketing is affected positively, because you can more effectively plan it.

Artistic directors can feel particularly at sea when faced with the challenge of grabbing hold of any financial problem, but your smartest move is to get

123

involved from day one. Don't be intimidated at the prospect of keeping track of money coming in and going out. Don't pretend you are so busy changing the face of dramatic art as we know it that you simply can't be bothered hearing about cash flow difficulties.

If you act like you're above caring about money, people will believe you and they won't tell you what's going on within your own organization. If you bite peoples' head off when they try to approach you bearing unpleasant financial news, they'll avoid you in the future. As a result, a hornet's nest of money problems can quickly accumulate. My mom always told me to face the truth about a problem head-on. If you know the true circumstances of a situation, no matter how dire things are, you've got a fighting chance to solve it. But if you duck the reality of a difficult situation, you'll never be able to see what you're dealing with clearly, and then you're sunk.

Rick Lombardo (New Repertory) concurs with this sage advice:

> I think the most difficult time was the first year after I came here. We had an operating deficit. We had lost a significant amount of cash, and things were difficult for a time.
>
> I think an artistic director needs to think like a producer about the financial aspects of his or her company. I solved the problem by doing that. One of my greatest achievements has been that ever since then, every season has had a surplus. Running a small to midsize theater company means you have to jump on every angle of a problem and seize every opportunity, short-term, long-term, operating by the seat of your pants. There's always extra pressure.

GOOD-BYE TO A FRIEND

The personal relationships that develop between the people in any theater company become quite intense. You forge a very close bond with your partners in crime—you laugh with them, cry with them, and ride on the same extreme emotional roller coaster of exciting performances, financial terrors, and one-of-a-kind magic moments.

The pain of having to let go of someone you've been through so much with is indescribable. Sometimes, though, it just has to be done. Michael Leibert, the dazzlingly brilliant founding force behind Berkeley Repertory, struggled with the problem of addiction. In the early '80s, he tried mightily to regain his health, and Mitzi Sales, in addition to the rest of the Berkeley Rep family, tried to support him.

Says Mitzi:

> Michael was getting sicker and sicker, and it was very hard.

Basically, he was put on disability, an opportunity [for him] to go get well. We had an acting artistic director, a member of the acting company. There was a hope that Michael could enter a program and could come back. That wasn't possible.

One of the strengths of the company throughout those early years was the core acting company. As Michael was declining, the acting company and directors were actually making a lot of the artistic choices. So it was interesting that during a particularly difficult time, artistically, the theater was continuing. It wasn't a marvelous high point, but there were some high points during that time, as fate would have it.

But it was a period of time of stopping and needing to regroup, having then made the decision to find a new artistic director, creating a search committee of the board of trustees, and hiring someone to manage that process. Hiring an outside professional to help us find an artistic director.

I agreed to serve on the artistic search committee, but I said I'd never vote because I felt like it needed to be the board of trustees' decision. They needed to utterly support whomever they chose. I had a very, very good, very close relationship with the board of trustees, and I didn't want my personal opinion to color who they might choose. I felt the artistic director needed their complete support. Very, very difficult time.

I sort of helped the process, and we got down to the final three candidates. They made the final decision and hired Sharon Ott, which was a terrific decision.

Basically, the hardest challenge was the final realization that Michael was not going to be able to come back to who he was.

Susan Medak continues the story, touching on the stress this situation put on the organization from a business perspective.

Michael's problems were a real issue. He drank. During those years, the company had a solid, respected reputation but was not at the forefront, as ambitious companies in the Bay area were, companies like the Magic Theatre, ACT, plus upstarts. Berkeley Rep was user-friendly theater, tangible theater, not theater on a pedestal, which was great, but in the late '70s, the company members began to aspire to expand.

With the help of the city of Berkeley, we planned a move to a space on Addison Street. This was a $3 million space with a shop, offices, a rehearsal hall, a deep-thrust stage. So here we could go from the audiences practically on top of the actors, from having very little scene shop space, very little costume shop space, from having to move empty seats to having a large audience. It was thrilling and terrifying to expand to a second theater like this, profoundly impactful.

Some people would say, "We loved the days where you could smell the actors!" because they were so close to the audience! Michael had personalized the theater by standing among the crowd during performances, talking to them after the show, putting faces to the subscribers. We still talk to them all the time, by the way; people can't love an institution if it treats them impersonally.

And we made a lot of room for opinion within the company. Many people felt we should conduct our growth with the artistic director, that it should not be solely them, what they think. But Michael's personality, although a very charismatic personality, made the decision to expand very difficult because of his alcohol problem.

Michael was fired by the board of directors in 1983. That creates insecurity within an institution, when a board of directors fires the leadership. But also, hiring and firing can galvanize an organization.

Sadly, Michael died three years after he was fired.

WHEN YOU COME TO THE END OF A ROAD

It can be very hard to know when it's time to change your focus and priorities within the scope of your company, for a number of reasons.

You may not see certain warning signs coming. Economic conditions may change and make the kind of production you want to do impractical. Perhaps you can't afford to do *The Coast of Utopia* during a recession, for example. If you didn't see the recession coming and you've already started work on such an epic work that you've already committed to, that investment could very well be money down the drain.

Another possibility: even if your company proves to be successful and long-lasting, as times change around you, you may find that the company has to change in order to continue to exist. This could mean that you have to update the original founder's "old-school" approach to the business.

Theater veteran David Fuller recalls how he elected to revamp Jean Cocteau Repertory in its later years:

I think it was in the twenty-ninth season—[there was a sense that] you could either move forward or go backward—I don't think you *can* stay the same; if you try to, I think you go backward. So, changing the thinking of an institution that's thirty years old is a big endeavor. I likened it to, if you're an ocean liner going in one direction, if you want to go to the left, you don't immediately make that turn. It takes a while to make that turn.

It pays to take your organization's internal temperature before making any sort of fundamental change or shift. Ask your colleagues for their thoughts;

be brutally honest with yourself as to whether conditions on the horizon make adjustments essential. Don't feel you have to act swiftly if you're not facing an emergency (financial or otherwise)—but don't sit tight too long, either. Slowly implement positive, progressive differences—that way, if they don't work, it won't be a huge hassle to undo what you don't dig.

GO WITH THE FLOW

Historically, many companies suffered a forced reworking of their sensibilities when the terrorist attacks of September 11, 2001, hit New York, and changed the business. Suddenly, doing shows replete with violence was seen as a dicey move. Likewise, super-frivolous, silly, navel-gazing material wasn't right for the times, either.

Perhaps your company has earnestly promoted a particular playwright's work, and the audience is staying away in droves. Or perhaps you've heard audience feedback that is most unflattering, bordering on verbally abusive—your production's values stink. This actor needs to be shown the door. That play was so long, I fell asleep, and now I want my money back. And so do these sixty-three friends of mine.

You might know there are serious problems that keep your company from making money and getting a better audience response, not to mention a better critical response, but you just don't want to admit it. You're in denial. You believe so strongly in your own bountiful genius, nobody can tell you anything. With that attitude, the odds are your company won't be long for this world.

You've got to be flexible in order to achieve longevity. You don't know everything.

Sometimes things change, and you don't see that coming, and that circumstance gives you only two options: quit or adjust. Quitting is beyond lame, isn't it? So that means you're going to adjust, and you're going to be glad about it, because changing artistic oars midstream may be the best thing that ever happens to your company. A fresh perspective, trying new things, letting what doesn't work just fall away—it's all good.

Susan Albert Loewenberg (LA Theatre Works) says:

> I think it's looking at something and saying, "You know what? This is a dead end." It would be a crisis point—a point where you feel a dead end. You feel it isn't going anywhere, you need some invigoration, and you figure out where you need to go.
>
> I think that's been the salvation of this company. It's enabled the company to move and grow, and it's sort of kept my interest.

127

STAFFING TRAUMAS

You have no staff, so you have to do everything yourself. You have a staff, but nobody shows up, so you have to do everything yourself. You lose great people. These are just a few of the many staffing upheavals every theater company has to face at one time or another, sometimes for years and years.

The ultimate compliment, of course, is that you build such great relationships with your staffers and offer them so much creative opportunity that they stick with you for a very long time. It's also a wonderful tribute to your company when actors return to job in with your company again and again, because they so enjoy the experience of contributing to your vision.

Wheelock Family Theatre has been paid these compliments and more. They've also dealt with much staffing drama, as has any long-term, successful company. Susan Kosoff goes back to the beginning:

> We had a very, very small staff. Tony and I never went to sleep. We literally stayed up, doing everything, and it was exhausting. So we came to the point where we were able to say, "OK, we have to have more help, and find ways to do that." We still are probably understaffed and are still trying to come up with ways to fix that.
>
> I think in terms of staff development, that's how we've worked, and it's been really hard. We couldn't pay our tech director what a place like ART (the American Repertory Theatre, located in nearby Cambridge, Massachusetts) can, so it meant that every few years we had to get a new tech director and adjust to that. I think we develop ways to deal with it, but it's a concern.
>
> The woman who worked on our business plan with us left after three years.
>
> She really wanted to help us get started and continues to be helpful; she did a million things. We're never going to be able to hire someone who is going to be able to do a million things the exact way she does. I think losing her and losing Tony Hancock (who passed away) were two of our biggest challenges.
>
> We've had those individual crises, like when we did *The Wizard of Oz* and one of the actors, who was playing the Scarecrow, didn't show up; we had to cancel the show. That's the only time we had to cancel a show but there was nothing else we could do. We've had those kinds of problems; I think every theater company has those kinds of problems.
>
> The second season, we did *The Phantom of the Opera*, and the guy who was playing the lead—his lungs collapsed. That's one of the fun things about theater!

FINDING FLEXIBILITY

Sometimes, the only way to really stay true to yourself, and to your theater company, is to compromise. This can mean a number of things. Maybe you'll feel the need to adjust or tweak your artistic sensibilities out of respect for the community you work in. Maybe you'll have to shift the way you like to do business in order to accommodate the style of a truly talented designer or director. When is this the right thing to do, and when is it selling out?

The answer truly lies within your goal set. If being artistically or practically flexible is a step you need to take in order to bring your company to the next level and taking this step doesn't violate your moral code in any way, consider giving it a try. By listening to other points of view, and trying other folks' ways of working, you may have a professional epiphany and learn a new, more productive way of operating. If not, you can always go back to the way you did things before. In heading up the Round Barn at Amish Acres, Richard Pletcher has been faced with a dual challenge of flexibility—he has needed to cooperate both in terms of his audience's conservatism and work with theater pros in new and necessary ways. Pletcher has managed to do all of this skillfully, as he elaborates:

> The biggest problem I've faced in running this company has been integrating traditional theater people into Amish Acres. I've really needed to concentrate on bringing in theater people who can adapt to a very different way of being—after all, I have an Amish carpenter who came to work here having never seen a play before. So getting used to, and being respectful of, that lifestyle is important, as is being able to adapt to the hard work we do here. Within our space, we have very difficult sight lines. We're not set up in the round, but our audience sits in the round. So you can't put up resistance to that, you have to work with it and a lot of scenic designers can't work with it—they're not flexible. I find, too, that many college theater programs don't prepare their students to work at the ground level.
>
> You also must be very adaptable to work here because we have a very unorthodox way of going about our business. First of all, we're indeed a business—I'm running a for-profit company. That doesn't mean I don't care about being artistic, but it does mean I have to make compromises to satisfy our audiences. Frankly, if there is a Bible Belt, we're in it—if John Adams says the word "damn" in *1776*, I'm going to hear about it from my patrons. My theory is, E equals E—expectations equal experience. We have two to three thousand subscribers per season, and as we prepare shows for them, we don't want to offend them with bad language or provocative material. We want them to feel that they've been here before and that they know the kind of show they're going to get and enjoy. A show like *Shenandoah* was very commercially successful and also, I think, *Big River* was one of our best—those are the kinds of family-oriented shows our subscribers always feel comfortable with. I always watch the reactions of our audiences and consider even opening night to

actually be a preview—I'm willing to change elements of a show, if necessary, based on what people like or dislike.

PERSONALITY MANAGEMENT

Theater folks, as a breed, are a colorful bunch, of course. In no other profession will you find such a colorful mix of personalities—and differing takes when it comes to ways in which your company should proceed. In reestablishing Bailiwick Repertory, Kevin Mayes clued in to the essential importance of getting all of his personnel on the same page, and speaks to the ongoing challenge this is for any theater company:

> From my perspective, my first major challenge was pulling together a group of people with very different priorities, viewpoints, and value systems. Dealing with all that raw material, getting to the point where we can work together for the good of each project, creates the essence of our organization and really will create the essence of any new theater company. I don't think you can underestimate the challenge of getting everyone in your group heading in the same direction! That's the most important first milestone. I used my own leadership abilities as best I could to actually put a lot of people out of their comfort zones—and that's a good thing, because you can't be held back by the ego and insecurities many artists have. You have to inspire people to rise above themselves to meet that common goal.

STRAIGHT-UP HONESTY

Another unfortunate fact of theatrical life: people are going to break promises to you. This can be disappointing on a personal level at best (a friend you counted on to step into a role says she will, but then flakes out in favor of a larger part in another show) and detrimental to your bottom line at worst (a major funder pledges cash your company is truly counting on, but ultimately doesn't come through).

How should you deal? By developing, from day one, a Teflon-tough attitude about your business. Prepare yourself for the difficult reality that anyone, even someone you truly trust, could let you down business-wise. Don't count on anyone but yourself. Separate business from friendship mentally. If you're working with someone you have a personal relationship with, that personal relationship must be left outside the theater. Always have a backup plan (like an understudy for every role and a second, dependable funding source) so you simply can't be left high and dry.

Gil Cates of the Geffen Playhouse stressed the importance of being prepared when dealing with anyone and everyone. Cates explained:

Theater is a three-act play. Ideally, theater is a place where people say what they mean and mean what they say, but sometimes you have to go through those acts to get what you want. It's just a matter of begging and pleading first, then getting your story straight so you can further your cause with donors and audience members who may respond with a lack of civility. Ultimately, though, if you get your act together and think around people, you can get what you want and need.

IGNORANCE IS NOT BLISS

Sometimes, a theater's problem has nothing to do with what it's about at all but is due to a larger problem in society as a whole.

In Jack Reuler's history as the artistic director of Mixed Blood Theatre, he has certainly had many more victories than difficulties. Reuler, however, has been rankled by a certain ignorance on cultural issues, specifically one that affected the perception of what he was trying to accomplish within his company.

Jack Reuler certainly wouldn't call this the biggest problem he ever faced, but he did consider it to be a significant issue at one point. Here, he talks about the problem of the term "multiculturalism."

> The expression that became identified with Mixed Blood was "color-blind casting." We were doing what we were doing for three years before anybody put a label on it. When we took that label on, and when I found out what it meant to other people, we stopped using it because it didn't define what we were doing. What we do we've come to call, needing a label, culture-conscious casting. What people are cast as is a "something"; it's not an absence of something. I think they bring that to the role. "Color-blind casting" meant you did it with disregard, paying no attention, rather than positive attention to people's differences.
>
> I don't think we changed what we did. We just changed what we called what we did. It was really an issue of "multiculturalism," a buzzword we tried to avoid. In education, business, philosophy, philanthropy, we saw it right from the beginning— it was going to be a passing fad. We needed to stay doing what we were doing before it came, and after it was gone.

Ultimately, Jack discovered that there's strength in displaying strength—which ultimately springs from your company's true core. Whatever you do, you can't go wrong letting your authentic flag fly. People will quickly tell you one way or another whether they agree with your hypothesis, which you can only control so much. Take care that it makes your mission statement clear. Jack did, and people got the point:

Trying to articulate this notion, that only really recently has come into vogue: when I sat down and wrote the mission for the organization at the age of twenty-two, it said, "Mixed Blood is a multiracial theater company dedicated to promoting cultural pluralism, individual quality, and artistic excellence."

Over the first ten years or more of the organization, people said, "What the hell is cultural pluralism?" Then within a week, it became a tired old buzzword. But what I wanted to do was create this world in which people could pay positive attention, not no attention, to their differences, and succeed in doing so.

It's always been important to me that we not be a "woe-is-me theater," that the material we do isn't victim theater. I didn't know anything except from being an audience member, and I'd been in some friends' directing projects. I put out an ad for directors, and got a ton of people who came in. There was a professor at the University of Minnesota, who out of thirty or so applicants, I chose to work with, who also had that unbridled enthusiasm and similar vision, and the very first play we did was *Status Quo Vadis* by a guy named Donald Driver. It was a class system comedy, and I'd seen it at the Ivanhoe in Chicago. The characters had different numbers woven into their costumes. The whole notion was that everybody's presuppositions about everybody else were the same. I read it again fifteen years later, and its politics were profoundly dated. But at the time, it was a great opening play choice.

THINGS WON'T CHANGE OVERNIGHT

There are other misconceptions of theater as a whole, of course.

People mistakenly believe that theater is elitist, exclusionary, and highbrow. Small minds and closed minds think theater is stuffy and boring. We know how many fabulously exciting and interactive productions have blown this theory out of the water, but still, old myths can persist.

In this pop culture period rife with dumbed-down movies and lowest common denominator reality TV, theater doesn't really fit neatly into the landscape. For the past few years, in fact, theater has been treated like the Kardashians' ugly, unloved stepsister.

Corey Fischer, formerly of the Jewish Theatre San Francisco says:

> The biggest problem is that our culture and society does not value theater as much as we do, or as much as most European countries do. The support isn't what it could be.
>
> Will things change and improve? I believe so. Why? Because entertainment culture is cyclical. Eventually, people will get sick of the stupid swill they've been force-fed and will look for fresh alternatives. Theater may just prove to be a very viable and attractive option.

Things won't change overnight, but I do think there are signs that society is smartening up and things are getting better. So keep on keeping on. Then when the masses are ready, you'll be there, ready to give them the thrill of a lifetime.

Woyzeck by Georg Büchner; adapted by Ann-Christin Rommen and Wolfgang Wiens
concept by Robert Wilson; music and lyrics by Tom Waits and Kathleen Brennan
directed by Mark Jackson
Pictured: Joe Estlack and Madeline H. D. Brown
Photo by Jessica Palopoli

Chapter Ten

The Biggest Victory We Ever Enjoyed

Now get ready for the good news!

A life in the theater is really, really fun. The adrenaline rush that washes over an actor right before he takes the stage is only one reason why. It's electric to be in your space on opening night after you've worked so hard putting together a show, no matter what role in a theater company you happen to play. If it's your very own company, the excitement is amped up to its highest power. (And the nausea you concurrently experience, perhaps. But I digress.)

Opening nights that go well are one great payoff, but there are so many ways victory can present itself. It can be that moment you recognize your cast is working together like a well-oiled machine. It can be a cash windfall at the box office. It can be consistently beautiful reviews. It can be catching sight of the collective joy on your audience members' faces as they watch the work you're presenting. It can simply be the moment when you know your company has made it over the hump, and is going to survive.

At the point you may be at right now, you probably think such positive proof of success will never present itself to you. But life can change in a second, you know. Also know this: There is a secret ingredient you can use when you're trying to cook up some victory. It's simple stick-to-it-ness. Hang in long enough and you'll see results. Make a daily commitment to refuse to let your company go away. Always find a way to keep going. When you ask somebody for something and they say no, go ask somebody else until you get a yes. Sheer willpower applied to any endeavor produces success sooner or later.

This chapter will survey a number of our subjects to find out what their respective big victories were like. Sometimes these events occurred immediately following a very difficult period in the company's history, or after a particularly sticky situation. Some victories were happy accidents. Some victories encompass the realization of a company goal. No matter what the victory might be, each of our experts deserves credit for hanging in long enough to steer their organizations toward achievement.

We'll discuss these big successes, proudest moments, and most exhilarating achievements, too, in order to inspire you. Just imagine yourself in the same glorious position of accomplishment and satisfaction—it's closer than you think. Just keep working hard and dreaming big.

WHEN SOMEBODY REALLY GETS IT

In that magical moment when an actor finds the truth onstage, the immediate reward that follows belongs to a number of people. First of all, it belongs to the actor himself. If he's been hesitant or nervous, then suddenly finds his groove, it's a major personal affirmation. Then to the show's director—here's validation that his or her skills and support have really helped in a big way. For the actor's fellow cast members, the unit is now more cohesive and creativity can flow between people much more easily. If the playwright is present, his or her material will now be able to be interpreted more ideally. And for a theater company's leadership, it's wonderful to know that all of this is happening not just before your eyes, but also under your auspices.

Paul Zuckerman always hires great people, but he realizes that even the most terrific actors sometimes don't have improv experience. He's seen actors break through many times, and every time it happens he regards those moments as major validations, not simply for the sake of his own contributions, but for the entire troupe's strength and unity. Zuckerman elaborates:

> Improvisation, which is created on the spot based on an audience suggestion—you can workshop the skill, but not the content, it's like a sport. Now, there's also sketch comedy—we're doing a lot of that at this point—and that is hitting us like a lightning rod. People are coming in with ideas. We do something that actually Second City had done, which is, after a show, getting suggestions from an audience, using that as a sort of a brainstorming possibility and then coming back with a series of pieces based on that brainstorming. You don't know where it's going to go. Your improvisational skills are molding it, but there is a little bit of a road map and that's how we wrote a lot of material as well. You try to go with the hot hand, because on different occasions, different nights, when the muse hits you, you don't want to not hear it. By the same token, you have to have a group of people who are oriented toward embracing each other's ideas to enable that. If you have a great idea and I'm

sort of going, "Yeah, yeah, yeah," but inside I'm going, "I don't think it's going to be that funny," you've lost out because I'm not helping and I've lost out because I'm not going to add much to the party. But if you have this orientation of embracing each other's ideas, yeah, once in a while you all die a miserable death because you embraced them. But more often than not, you'll discover something that neither of you would have come up with independently.

Collaboration is a very strong part of the energy and the reason why our group stays together. We always talk about the ability to anchor a show. If we take our great cast members, I can take someone who's never improvised, put him on stage with us, and you might not notice it. If they follow what's going on and keep their mouths shut, generally they'll be OK. But that person can't be the leader—he doesn't have the skills. That's sort of the individual affirmation—this guy or gal who maybe a year ago took second billing because they were tentative or whatever, all of a sudden they're in command, they're dragging a scene along, they're leading it—that's a very satisfying feeling.

FINDING STRONG ORIGINAL WORK

Outside of the immediate and specialized realm of improv, finding a good original play to produce can be surprisingly difficult. You would think that with the vast number of aspiring, hungry playwrights out there, new American plays would be plentiful. Discovering new writers, too, is always important to do, since they are the lifeblood by which the theater art form will ultimately live or die.

Another roadblock to finding quality new material when your company is just starting out: Nobody knows who you are yet, so why would playwrights send you scripts? It's sometimes simply a matter of time until you establish your name, even nominally. Since we know there are lots of writers out there just waiting for an opportunity, at that point, after you've produced a few well-received shows, you just might get lucky and find that talented writers with good scripts are starting to approach you.

Producer Leslie Jacobson found herself in that precise position when heading up Horizons Theatre. She discusses how producing new works was a real boon, artistically, to her feminist theater organization:

The reason that we had created our own work initially was that we weren't finding a lot of plays by women that had the range of ideas and characters that we wanted to present. But by '83, people were more aware of us and we were more aware of playwrights out there. We were able to start developing relationships with playwrights from other parts of the country and playwrights from DC.

We were able to really pick seasons. We still did some original work from time to time, but we were also able to do a lot of area and world premieres of already-

137

existing plays by women playwrights. We commissioned a work by a playwright in Minneapolis at one point, we did a lot of staged readings, and we were able to bring playwrights into opening nights and productions.

It was a very positive experience, doing that.

SHOWS THAT STAND OUT

It's not unusual for a theater company to recall a particular production as a most memorable moment, and why not? It's a rare and beautiful thing when all the elements of a production come together perfectly—dramatically, technically, in every way. Those times when it's exactly the way you envisioned it deserve to be remembered, so you can use them as a sort of divining rod to help you catch lightning like that again.

Not that Rick Lombardo needs any help catching lightning. His determination to expand the reputation of New Repertory Theatre helped fuel the company to huge achievements, and the high-quality stamp he's helped put on so many New Rep projects is most evident. Rick Lombardo says:

> Artistically, the 2000 to 2001 season was the biggest, huge! We did the New England premiere of *King Lear* with Austin Pendleton, which was untried, a challenge, but a success.
>
> The Boston-area critic Ed Siegel once noted that one of the things lacking in this area was a midsize theater—a "Steppenwolf" of Boston. New Repertory Theatre has clearly cultivated a literate, sophisticated audience.

Likewise, David Zak recalls with pride a particularly jubilant and sweet moment, when a Chicago critics' poll took notice of his company's fine work. "Our production of *Pope Joan* by Christopher Moore beat out all of the big Equity houses as Best Musical in our eighth season."

BEAUTY IN A STOREFRONT

When material works, it works, and you know it. It pushes aside, for the time span of a performance, all of the worries and difficulties and struggles you're dealing with and confirms your faith in your company's existence and future like nothing else. Mitzi Sales recalls having this transformative experience in the early days of Berkeley Rep:

> Michael was a great collaborator. I think that was one of his great primary skills. He could recognize talent. His ego was not such that he had to make every single decision and control everything. He very much worked collaboratively with Doug

Johnson, who was the associate director at that time. There were a couple of other directors he worked with from the university, and some of the actors.

He would talk about what plays would work best with the acting pool that we had, with the directing pool that we had. I think that the choices that were made during that time just got better and better. They were more astute choices, because obviously in a really tiny space with very little technical ability, you needed to choose plays that would really show off the skills of the actors, the intelligence of the director.

It was great. The very first season I was there, the '72 to '73 season, it was dawning on me, "What are we doing here, the cash flow is a joke." I was sweating bullets every time payroll came around. When the phone rang, I would disguise my voice, in case it was a bill collector—I was ill-prepared for this. And we did a production, *Dance of Death*. It was breathtaking! And at that point, you just think, if this can happen here in this little storefront in Berkeley, who am I not to work as hard as I can and try to make a go?

UPHEAVAL LEADS TO TRIUMPH

At Berkeley Repertory, as well, one other production historically stands out as exceptional in a long line of tremendously exceptional shows. This play was not simply well done, but very key in terms of the fact that it came in the middle of significant upheaval and seemed, in many ways, to define the positive results of this sea of change. In Berkeley's case, the show led to a new strength of determination, which subsequently led to the theater creating for itself a new facility.

This anecdote brings up a very interesting point about change as well; it's rarely not chaotic, especially if it is truly needed. Oftentimes, change within a theater company will come about because there is really no choice but to have it. Events and issues start to converge and snowball to the point where things are changing whether you want them to or not. It's never just about you—it's always about the communal force of your company's energy as a whole.

So you shouldn't stand in the way of change, even if you didn't want it in the first place yourself. The only thing you should do is try to guide your organization's shift in a positive direction, and make sure something really good comes out of change you can't prevent or control.

Susan Medak explains how this dynamic worked within the changing times at Berkeley Repertory.

In 1990, I came on as managing director. It was a big transition period from the founding board philosophy—an agent of change. The perception was that I was somebody who was an activist. It also became interesting between me and the community—I wanted to build my long-term, external relationship with it.

So a very large signature of this time period happened when we did *Woman Warrior* in 1991. It was a $1 million project and it broke us out of the box, expanding the universe we were in. It also changed our ambition, gave us an enormous appetite, illustrated our commitment to working outside of the mainstream.

The production was visually spectacular and it was about our community—it came from a local writer and would sing here as it would not sing in other places. It pushed us as artists, and as a theater, and made us see that anything we decided to do, we could do!

Building a new theater was a huge touchstone as well. The building renewed our sense of community. When we first began to talk about building a new theater, people were enraged! But we couldn't remain the same and still grow to be all we wanted to be, to be all our audiences want us to be. I see myself as an interpreter for the layperson—I interact with the city and we make ourselves indispensable to it. So once people got that we would open up the building to other organizations and events, all that we, as a company, were about to experience became something that was for everyone, and the community got that sense of ownership, not stewardship. Urban pride is a linchpin in this city. Thinking about the new building in terms of urban revitalization—downtown Berkeley had declined—made everyone seize the moment and start a new way of thinking.

We received $4 million from the city and we were all so proud—we as a community had done this, placed this theater as the new center of our community. So not only did the new building expand our vision artistically, it redefined what our relationship had been to the community.

SMART MOVES

Back to Steppenwolf: for this company, making intelligent moves at key moments has brought big dividends. Physically, in terms of taking their work out to new audience populations in the world, the company's movement led to greater acclaim.

Artistically, as well, the initiative to tackle some magnificent material translated that material into legendary Steppenwolf stage works. Michael Gennaro elaborates:

Probably in '82, they had done *True West* and they got the chance to go to New York. That was a big, big conversation within the company because it was kind of like, "Well, we're moving from Highland Park down into the city, and now we're moving out of the city? This is too big of a thing, it will splinter the company, that's not why we did this."

They ended up making the decision to go and, of course, that really set them on the map. It kind of led to the ability to make the move, in '91, down to the space we're in now. Clearly, the moving into the city was a big step; clearly, the move to *True West* was a big step; the move here [to our current space] was a big step.

The other thing that probably set them on the map—there are probably three plays, in my opinion. *True West*, *Balm in Gilead*, and *The Grapes of Wrath*. *Grapes* was a long journey, but one of the things it did was take us to London. When we've gone back now to London, people have never forgotten *The Grapes of Wrath*. It got the Tony, and then they got the Tony for regional theater.

At the same time, all of those moments have their challenges and their victories, because they all influence and affect the company.

THEATER THAT TOUCHES PEOPLE

A theater company that strives to specifically address the human condition in positive, proactive ways can enjoy unique affirming victories.

Wheelock Family Theatre is one such company. How Wheelock uniquely operates is from a humanistic standpoint, in terms of being especially conscious and considerate of its audience members' needs. Some of these needs are specialized and, in general, are as diverse as the many different types of people who love the company's productions.

Susan Kosoff expresses her delight at Wheelock's creative successes, then goes on to mention some memorable highlights confirming that Wheelock really cares about its audience.

I think there are shows that are emblematic, when everything comes together well and we're proud of the results. The audiences like them, the critics like them—they go well and it's fabulous.

Some of the individual accomplishments of some of the kids [Wheelock works with] are heartwarming. Some of the recognition we've gotten—we received an award from the White House for one of our programs. We got an Actors' Equity award. We've really gotten some important recognition nationally and regionally. Just this year we got an award from the African American Theater Festival in Boston.

What can I say? It's affirming! I think about people in wheelchairs who have never seen live theater—they are seeing it and loving it. It keeps you going. The first few times I was there to see blind people, people with seeing-eye dogs in the audience, it's such a great feeling for them to be there. It's just great.

A BREED APART

Lots of theater companies claim that the work they do is groundbreaking, but not as many can prove it with as many different forays into creative expression as LA Theatre Works.

Says Susan Albert Loewenberg:

In the beginning phases we broke new ground.

We did a lot of the kind of work that's lauded today, but we were really pioneers, creating plays organically within the community, targeting specific populations, and really being creative within that.

We actually made a film in 1976 about creating a play inside the prison walls, a documentary. We got a grant from the Endowment to do it, and we actually followed ourselves doing a production from start to finish. It was interspersed with talking heads; people would actually interview people in the workshop about their lives, who they were and what they did. You'd see this person doing this fabulous vignette, being perfectly charming and wonderful, then telling you how they did a bank robbery. So it was an interesting film that basically celebrated the human spirit and the ability to find creativity everywhere, how positive an experience creativity is.

I think that when we did our prison work, we achieved our highest level within that work. We really did it well and we were recognized for it. We were financially rewarded by major grants, we had critical recognition. We achieved the highest level of excellence and we were recognized for that.

When we started producing professional theater, working developmentally, discovering new writers, doing highly theatrical work, we also achieved a high level of recognition. We received the highest award for several of our productions from the LA Drama Critics Circle. We got great recognition. It was not easy for a Los Angeles theater company to get money from the theater program of the Endowment.

Through the years, I think the Endowment has supported us incredibly. We've had major, major grants from the NEA for all of our endeavors, which is, to me, the highest recognition. It's really your peers judging you, and it isn't filtered through corporate objectives and who you know. It's really about merit.

When we started our radio programming, I think we've achieved a unique position, in that we have the only library of its kind in the United States. So I think that at each level, we've done quality work and fairly unique things.

I think in general, we have a very good reputation for quality.

Loewenberg has also discovered a tremendous amount of brilliant talent over the years, due to her keen artistic eye and mind-set: "What happened was, around 1980, we became more interested in being a more traditional theater company, working with professional writers and producing plays," she explains.

We were really developing new work, and we were only interested in that—highly theatrical work.

I introduced Steven Berkoff to the United States, for example, with a production called *Greek*, which became kind of a legend in Los Angeles and went on to off-Broadway. Major British playwrights. I gave Tim Robbins one of his first shots. I had a little workshop theater downtown for new American work—I discovered Jon Robin Baitz, produced his first play.

Milcha Sanchez Scott—she's a leading Chicana playwright, she's half-Chinese, half-Mexican, actually. She was an actress and working at an employment agency for domestics. We hired her as an actress to supplement a workshop we were doing at a women's prison. The ride out to that prison was humongous, it was like an hour and a half each way and she would tell us stories about working in this domestics agency and how conflicted she was. She said she'd kept a diary of her experiences, and we asked if we could see it. We all looked at it and thought, "God, what a great play." One of the directors worked with her to develop it as a play, and we presented it as a professional production in Los Angeles. It was called *Latina*.

It was very community-based, very organic. Then there was this utter stream that started of very sophisticated, very avant-garde British writers we were doing. We became known as a company that was playwright-centered, developmentally oriented.

A NEW LEASE ON LIFE

It can get frustrating, waiting out the months and years it sometimes takes for your company to become more financially stable. You're working your tail off, but you never feel like you're really getting anywhere, at times, because money is perpetually so tight. It takes a lot out of you, because you're a human being before you're a worker bee, after all.

What's super is when money materializes out of the blue, money that will allow you to really obtain something that gives your company stronger legs to stand on. This kind of miracle does happen; it happened to Berkeley Rep.

Says Mitzi Sales:

There's the story that's been told over and over again as a high point.

Here we are, a 153-seat theater, a fledgling, neighborhood-based theater, and we're going to try to raise $1.2 million or something silly to build a theater and move downtown.

We actually got word that Mark Taper, who was a banker—the Mark Taper Forum was named for his philanthropy—had heard that we were building a theater up in Berkeley and he might be interested. I guess that the negotiation, and the final getting of $250,000, was unbelievable. It was just breathtaking, it was celebratory, it was, "Oh, my gosh, I guess we can do this." I think our largest gift up to that point had probably been $10,000.

Revenue was coming very, very slowly, very painfully. We thought we'd never make it. I think we were feeling downhearted, so this gave us a great shot in the arm, a great impetus to go forward. So that was probably the high point.

Let me just also say, on an extremely personal level, every time we opened a new show, and I read a great review, that never got old. Opening night, being in the theater! I would actually stay away from most rehearsals, and part of the reason I did that was because I felt like one of my own values to the company, the artistic director, the director, whomever, was to come as fresh as I could to the final production. Not that I ever really could—who was I kidding? But I would come to the opening night and watch the show, feeling those feelings, seeing if it's working, cringing every time a prop fell apart!

THE REWARDS OF TEAMWORK

Lyla White, formerly of the Pasadena Playhouse, feels that many of her most successful theatrical enterprises at the Playhouse have worked out so well because of the contributions staff members and friends have made to their execution and success. She believes strongly in the concept of teamwork and is eager to give credit where credit is due.

People came up with creative ideas of how we can promote in different ways.

For instance, the play *Life in the Theater*, at the Pasadena Playhouse. A woman who worked with us part-time in artistic development came up with an idea of inviting people who have lived their lives in the theater to come and talk to the wider community—high school students, members of the community—about their lives in the theater. We said, "That sounds like a good idea," so she sent out a letter. Gregory Hines said he would come and he'd bring his tap shoes and talk about his life in the theater. Sheldon Epps said, "All right, I'll ask Michael York." Michael York said, "Well, if Gregory Hines is going to dance, I'll sing a little and talk about my life in the theater." He had a book coming out, so there'd be a book signing on the patio, we'd make that kind of a day. Carol Lawrence agreed to come and talk about her life in the theater.

So we had three weeks of that six-week run during which, on the weekends three weeks in a row, we had a program. The important part of that program was, [this idea came from] a woman who usually sits at her desk and sends out emails. Everybody got behind this; we decided to do it together.

The play before that, *Do I Hear a Waltz?*, another staff member, a publications editor, said, "I think we should roll the prices back to what they were when *Do I Hear a Waltz?* came out in New York in 1965." We did some research, and that was $9.60. So for one day only, we sold tickets for three of our previews for $9.60. We had a line around the block and we were all involved with it. That is a grassroots idea.

IT SHOULDN'T HAVE BEEN A CONTENDER . . . BUT WHAT A CONTENDER!

Sometimes you hear about a particular show and think, right off the bat, *That's a sure thing*. You look over the list of elements it boasts—experienced playwright, gorgeous house, and more—and you just know the thing is a go.

There are other times when nothing about a show remotely shouts success, at least at first glance. Then it turns out to be fabulous. Who knew? Nobody did, but one thing you can bet on is that lots of people who weren't involved will leap right up on the old bandwagon and claim they called its genius before anybody else.

Now Jack Reuler is a guy who can honestly lay claim to recognizing a number of diamonds in the rough. Yet even he was flummoxed by the success of one show that never should have worked. This show came up in Jack's mind again recently, when he was asked about which productions he'd done that he lists among his biggest successes.

"It's like asking a parent which kid they love the most," Jack laughed. "There have been so many things that I just go, 'This is fabulous that this happened.'"

Here's one: In the big picture of the history of the organization it's somewhat minor . . . but there was a guy, he's Chicano, and he wrote this play called *King of the Kosher Grocers*. He'd never written a play; he's a successful restaurateur. I saw him and I got him to be in a couple of plays, and he was really good. He wrote this play like in two weeks. I said, "We should develop this and do it." It was so much about the north side of Minneapolis; every city has a part of town like this, that became the "bad part of town."

We rented this abandoned supermarket and turned it into a theater, and did it there, so we could try to convene the people who'd left the north side with the people who'd come to the north side with the people who'd stayed on the north side. It was a huge hit. Who the audience was was exactly what we wanted to have happen, and Marion McClinton directed it, who's gone on to have a great career.

145

There was no reason it should have worked. It was a first-time playwright doing a play in a space that had never been a theater in a part of town where generations of people had never gone to that corner, who would do anything to avoid going to that corner.

The ridiculous part of it was, I thought it was so important to do it there, because who else would care? But the Old Globe did it. It's been done all over the country. I kept second-guessing myself—is this the right thing to do? And it ran for months. It couldn't have been righter.

IT'S CALLED SURVIVAL

The biggest accomplishment any theater company can hope to have: that its work endures. In theater veteran Corey Fischer's opinion, encouraging new talent, then pulling them into an organization to keep that company evolving with a purity of mission, is what it's all about. "The whole notion of bringing in a younger generation begins to become a sign that the theater will keep going," he says. What's more, if a piece of your company's work becomes a lauded, memorable classic, and other companies hope to do it? Not only have you been paid a giant creative compliment, but you're beginning to cement a lasting legacy.

Artistic endurance and survival is the ultimate victory.

Chapter Eleven
Adapting to Growth

Signs of success and longevity are what every theater company strives for. When you start to realize your hard work has paid off to the point where you've outgrown your best-case, big-picture scenario, it's tremendously rewarding.

A savvy theater head is never satisfied, though. He or she wants to always keep going for it, accomplishing more goals once original ones have been achieved. This can be a fresh motivator for staffers and company members, sure, but it can also be a little daunting. How is a company really affected or changed by growth and success, after all?

You have to assess a number of factors—business planning, material choices, marketing, and more—to make sure these things are serving your expansion as effectively as possible. If you need to make changes in these areas, you make them. However, you have to make sure you're not biting off more than you can chew. Overinflating the importance of your position in the market, your financial situation at the present moment, or your creative influence on the universe can be hard traps to avoid when you're feeling a little power. Yet to do any of that would be most unwise.

In this chapter, our experts will relate their strategies for adapting to growth intelligently. Sometimes, their particular situations called for taking on a little risk to keep moving forward—but even that risk was strategic. Sometimes adapting to growth meant diversifying as an organization. Sometimes it meant revamping finances, or realizing that the organization had become a little too loose, so more structure needed to be added. Every organization has faced different challenges.

The common denominator between them, however, is courage to push their individual organizations to the limits of being the best that they can be. Long-established company personnel are not afraid of much—they've been through so much on the way up, a certain self-assured defiance in the face of change tends to develop. Rather than worry, they just get on with business.

Another trait these successful companies have in common? There came a point where they refused to be comfortable. A lot of less ambitious troupes would be satisfied with staying at a certain level that offered few surprises but was never going to allow greatness. Our subjects dared to be great.

LET'S GO

Paul Zuckerman knew his group could do so much more than its geographical boundaries dictated, so his group made a radical move, taking a fateful road trip that changed its destiny for the better. Paul tells of Chicago City Limits' early growth:

> Chicago, all of a sudden, didn't seem like the ultimate goal anymore for us. We needed to keep evolving. The bars in Chicago weren't gonna do it for us. Second City is gonna hire me? If you go back deeper into those groups breaking up and forming, you've got people like Jim Belushi and Tim Kazurinsky who worked with members of our group, so what happens is, a group like Second City's hiring some of the best people as well. So you've kind of got this sense that, "We've got something, and now all of a sudden Second City becomes less of an appealing alternative, because we *do* have something." The aspiration becomes, "Well, what's next?"
>
> The way we handled it? We went on tour. We went on the crazy tour, seemed pretty crazy at the time, out west in 1978. We were basically a bar group at this time—I don't think we'd worked anywhere except bars. We go to Las Vegas. Joan Rivers was performing in Las Vegas. At her show, George [Todisco], our founder, slipped a waiter twenty bucks to send a message back to Joan: "Hey, we're from Chicago"—she's a Second City alumna—"we'd love to meet you." She sends a note back: "Where are you performing?" George immediately writes back, "The Jockey Club tomorrow at nine o'clock." We had no gig there.
>
> So we called the Jockey Club and said Joan Rivers wanted to see us there, got a spot? Of course they had one. She walks in, she sees us, and boom! There's a buzz about us in Las Vegas.
>
> We were invited to go out to Los Angeles and perform at the Improvisation, and at a club called the Ice Palace. We were doing pretty good! So about getting your foot in the door—there's hundreds of doors, most of them locked tighter than a drum. You've got to be ready, but once you're ready, you've got to act.
>
> Bud Friedman, who owned the Improvisation in Los Angeles and the Improvisation in New York, had been divorced, and I think his wife got the New

York club. He said, "Why don't you go to New York? You'd be great at the Improv there." So we drive to New York from California. We're going over the George Washington Bridge at night and we're from New York, a lot of us. We just walk into the Improvisation, let them know who we were, lo and behold, ten minutes later we're opening the show that night. It was unbelievable. We didn't expect it and we killed! There was this instant buzz about "these guys from Chicago."

We spent about a year performing in the clubs around New York. At this point, we kind of in quick succession cut big with Chicago. We quit jobs, a couple of relationships fell apart, and we relocated.

This solidified us—and almost destroyed us. The problem with the clubs is that you can't develop material. You have to be doing your A material at all times. No club owner wants you to come in and sort of work something out. He wants you to come in at ten o'clock, at Catch a Rising Star, and those twenty minutes better be the funniest twenty minutes you can do. So OK, we were good at that. But a year into it, we haven't developed much material, we're working three, four, five clubs a night, not making any money. We can't do this.

The realities start to hit you. We started looking for a space. Not that we got our inspiration, but years later, reading Stanislavski, one of the things he really talks about is that an actor more than anything needs to find a situation where he's working, not looking for work. That's how you develop your craft. So we have a need to find a space, mostly artistically. We want to be able to develop material. We want to flourish as a theater company. We find a space on West 42nd Street.

Now at this point, we start to expand as a company as well. We need to train people for the future. They were not out there—quality improvisers just weren't there. So we start workshops, at some level to raise some cash but, really, to develop what turned into our national touring company, so we can start to develop a business and start to get people trained to come into our show and evolve our show over time. That happened probably the first year we had our space. We started the workshops and we had some very promising students. We had very few understudies; people would perform in those days under incredibly bad physical conditions. But once in a while, if we needed to cover somebody, we could use one of these people.

By 1980, our national touring company was actually performing shows at colleges and regional theaters; that continues today. It's been almost a constant source of cash replenishment for the resident company over time. And the workshop program, which has evolved and been developed, is basically where most of these people are trained.

There was no active desire to infuse new blood but there were a couple of changes in our casting. George, our founder and artistic director, died at the age of thirty. Very tragic, but in some strange way, further solidified this odd commitment and religion, if you will. We added our stage manager to the show, who was an actor but at the beginning, did not have the stage skills he later developed. But pretty much, that ensemble, barring George's situation, performed together as an ensemble throughout the mid-'80s. One cast member had a child, one eventually moved to California as a writer, but there was a very slow attrition. People did develop and evolve their careers, yet stayed a long time.

Evolution becomes a challenge over time. It's like anything: What have you done for me lately? It's like a restaurant—you can go ten times and it's great meals, then go the eleventh time and it's lousy, and I think theater is the same thing. So the constant challenge is to evolve the show in a way that reflects the skills of the current cast, doesn't throw the baby out with the bathwater, but doesn't hold on to something that no longer should be held on to.

You might have a cast that's very strong vocally, which will naturally take you into doing more musical kinds of things. When that cast turns over, and maybe the next group of people aren't so vocally gifted, you're hitting your head against the wall to try to develop music with them. You make your adjustments. I've always felt the strength of the group is diversity, but you have to see it, acknowledge it, and utilize it.

THAT AGE-OLD CHALLENGE

Even when your company is known and established, giving your creative work and your business concerns equal weight and attention can still be hard to do.

Certain decisions can tend to provide you a shortcut to solving this imbalance. For example, some companies make a great effort at an obvious point of growth to rework their financial plans, in order to create more stability in terms of consistent income. That solid financial base can allow you the freedom to get a little crazy artistically.

Other organizations hire more people to keep an eye on fiscal growth, so key personnel can be free to focus more attention on creative output. Such a plan has its pluses and minuses. On the plus side, if you hire great money minds you can trust, the company can quickly become more organized and profitable. On the minus side, if you make a dumb move like hiring your stage manager's cousin Bob, who was reputed to have attended a top business program but in reality proves to you he couldn't manage the profits from a Girl Scout Cookie fund drive, you've got more headaches than ever.

If you're used to hand-to-mouth survival, it's possible that deep down, a part of you likes a little struggle. Maybe you're still a little split-focused on merging your creative and financial sides seamlessly because you don't want to get too "professional." This may sound totally beside the point of why you would go into business in the first place, but it's a very, very common attitude. It's almost a point of pride for some theater companies, in fact.

If this is your outlook, you've got to know something: you've peaked already. You can't grow any further. You've got to be willing to merge your creative concerns and your business concerns to attain a larger profile, which probably sounds all corporate and boring and smacks of becoming part of the establishment and all of that. Yet it doesn't have to be that way at all—you can retain your artistic principles and still make more money.

Berkeley Rep has always done just that. Susan Medak emphasizes that a strong contributing factor to the theater's ability to expand on all gears has to do with accepting fluidity. Medak observes:

> I don't think of "growth" as being the operative word for the next few years. I think "change" is a more accurate word. Our short-term goal is to maintain the quality, energy, and ambition of the company, even as the national economy is uncertain. Our long-term goal is to have the organizational capacity to evolve as our artists and audiences evolve. This probably includes a greater focus on internationalism, an increased capacity to deal with new media and new technology, both onstage and offstage, and what I fully believe will be a renewed value placed on live, authentic experience.

MAXIMIZING POTENTIAL

La Jolla Playhouse is known for its smart and entertaining franchising strategies. Very few regional theaters can claim the track record the Playhouse has, in terms of sending so much quality work out into the world and having its investments, both artistic and financial, come back tenfold. Huge box office, critical raves, Tonys, long smash runs, you know the successful end results.

Another priority for the Playhouse is, of course, meeting the ongoing, welcome challenges of constant growth on the home front. Terrence Dwyer always had an expert eye for recognizing how to maximize the potential of the Playhouse's many assets to compliment its ongoing artistic and business expansions. He also knew just the right moves to make to create growth wherever the organization wants it to occur.

"Improved staffing in 1993 enabled us to grow," Dwyer explains. "Before that, there had been fairly limited progress in terms of growth and meeting financial challenges.

> A staff must also remain constant in terms of belief in the artistic mission of a company. So recruiting more staff, plus adding more members to our board—sustaining and building with good people, everything flows from that.

151

Another piece of the puzzle: we do a lot of musicals and, entrepreneurially, to get rid of our debt, their success positioned us well. That was leverage for us and very strategic in terms of driving a subcategory of productions we are involved in, shows that go beyond our company, to Broadway, etc.

Artistically, another strategic move was to get rid of our old menu and try flash performances. Flash performances are artistically exciting show runs of one to seven performances, and we scheduled them at times when things were dark. These works have integrity—they feature such artists as Sandra Bernhard, and they've been very successful.

More visibility, a broader artistic scope, and good cash flow produce growth.

TAKING MATERIAL, AND BUSINESS, IN A NEW DIRECTION

Back to Berkeley Repertory: after Michael Leibert's tenure ended and Sharon Ott was selected as the company's new artistic director, it was natural that adjustments and changes would be made.

In such a situation, when a new leader takes over, it's always smart business sense to keep the great things that work about a company's artistic statement and modes of operation. It's also very important that the company's new leader express his or her creative self regardless of monetary concerns, to a certain extent. A new face at the top should mean that the company's work feels new and fresh and that this leader can put his or her thumbprint on the theater's artistic offerings. Audiences rarely reject this—they want to know how the new company head thinks. They're interested in being challenged and don't want to be bored or disappointed by a company playing things too safe after such a major change.

Susan Medak came into Berkeley Repertory as such artistic adjustments were happening and she felt inspired by the atmosphere of change. In her position as the company's new business manager, Medak wanted to deal with the issues of financial expansion in a new way. She explains how Ott's new look at the company's creative scheme, plus her own business philosophy, took the company in a new direction:

Sharon Ott was interested in the development of new works, in eclectic programming. She used short-run shows, collaboration with companies, as a way to begin to introduce the idea that new work could be as interesting as classic work.

The company began a parallel season of works that played with form and structure, in addition to the regular season. The subscribers were offered a "grazer's package" for those who saw themselves as more adventurous and wanted to sample the more eclectic work in addition to the more traditional productions. It blew up!

Out of six thousand subscribers, more than 50 percent were attending both seasons. We now have two theaters.

Sharon was not interested in a resident pool of actors. She wanted to work more with artists of color, to have much more of a director's theater, more focused on physical design. The shows were [things like] the Eureka Theatre [did]—gritty, intensely politicized, very vivid, very elegant approaches. Sharon's hallmark and aesthetic sensibilities matched the core values of the company, though—quality and flexibility.

We came to understand that you deal with artists on their own rhythm for finding the truth of the material. We found our own rhythm for producing work, too. Our intention is for artists to do their best work within our theater, so they must be surrounded by support. Support from the production staff—you must assume that duty for each member of your company. Your job is to help them do their job the best they can, to be respectful and responsible for the work the artist envisions. And as far as jobbers are concerned, they are also invested in this company, whether they're with you for two weeks or ten weeks. It all goes back to those core values repeated.

Oh, and here's another core value to add to those I mentioned: comfort with ambiguity. People who want absolutes do not always feel comfortable here. For us, living in the gray area is most interesting. Because with Sharon, we became much more of a risk-taking organization, taking risks onstage and taking financial risks, too.

Mitzi resigned eventually, because even though she was flexible and prudent, she couldn't solve the fact that our budget was not reflecting the expansion—not because of anything to do with her, but because the resources weren't immediately there. Since 1985, we've lived with a degree of financial risk. We've had years with surplus and years with debt. But without risk, without taking large leaps, you can't grow. That's a price I choose to pay.

You've got to always think you can do it. Leaps of faith and acts of will! Every day, I come into work, open the doors on the first day of rehearsal for a show, and I believe that show will be great.

REINVENTION LEADS TO GOOD THINGS

It ain't over till it's over; just ask Kevin Mayes. This respected Chicago theater artist was a longtime member of Bailiwick Repertory and greatly proud of his association with the company's daring, lauded works. Then, in 2008, things changed—Bailiwick Repertory lost the performance space it had used for fifteen years because of financial problems. Mayes picks up the story from there:

Bailiwick Repertory had to close because of financial and legal reasons. It wasn't a sudden thing—it happened because of a lot of precarious financial circumstances.

153

In December 2008, David Zak left the theater's space on Belmont; attempts were made to sustain the company in a kind of floating capacity, without a permanent space. In terms of funding, though, it was like going to the same trough over and over again for money, as not enough effort had been spent on expanding the donor base. I think, too, that a number of risky projects didn't pay off, from both an artistic and financial perspective. Finally, the board of directors and David decided to close the doors.

A group of us who had been active in the company—actors, directors, designers, etc.—really decided we wanted to continue, though, so I approached the board about the possibility of using the Bailiwick name. After all, in Chicago, there are approximately 200 active theater companies—brand awareness is half the battle! Artistically, from a mission perspective, we wanted to expand upon the previous work Bailiwick had done. We just thought, "Let's take a stab at this; let's see if we can regenerate, using a fresh, artistic-led approach."

We started up officially as the new Bailiwick entity in the fall of 2009. Calling ourselves Bailiwick Chicago, we established ties with a completely new board of directors. In its previous incarnation, Bailiwick had pursued a strong GLBT programming focus, and while we still wanted to do that work, we wanted to expand into further diversity as well—in effect, we wanted to tell stories about people whose stories are not being told. African American stories, Latino stories, Asian stories—and to this end, we wanted to work with organizations that serve different communities as well as organizations that serve the GLBT community. For every major project, we partnered—for instance, on our production of Elton John's *Aida*, we partnered with a wonderful African American dance company. The core of our mission became to partner—this furthered our dedication to developing new works as well, as with the musical we worked on that's modeled off of the O'Neil Playwrights' Conference.

The way we decided to work is as an ensemble, or as we call it, the Collective.

The Collective is responsible for pursuing our artistic mission as a whole; we amassed thirteen permanent members, and twenty artistic associates, plus expected more to join over time. We have to be careful when it comes to size, so our group won't get so big that things get unruly! Everyone in the Collective had some working relationship to the old Bailiwick; we've also looked for diversity in terms of skills, age, cultural experience, and ways of thinking.

THE IMPORTANCE OF A BOARD IN THE GROWTH PROCESS

The members of the Steppenwolf ensemble have, of course, always been ahead of the curve. The Steppenwolf board is also brilliant at foreseeing the future and the changes that must be met to meet it.

Choosing Martha Lavey, Michael Gennaro, and then David Hawkanson to head Steppenwolf was one such well-strategized move. Another very important step the board took was to completely examine where the company could go next, in both artistic and business aspects. The board handed its proposed plans to its new hires, who deftly carried out the changes, and took the company on to even greater achievements.

But what's most unusual about this story is the way the board reevaluated itself to benefit the company as a whole. Michael Gennaro remembers:

> In the process of bringing Martha Lavey and myself on, the board worked on a strategic plan to get a sense of what they wanted [us] to change, expand upon, whatever. All of those [things] were accomplished in just about three years.
>
> At the same time, things started to happen, like getting the National Medal of Arts and the Illinois Arts Legend Award. A number of things mounted on top of each other from just doing the work. We also expanded the spaces. We also expanded the amount of real estate we have to support what we're doing. I think what's interesting is, the board kind of looked around and said, "Wait a minute—we challenged the administration and the artistic office to do a bunch of things, and now they've done them all. We've kind of fallen behind. Now we need to step up and regovern ourselves, put a plan on the table to change the structure of the way we do things, so we can catch up and get back on course." Which they did. So there was a kind of stepping up of everything around us, and I think to get to that place, for the organization as a whole, was a great accomplishment.

DIVERSIFICATION

Sometimes, in order for a company to be at its most productive, it has to be willing and eager to wipe the artistic and business slate clean and start over.

Susan Albert Loewenberg explains how her company has progressed through her willingness to fully embrace changes in her environment, as suggested by her esteemed collaborators and as a unique means to the end of securing the organization's ultimate longevity and excellence.

> I think the reason I've succeeded is because I've kept moving. By my nature, I'm a tenacious person—you'll notice I've been with the same company for twenty-seven years—but I've reinvented the company. I think that rather than go off and do something else, I stayed within the same structure and just made different businesses.
>
> I think that my skill is, I'm able to see an opportunity and go with it, move on.

Producing theater in a ninety-nine-seat situation was a great learning experience, but it's not something I'd want to devote my life to. I mean, in LA, it's silly. It's for young people to stretch their wings. It's not a lifetime career. It's just not.

We were never really able, for whatever reason, to fully realize this company as a theatrical performing company. Not because of the actors—we just couldn't raise the money. That's part of the problem with Los Angeles. Los Angeles, particularly at that time and probably just as much today, it just doesn't step up to the plate. It just doesn't.

To me, the fact that it never professionalized was its death knell. The fact that we don't have a coterie of general managers and advertising agencies—it's impossible to advertise in the *Los Angeles Times*. There are all kinds of reasons why, until recently, it's been a one-show town with the Taper. It's been too difficult. Too many things conspire against being taken seriously.

Plus, if you saw what happened in New York [after the World Trade Center attack], you realize how dependent even that city is, frankly, on the bridge-and-tunnel traffic and the real tourists, the out-of-towners. You can't support the theater just with the people living in New York City.

People don't come to Los Angeles to go to the theater. We don't have that advantage, so we have to depend entirely upon our indigenous population. And it just doesn't work.

But be that as it may, we continued as a group. The fund-raising for this idea was kind of languishing. We had actually built a beautiful, gorgeous space for a workshop. We would meet regularly and work on pieces and stuff, and Richard Dreyfuss said one day, "You know, I've always wanted to work on the radio, do a radio drama." I said, "I'll go and see Ruth Seymour." She got very excited about it—she's a very adventurous [radio] programmer. She thought it was a fabulous idea, and said, "Let's do something big." I said, "Why don't we do a book?" We then began the search for a book, and my idea was, all thirty-four people have to be in this thing. We came up with Sinclair Lewis's *Babbit*. It took us a year and a half to record and edit. We did it in the studio, put the whole book up on a computer, and figured out which characters were in which scenes. There were ninety characters played by all thirty-four actors; the main characters, of course, were only played by one actor, but the minor characters, they doubled. We split up the narration. It was a twelve-and-a half recording. Lynn debuted it in 1987 on Thanksgiving day as a marathon, all day long, and it became a huge hit and instant cult classic.

National Public Radio picked it up and ran it all over the country. It is still a magnificent recording. I mean, we had absolutely no idea what we were doing, but we had a fabulous editor who was a real radio pro. And Gordon Hunt, Helen' s dad, a terrific guy who was the head of recording for animation for Hanna-Barbera at the time. The BBC heard us and contacted us. They came over—it was the occasion of the UK–LA Festival 1987. We did two plays with them—*The Crucible*, starring Stacy Keach, Richard Dreyfuss, Hector Elizondo, and Michael York, and *Are You Now or Have You Ever Been?* as a companion piece. The BBC, Martin Jenkins, came over, and it was a big task. We were doing it on a soundstage, not in front of people. And the programs came out brilliantly—the BBC paid for everything. Ruth aired them, the BBC aired them, we got paid for our time, all the actors got paid, and it was a fantastic launch.

We have since done many programs in collaboration with the BBC. They usually come over—once, we went to England, to the BBC studios. Some of the best work we've ever done, we've done with them.

This began slowly taking over—we were still doing a little theater production, but by 1992, I think I did my last [stage] show, my last regular theater piece. We had a little program of play readings that we usually did in our office. It was becoming too crowded—it held about seventy people. Ed Asner called me—I was on vacation in Europe—and he said, "You've got to meet with these guys! A partner of mine is staying in this new hotel, and we should do something in their ballroom!" I thought, "Yuck, Ed, I don't want to do something in a hotel ballroom." But he kept insisting.

I came back, and I said, "OK, it's Ed, I've got to do this." So I went and met with the hotel manager of the Guest Quarters in Santa Monica, which later morphed into Doubletree, and then became part of Hilton. Long story short, we're having this meeting, and they wanted to build up the hotel, because they'd just opened in Santa Monica. Suddenly, a lightbulb went on in my head, and I thought, "I could record plays live in performance, just like we did at our benefit."

I had no idea whether this would fly. I contacted Ruth, and she thought it was interesting. We agreed that we would do six plays, send out a little brochure and see if anybody was interested. We got a terrific response back. We did each [play] over one night, no idea what we were doing. We hired a recording engineer who brought in equipment.

I remember the first show we did was a Molière play. The actors were all grouped around one microphone—it was terrible! But people seemed to like it. Over the course of those six plays, we actually began to figure out how to do it, and we were stunned—people loved coming there. They loved coming to the hotel, having dinner there—it was a package deal, it was easy to park. It worked for Los Angeles.

It was very strange, because everything worked. You had famous actors, you had a limited time frame for them, you had a kind of interesting, car-culture-friendly venue situation. It was a very odd thing. We actually started, by the second year, doing some good work. We figured out how to record, we figured out what to do.

157

The thing about Doubletree was, they were a fantastic corporate sponsor. They paid for everything—all of a sudden hundreds of people were coming to their hotel. We were with them for ten years—we went from one show to four shows, the ballroom held about four hundred people. They paid for the brochure, they really got us going, and we got a grant from the Irvine Foundation, which also helped us.

We built a subscription audience. By the time we left the Doubletree in 1998, we had a huge subscription audience and a fantastic program. By that time, we were doing fourteen shows a year, four performances each, so we could make good recordings, but we realized we had to do a lot of performances to get a good recording. Now we do five or six, so we cross-edit and get a very superior product. We built this incredible reputation, we were on KCRW, the centerpiece of KCRW Playhouse. We were on twenty, twenty-five times a year, we were promoed every week, if you said "LA Theatre Works," everybody knew what it was because we were on the radio all the time.

Around 1994, I began to realize, we ought to sell these things. So then we had to go back and get all the rights for audio sale, which was an interesting process, and start another business, which was the audio publishing business. We got a great start-up grant from the Endowment for about $100,000, developed a catalogue, developed packaging.

We basically started a whole huge other business, which was an enormous undertaking,

I cannot begin to describe it. I mean, we are audio publishers, and radio has been a very interesting vehicle for us, but it's not the end of the story.

WHEN FAITH AND FORTUNE COLLIDE

Sometimes, when faced with whether to take a risk in the name of growth, you just have to believe it will work. Even when you're not sure it will.

If you're lucky, you'll build an ever-enlarging audience support base. Sooner or later, that's going to lead to a need for increased space requirements. So you'll be looking at a move to a larger venue.

At a time such as this, when growth is going to be necessary in order to make more revenue, people tend to panic. What if we pick up and move and our loyal audience doesn't feel like making the trek across town, or down that extra three exit ramps on the freeway, to come see us? What if we overcalculate seat numbers, and every show has an audience deficit? "What ifs" tend to multiply in your mind like unsupervised bunnies in a pet store, you know.

Unless you refuse to indulge that sort of bunker mentality in the first place. Here's how to get a hold of yourself: What is your alternative? To stagnate? Of course not. If you are truly committed to the ongoing progress of your organization, don't chicken out. Just tell yourself your move is going to work spectacularly well. If you don't quite believe that yet, stay close to your partners who do and let them brainwash you with their positive, can-do attitudes.

In those beautiful early days of Berkeley Repertory, Mitzi Sales and Michael Leibert both believed in the future growth of their organization against very high odds. They made a move despite the risks, and it paid off in spades. Mitzi Sales remembers:

> A very interesting experience, actually, a wonderful, sort of alarming, funny thing: There was a minor joke when Michael first looked around and found the space on College Avenue, my comment was like, "Build the space and they will come." When we built the space in downtown Berkeley, that actually happened!
>
> We had this subscriber base; we were practically sold out at 153 seats. But when we built this four-hundred-seat theater, I thought, "Oh, boy." My experience was how long it took us to build up the audience in the College Avenue space. We built the theater, sent out a subscription brochure, and the unbelievable number of subscribers! It grew—kabloom! People were buying subscriptions who had never seen a show. It was like, "What?!" It was remarkable.
>
> You've got to prepare yourself for a lot of lean years, to build your reputation, to make your mistakes. But it did help, in those early years, that there was a foundation for the expansion and development in theaters in those days—it actually did help that there were those organizations, that they would have meetings and we could come together with other people who were struggling. We could all figure out where to go to get some money, how to market with no budget and no money. There are resources.

JOB SATISFACTION

A good artistic director wants to make his employees happy—every employee, including actors, directors, technical staff, design staff, administrative staff, the lot. A good managing director helps the artistic director make this happen.

When your company has a high job satisfaction percentage, the company moves forward. This can be tough to accomplish in the theater, by the way. As you probably know, theater folks love to be dramatic and complain. Some live to be long-suffering.

So know this in advance. When it happens to you, stage a preemptive strike: when you hear rumblings of discontent, address them directly with an employee before the discontent starts to spread. Often, employees will try to enlist other coconspirators to agree with their complaints, and you don't want to have mutiny on your hands. So try to give in on little points when you can. Make a pleasant working environment for your actors.

159

Still, don't be a pushover. You can't allow your people to go diva on you. You also have to make sure that folks don't get too comfortable after a while in the routine of working for your company. Find novel ways to discourage laziness.

As a theater veteran, Dona Lee Kelly, former managing director at Jean Cocteau Repertory in New York City, believes that it's key to always be aware of the message you're sending out. "Ultimately, it's art that's going to bring people into the theater, not how well you manage, even though I'm saying you'd better manage impeccably well," she says. "But that's part of management, making sure that the art is very focused and everything it's saying is prioritized.

People have to understand that management is not just crunching numbers. It's really making sure that the organization is defined, handled well, and positioned well artistically within the community. That's part of being a producer.

SMALL STEPS FORWARD MEAN A LOT

When charting the growth of your organization, you may feel a bit discouraged if you only see small improvements happening slowly. You've probably got your heart set on big, explosive, visible changes you can brag about to your family and friends, like four-star reviews in the *New York Times*, riots breaking out in the unruly patron lines that routinely ring your block, and Cate Blanchett calling every hour on the hour, dying to know when you'll be casting her in a classic.

OK, back down to earth. That stuff is very nice indeed, but much more realistically, growth should be measured in small increments. Set mini goals you can meet fairly quickly—it's a real boost, plus every drop in the bucket gets you closer to your ultimate dreams fulfilled.

The best way to make early progress, which carries you through to the next level, is to decide what is important to you to achieve within your company. Also, surround yourself with capable people, who know what they are doing on a regular basis. Both of these things are key, because what you decide is really important will be something you get going on trying to implement from day one, and you'll soon see little signs everywhere that what you want is starting to happen.

And the progressive value of people who know what they're doing? They get busy doing it and slowly but surely that lightens the load of your theater's ongoing to-do list. Really, capable people are the greatest sigh of relief you'll ever breathe.

Susan Kosoff followed a similar slow-but-sure strategy at Wheelock. The company began by focusing on its interest in theatrical education.

In the second year, we started having classes. That program has grown tremendously over the years and has become a substantial part of our budget. But we only started it as an educational enterprise.

It took us a long time to get a full-time educational director—it's only been in the last couple of years that we've had that.

I think in the beginning, every power tool we bought was a big deal! But I decided early on that we were going to put money into permanent equipment rather than rent it, and that way we built things up. There are always ways that you want to build up a space, and I think that there continue to be. But it's a very different facility, much more current, certainly than it was twenty years ago. This year, it improved. Some of that is that, over time, we've worked with some very good designers, tech directors, people who make that happen.

MARKETING MILESTONES

There are as many theories of how you can use marketing to power your company along as there are members of the Osmond family. Yet I feel there's only one way that really helps you determine whether you are on the right horse: don't compete. That's when you make true progress.

Crazy? Not at all. When you're marketing something at your theater while looking over your shoulder to see how the guy next to you is marketing something at his, you've already lost your edge. You've stopped paying attention to what is great about the show your company has to offer.

Pay attention to the reasons you love the play you're presenting. Why did you choose this material in the first place? What blew you away at auditions about the actor you're casting in the lead? What took your breath away about the set the first time you saw it? Review your enthusiasm and when you figure out what you loved originally about this work, and continue to love, use marketing to tell your potential audience about it. It's that simple.

The key to marketing progress is to polish each product you offer your audience, as you go along, into the best product it can be. Then tell the world about it and collect your money. Not every show will be a winner, but if you're trying your best to make each current offering the most it can be, you will be learning more with each show you do.

Jack Reuler (Mixed Blood) has this very healthy take on marketing:

I don't believe that we're competing with other live events. I think if you go to a live event and have a good experience, you're going to go to another live event. In terms of subscription, what we've done is say, "You can come and see all these shows that we're doing, but then you can go see culturally specific programming at these other institutions." I'm real excited about the possibility of that. I don't know if I have the marketing chops to get enough people to buy it, but I'm sure going to try.

We're getting a good audience—it's who we want to have. We're getting a good mix of audience members. So that's looking good. I think we've had really good luck, in a city like ours. A number of theaters in different cities have done bilingual work. We do a show each year in Spanish and English—some nights it's in Spanish, some nights it's in English—and we've done very well with that in terms of attendance. This last year, we actually did a show where the characters were bilingual and depending on who they were talking to, they actually kept switching during the course of the production. It worked out really well.

We're sort of finding our way in that area. My current intention is to become the theater, in our area, of new populations—primarily immigrants and refugees, of which there are many. The programming reflects that.

So between doing new work, which I feel strongly about, and giving the voice of the great writers and others the place in which they can be heard, and trying to reach these new audiences—again, whatever we do, it's the very nature of doing race-based things. Whenever anybody who isn't white gets onstage in America, there's some political statement made. Because of that, you need to be that much better than everybody else doing it. So really, to maintain high-level standards of quality while doing what we're trying to do in terms of substance and content is really important.

The '80s, in many ways, were a huge success for us. I think that a couple of those theater critics who completely bought into us were directly responsible for that. It wasn't genius marketing; we'd open a show, we'd get a rave review, then we'd get more support and word of mouth. I thought that's what marketing was.

Jack's right—that is, in a nutshell, what marketing is supposed to be.

He defines his idea of progress very personally, and so should you. Your company is not like anybody else's, so to compare yourself to others is a futile exercise. Don't do something if it doesn't mean anything to you.

To really make the most of your company's growth, that growth has to be for a purpose. Every step that forwards your company's mission is the growth that counts.

PART THREE

NOW AND FOREVER

Phaedra by Adam Bock
directed by Rose Riordan
Shotgun Players 2011 Season
Pictured: Catherine Castellanos and Keith Burkland
Photo by Pak Han

Chapter Twelve
Navigating Financial Realities

"The main ingredient of any theater company, more than money, more than knowledge, more than connections, is passion," said Gil Cates, founder and producing director of the Geffen Playhouse.

> You need to have that extraordinary desire to help you face down tremendous obstacles. You'll face issues with programming, finding physical space, planning the direction your company will go in, but if you don't have that passion, it's not worth the effort—just don't do it. Every wonderful theater artist I work with is motivated by this passion—actors ranging from Annette Bening to Frank Langella to Peter Falk, as well as our own staff and crew. Passion can help get you through.

Mr. Cates was known throughout the entertainment industry as proof of his own philosophy—his love of theater clearly drove him to the highest achievements possible. And in today's ruthless financial climate, passion *is* the crucial fuel you need to keep moving forward. In many cases, passion may seem like the only weapon you have when fighting to establish, or maintain, your theater company against incredibly tough odds.

A report by the NEA found that there was a 12 percent revenue drop for nonprofits after 2001, nationwide. Even the most admired, longest-enduring national theater companies haven't been immune to recessionary impact. In the first edition of this book, published in 2002, I profiled fourteen companies—five of those organizations have since been shuttered. Add in the scores of lesser-known nonprofits forced to terminate business across the country and it's crystal clear that times are as tough as they've ever been.

Is your company doomed to fail, then? Should you give up on your dreams before you even put them into motion? In a word: no. If you approach your company with the right balance of information and ingenuity, of course you still have a shot! It all boils down to being realistic—and honest. I've noticed that a great percentage of the theater companies that have gone under recently were actually suffering in silence for some time before their problems became public. Crushing debt, low ticket sales, and cash flow difficulties are bound to overtake you eventually if you remain passive about them—but if you voice concerns and take action early, you have more financial control than you know. To start your company or keep your company alive, the most important thing to do at all times is to be honest with yourself about your circumstances—and face them down, no matter how hard that seems.

In this chapter, our experts frankly discuss financial issues with a view toward staying proactive, not daunted. Apply their examples and philosophies to your own situation, mix in that all-important passion, and vow to accomplish all you can.

BACK FROM THE BRINK

When it comes to finances, even the most mindful theater organization can get caught off-balance. Sure, you're fiscally conservative as much as any company can be—you cut corners on props, curtail your ad dollars smartly, maybe even ask your staff to take a pay cut (and take one yourself, of course). Things are manageable—until your audience members have to choose between buying a ticket to your new show and buying groceries and are forced to stop coming to your theater.

When your best-laid plans and tried-and-true strategies stop working, stop using them.

Step back and reorganize—it's a simple concept but can be incredibly hard to do. You need clarity to see where things are precisely going south, so put a number of heads together. Sit down with your staff, lay out your worst fears on the table, and back them up with budget and box office figures. Crunch and recrunch the numbers together—chances are good there will be some wiggle room for allocation of funds somewhere. But be up front with each other. Should you think about an immediate reorganizational plan? Are things so dire that you need to go to your funders, board, even community?

That idea may drop your stomach to the floor, but it can actually be the best move to make. The Jewish Theatre San Francisco was reborn just this way. "I believe the company survived thanks to the perseverance and ingenuity of Aaron Davidman and Sara Schwartz Geller," says Corey Fischer.

They were TJT's second generation of leaders, who, in a sense, completed their "initiation" into full-fledged leadership during TJT's worst financial crisis ever in 2008. Aaron and Sara recognized that the business model, or lack thereof, that TJT was laboring under was no longer sustainable. Debt load, lack of cash reserves, limits to earned income, growing fixed costs, understaffing, and more were killing us. Aaron, Sara, Naomi, and I decided we had one last card to play: reveal the truth of our dire straits to our funders and community, along with a credible plan for a sustainable future, that would make it clear we would be making considerable changes to that end.

I drafted the original new strategic plan, which was then edited extensively by Aaron and Sara. This was also one of the hardest moments for me in thirty years of TJT's life: the major changes entailed reducing full-time salaried employees to two—Aaron as AD and Sara as ED. As ED, Sara also did the work of development director and marketing/PR director with some outsourcing. [We also budgeted for] one half-time administrative assistant and a bookkeeper at quarter-time. Naomi and I went off salary, no pension, although TJT committed to continue covering our health insurance, no small thing. We then since worked on a project-to-project basis and I also did freelance grant-writing to assist Sara.

The other hard call was to move away from TJT's thirty-year commitment to the creation of collaborative ensemble works—new plays, Bay area premieres, reimagined classics—unless Aaron and Sara presented our case to a group of local foundation people who had funded us fairly consistently, convened by a program officer from one of the most supportive foundations. They responded by agreeing to an extraordinary joint grant that would do a great deal to get us out of our debt, which was mainly left from cost overruns in 1998 when we renovated our theater, and give us a good start on the following season. This was done on the condition that we raise $150,000 in the following three months from our board and community. We did it; the grant followed.

Maintaining a financial reorganization is tough—but it buys you a lifeline. It's very important to change your expectations to fit what you can do for the time being and avoid pie-in-the-sky thinking. This doesn't mean you can't again one day pursue your most desired objectives, like dream productions or being able to afford employing that wonderful guest artist for a season. It does mean you may see new avenues you want to pursue that might never have occurred to you before.

Berkeley Rep has, in recent times, made these kinds of necessary, positive adjustments. "This recession has required us to rethink our priorities," says Susan Medak.

It has given us a chance to jettison some practices that we were wedded to, but that no longer make sense. It has given us a reason to leap with more urgency into new technologies that may help us reduce costs in the short and long terms. Overall, this financial challenge has made us focus on our core competencies, and has required that we be willing to effect real, fundamental changes in areas that have hitherto been sacrosanct. We've become much more opportunistic; by that, I mean that we've become much more attuned to a behavior in which we try to take advantage of opportunities that come our way.

TO CONCEDE OR NOT CONCEDE

OK, so you've got some stability. How do you get more? For a growing number of companies, the answer is: sell out creatively. It's a shame, but it's happening way too often.

Not to be a gloom-meister, but all you have to do is take a look at the state of today's Broadway to smell the coffee—it's revivals, revivals, revivals. Of course, a big reason for that is the tourist dollar—producers are looking for shows that are familiar, sure bets, especially following the challenging times the business has faced from September 11, 2001, all the way through to today. Beyond Broadway, things are equally tough all over in this respect. A major reason why is also economics—following the Broadway model, many regional and small theater companies are choosing well-known shows that will minimize their financial risks. To make a buck, you need a jukebox musical or a big honking superstar as your lead, or a jukebox musical with a big honking superstar as your lead.

Not to say this is always a bad thing—populist fare rocks when done right. David Fuller, former artistic director of Jean Cocteau Repertory, says, "I don't discount plays just for their entertainment value. I've always felt that there's a place for a play that truly entertains, because you have to temper a production schedule with some levity. Laughing at ourselves is also part of looking at the human condition."

On the other hand, you don't always have to stick to conventional choices in order to attract an audience. Many times, a company's most successful move in terms of material turns its audience's expectation on its head slightly, while still retaining the basic germ of quality and what the company stands for thematically. So can you afford, for instance, to still take a chance on a new work by a promising playwright, even if that artist isn't a name yet? I think you can, if you let quality be your guide and if you're prudent about the development process.

Here's an example: Let's say you've got such a playwright in your circle who's been writing drafts of her script for seven years now. You're interested in the work as it reads, yet she recoils in horror at the thought of your company actually producing her play because it just isn't perfect yet. Should you give her more time to rewrite, then do the play, the delay causing a possible financial loss? Or should you pass altogether, with a view toward financial feasibility?

I would pass. After a certain number of rewrites, material becomes little more than an exercise in typing. Can you think of a bigger time waster and commercial risk for your fledgling company? Your best bet, both creatively and financially, is to go with that neat new work by that undiscovered playwright who's willing to collaborate with you, won't suck dollars out of your coffers "improving" her already fine work, and whose writing voice feels fresh. Offer this writer a fair financial deal that won't bankrupt you, and you could have a truly cost-effective, high-quality hit. As producer/director/performer Ralph Remington puts it, "You take chances on material that wouldn't ordinarily be used. I think what happens in the American theater today is that we develop plays to death. All the life is beaten out. The original impulse, the original energy, the original excitement gets stale."

And impulse, energy, and excitement are the elements audiences *always* want to pay money to see.

COST-CUTTING 411

Belt-tightening may not be a lot of fun but doing a cut-rate job is an even worse option.

Remember that community theater production of *Brigadoon* you sat through, repulsed by the tacky costumes and flimsy sets? Know when to scale down rather than cheapen your product and overall reputation.

If you can't do a particular play because you don't have the money to stage it properly, then don't attempt to put up a lesser version. Shelve the show for now. Your company will look the better for it. This is good advice any time, not just during your start-up period. Seek, instead, material that fits your company's size at this moment. If you can't pay six actors, do a play with four parts, then make it up to whichever actors in your company can't be in the show next time. Choose a show that doesn't require a huge set if you can't afford one. Just follow your common sense.

Go over your receipts, essential monthly expenses, and payroll, and see where there's fat you might be able to cut. Ask your department heads for expense listings and, with their input and advice, reshuffle some budget numbers. Put a generic-brand paper towel in your restrooms. You get the drift—be practical. "Theater is always a challenge, even in good times," say Paul Zuckerman of Chicago City Limits.

If you have the right creative team, you need to strike when those stars are aligned. But given economic realities, try to eliminate as many fixed costs as possible—say, work out of a home instead of an office. Find a partnership with other companies to share performing space rather than being the sole rent payer. Keep staffing at a minimum.

Which brings up the uncomfortable topic of layoffs or outright position eliminations. If you have to let people go, how do you do so most humanely? Again, it all comes back to honesty. Sit your staff members down collectively first, and explain the financial issues your company is facing in plain language. Express your admiration for each staffer and your appreciation for their talents and commitment. Promise that you will speak to each of them one on one and openly, in detail, as soon as you're aware of any need to let anyone go.

Then, if push comes to shove, do just that. If you have to lay someone off or cut a job, talk to him or her privately and respectfully. Try to offer this person options: Is there any chance, for instance, your box office manager might be able to do the job on a limited or show-by-show basis? Could you give a concrete date at which you might bring him or her back to the company? Could a former acting company member stay with you as an understudy or swing? Try to find any way you can to offer support and future connection.

Be very careful, however, not to make promises you may not be able to keep. For many companies, it's very hard to see the future with complete accuracy right now. "I'm not really a five-year planner—I don't think, in this economy, you can be," says Richard Pletcher of Amish Acres.

> You have to focus on surviving financially and being practical. I run our budgets very closely and have cut thousands by figuring out how much outside work we can really do in-house. We have worked with a lighting designer from New York, for example, who was excellent, but we can't do that hiring anymore feasibly, so now we do our own design. President Obama stated in a speech that our area suffered the highest unemployment rate in the country—20 percent of our county is jobless. So, of course, theater dollars are going to be the last discretionary amounts anyone here is going to spend.

LET'S MAKE A DEAL

To stay in business, it's a must for your theater company to honor its financial commitments. This can seem impossible, though, when you're swamped by commitments to unions, cast, crew, creditors—it may seem like the whole world has its hand out. In cases like this, you may be tempted to fudge on a few payments. Don't do it.

Even if you think a missed payment won't be noticed, it will be. Never, ever, for instance, try to cheat a publishing company out of royalties. Even if you're putting on a play in a dilapidated shed out in a cornfield in the middle of nowhere, word of mouth might spread. Stranger things have happened. You just never know who might get wind of the fact you're presenting a play you haven't paid the piper to present. So don't take a chance.

If you really don't have the money to pay royalties on a show you've got your heart set on, it's better to choose free material or material at a lower royalty percentage (if you can swing that). Know this, though: you can negotiate! Call the play's publisher and plead your case as nicely as possible. Many of the folks who work at companies such as Samuel French are very helpful. That's not to say that you'll get to do the play you want at a lower royalty rate, by any means. But either way, by getting in touch, you will develop a friendly relationship with a contact at a publishing firm and impress him or her with your straightforward honesty. In the future, that could help your company out a lot. This strategy can also work when dealing with unions and vendors, especially if you contact these folks at the very first sign you may be having a financial issue. Susan Kosoff of Wheelock Family Theatre reiterates, "Be in contact with a company ASAP, so that you know what's involved. And don't be afraid to negotiate, based on the specifics of your organization."

If you're having problems cutting paychecks, it's essential that you tell your employees right away then give them a precise date on which they will receive the money they're owed. Never duck a phone call. Never fib regarding someone's salary. This advice should go without saying, but a very offensive trend that's emerged in recent times all over the theater world is simply stiffing hardworking artists and techies, with no warning or explanation. You're better than that, period.

IGNORE THE NOISE

Whenever rough financial waters need to be navigated, many theater company heads become too aware—OK, obsessed in some cases—with what the company across town is doing. This paranoia can be chalked up, to some extent, to the dog-eat-dog nature of the business as a whole or to good old-fashioned insecurity. As we touched on previously, whatever the cause, try with all your might not to get caught up with how your competition's faring.

A true winner, as we've previously established, knows only to compete with himself or herself. This means keeping your nose to the grindstone, focusing on what your company does best, and doing that even better. So don't decide you're going to better a play a rival company has done, and made money with. Why? It makes you look petty. It's bad karma. It's a bad business move even if the first show was a hit. You'll need to top its commercial and critical success handily, or your show will look like a dud.

Yet you'd be surprised how many companies play bumper cars like this with their competition's shows. You'd also be surprised how many companies never bother to research what productions have been done in their area recently, so they don't accidentally schedule the same material. Follow this example instead, from David Zak regarding the early days of Bailiwick Repertory:

> We were selecting slightly off-center plays. Plays not done by others in the city. Too often, I think, theaters choose plays they want to do, disregarding the production history of those scripts in the city.
>
> We started doing classics. *The Country Wife* was followed by *Pygmalion*. Only then did we add new works to our artistic agenda.

Even in the worst monetary times, you need always to define success your way, not measure it through externals. Here's a good case in point, brought to us by Terrence Dwyer regarding La Jolla Playhouse. In the early days of the Playhouse, challenging classics became the sterling standard of fare presented regularly to audiences—1953's *The Dazzling Hour* and 1958's *The Skin of Our Teeth* being just two of many examples. For their time, works such as these were considered daringly brilliant.

Throughout the years, La Jolla Playhouse continued its dedication to innovative material. Some years back, Des McAnuff, who is a great fan of meshing pop culture with art and social culture at large, commenced work on *80 Days*, a large-scope musical à la *Around the World in 80 Days*, infused with the genius of Ray Davies of the rock band the Kinks.

It was original stuff, to be sure, but wasn't one of the Playhouse's biggest commercial hits. No matter—McAnuff considered it to be a success. His perspective to this day is that a show can be an ultimate artistic success regardless of its box office take.

Do you agree with that viewpoint? If not, be brave, take that leap, and believe. You've got to have the confidence in yourself to think like Des McAnuff. You may be thinking, *Huh? He's a theatrical god, and I'm a pipsqueak with a brand-new theater company.* Yet having faith in the choices you make for your company means you won't be constantly second-guessing yourself and beating yourself up. Really, it's about setting your own standard of excellence.

Be true to that standard and you'll always be satisfied with your company's output.

Don't take wild, crazy, unnecessary risks at a time when your budget is strained, but don't hold back against your best instincts, either. Also, ignore rumor and doomsaying, which has exploded across the theater community during this period of fiscal uncertainty.

Yes, some companies aren't doing well; some have folded. Yet many companies are on track to survive and there's no reason why yours can't be one of them.

DON'T PANIC

Yes, indeed, perspective is your best friend when faced with difficult financial problems. It's very, very important not to let your mind automatically go to worst-case scenarios. After all, there have been numerous times in the theater, and in the world as a whole, when recessions have come and recessions have eased. "I don't believe there was ever a 'good old days' when financial times weren't difficult," concurs Mixed Blood's Jack Reuler.

After thirty-four years, I've never heard anyone speak in the current tense about comfort, overflowing coffers, or the absence of financial struggle. That being said, my advice is, mission, mission, mission, planning, and analysis. While a theater or nonprofit should always let mission, vision, and values drive its every decision, this is especially true in more difficult financial times. As foundations' portfolios collapsed, corporate profits disappeared, government budgets evaporated, and individuals' savings were decimated—all impacting giving power—some theaters decided to try to replace contributed income by producing work with stronger box office potential. Often those ticket sales never materialized, and when philanthropy rebounded, those organizations were penalized for losing their way.

Never confuse financial stability for institutional health. That health is driven by the organization's attempt to realize its mission. As times get tight, dig into mission. It isn't a fund-raising tool—it is something to achieve, and when achieved, to close the doors, as mission is accomplished. Survival is not the end, it's the means to the end. Theaters that stick to purpose in the hardest of times will ultimately either thrive or go out of business, but it will have been on their own terms. Short or long, that is a career worth having.

Similarly, planning—strategic, communication, succession, whatever fits—and assessment reveal themselves to be the most valuable in hard times. Priorities have been set that can also allow for entrepreneurial opportunism. Keep records and follow the data for analysis that allows for smarter planning.

PUT YOURSELF OUT THERE

Which brings us back to Gil Cates of the Geffen Playhouse. He was a strong believer in putting out maximum effort to get returns and there's no better advice to help you weather financial challenges. "I think that many of the people who start a theater company raise their money and then say, 'I just want to direct.' You can't direct, or sustain your company, unless you put yourself out in the world and get the support you need," Gil stressed.

> This means making calls to people who can give you money, and going to lunches with them and hearing no for an answer, but then getting right back on the phone and calling someone else for lunch.
>
> You need a rhino hide to survive, because running a theater company isn't just about managing one enterprise. It's about managing many enterprises—financial, artistic, and more. You need energy and insight into many different things to do the job well.

As Gil told us at the start of this chapter, it comes back full circle to passion. Regardless of your company's financial situation, never let that unbridled enthusiasm dim. Jump in and get the job done.

SUCCESS SECRETS: FIVE TIPS FOR STAYING MOTIVATED

1. Take one hour a day to recharge your mental batteries. Exercise, read gossip on the web, eat a nice relaxing meal—do anything that takes your mind off running your company, because briefly recharging your battery will prevent burnout.

2. If you're working on something creative but just aren't feeling it—as in, you know you need to fix a scene with your team in rehearsal but you've watched it so many times you can't see it anymore—bring in a pair of fresh eyes. Preferably, this set of eyes should belong to someone who has no knowledge of the scene or your issues with it—the FedEx guy, an actor's girlfriend who just happens to be visiting that day, etc. Ask this person if the scene makes sense to them, and use their opinion as a tool for added clarity.

3. Only do one task at a time. When your day is extra heavy duty, it can be very easy to try to juggle twenty things at once. Slow is beautiful—take a deep breath and then focus only on what is directly in front of you. You'll actually save time if you omit other distractions and feel less frustrated.

4. When you're thinking your heart just isn't in the hard work you need to pour into your company anymore, don't make any rash decisions. Call your mom. Or

your dad, sister, brother, best friend since kindergarten—tell this trusted soul that you're losing steam and motivation. Then really listen to their response: no doubt they are going to remind you about who you really are—how strong, talented, and determined you have always been about your company and how much you love your work. No doubt they're going to let you know how proud they are of you, too. Bet you'll be feeling more energetic and motivated in no time.

5. It's a simple fact, but it's always key to remember: Sleep is the enemy of motivation. It can be really hard to get eight hours a night when you're spending all of your time planning, producing, and fund-raising, but you need to make time. Add two twenty-minute naps to your day—one mid-morning and one mid-afternoon; that brief respite curled up in a comfy spot, in your office or in an house seat if necessary, will help clear your mind and fire up your mood.

Shipwreck by Tom Stoppard
directed by Patrick Dooley
Shotgun Players 2013 Season
Pictured: Patrick Kelly Jones and Caitlyn Louchard
Photo by Pak Han

Chapter Thirteen
Creating Great Partnerships

Teamwork—it's the glue that holds any theater company together. By now, you know and trust your company members, the folks you're in the trenches with day in and day out. When your company starts to make a solid name for itself, you'll also be afforded the opportunity to work with new associates—people who admire what you're doing and want to collaborate artistically, for example. Or a corporate sponsor may have come calling—should you take the leap?

Maybe you've produced an original play that's done exceedingly well, and you (and your playwright) feel it's time to license the work so other groups can perform it. You'll need to partner with a publisher/license group—so you need to understand the way that process works. Similarly, a producer may be hovering around your latest production as it runs, dangling carrots as he expresses over and over how much he wants to pick up your show. How do you really know if you should hook up with this guy?

No matter what type of outside partnership you're considering, it's crucial that you *always* listen to your gut.

Your intuition is the greatest guide you have when it comes to filtering through the noise and determining if any partnership is truly in your company's best interest. Let's look at a variety of partnership situations you may find yourself evaluating, to see how you can best determine their value to your specific goals.

CORPORATE TEMPTATION

If your company makes a big splash—meaning your reviews are stellar, you've racked up a number of significant awards, and you have well-known actors as company members or company associates—then corporate sponsors may show interest in funding you. This may seem like Christmas and your birthday wrapped up in one big, cash-lined package, right? Well, hold on.

Forging an agreement with a corporate entity, either fully or partially, works well if the exchange you make is fair, and not suffocating. A sponsor who will fund a specific season in return for advertising on your website and in your audience materials might be offering you a fair deal, provided you negotiate only for a certain portion of time, and limit any input the sponsor has into creative decision-making.

A sponsor who wants a long-term deal with you, though, and offers you more money if you allow it to screen material is almost never worth your time, though. A sponsor with a certain commercial image, say for family-oriented products, could very well obtain the right to censor your work if you unwisely or unknowingly agree to this.

If a corporate entity approaches you, don't be dazzled; lawyer up. That's just good common sense, but it's amazing how many theater pros think they can negotiate on their own. Don't talk to a corporate sponsor at all unless your lawyer is present; then you can begin a constructive, positive dialogue while protecting your intellectual and business property, and pursue all of your options with an expert's perspective.

THE LAWS OF LICENSING

When it comes to licensing a new play you own the rights to—either solely on your own, or with a playwright—there are a few ways you can proceed. A producer will most likely be entitled to a percentage of performance rights if he or she produced the first full production of a play or musical, FYI; individual circumstances vary greatly, though, so you and your playwright should work out the terms that work best for both of you when negotiating a pre-production contract.

Most writers and producers, when applicable, send their material to publishers who act as licensing agencies. (Samuel French, of course, is one of the biggest players in this aspect of the industry.) A publisher will agree to publish the play, and will then negotiate performance rights with any venue wishing to perform it; you split the profits with the publisher. Here are the basic categories of venues that seek to perform published original work:

—AMATEUR—EDUCATIONAL PRODUCTIONS, or community theater productions with nonunion, amateur actors and director. Houses are usually less than 500 seats, and contracts are most often per performance only.

—**PROFESSIONAL**—regional or professional productions with union or nonunion actors and director. These venues are often larger than 500 seats, and a cut of the door is often paid in addition to contracted licensing fees.

—**BROADWAY/FIRST RATE**—New York legitimate or West End legitimate productions with all-union personnel. Royalties based on ticket sales are usually structured into these agreements.

—**COMPETITION/FESTIVAL**—productions that are limited runs in this category have specifics that vary widely.

Can you keep your rights yourself, and license your show without involving a publisher/licensing agency?

You can, but it's not advisable. Why? It marks you as an amateur, and gives off the message that you'd rather make a buck than act according to industry standard. Also, practically, do you want the hassle of watching door receipts, and double-checking all of that bookkeeping for every venue that performs your play?

Didn't think so. Choose a great publisher who wants to work with you, and have an entertainment lawyer check over any prospective licensing deal.

ART FOR ART'S SAKE

Artistic collaborations can be thrilling and rewarding—or soul-crushing and messy. How can you tell whether joining forces with another creative artist or entity would really be a good fit for your company?

That question is a real double-edged sword. You could say that working with a creative entity that shares your vision to a T is the ultimate—but then, a company coming at their work from a polar opposite perspective can challenge and reenergize your process invaluably. Most successful theater collaborations, I've found, work best not so much on whether the same artistic approach is shared, but if a specific *goal* is set. What do you both agree the audience should gain from your collaboration? If you agree on the answer to that question, you're off to a grand start.

Lily Tung Crystal believes in this precise factor when she chooses artists to work with. Crystal explains,

> Our group vision has really been to touch people, to create work that sticks with people. That's beautiful to me. Because of this vision, I really feel it's important to wait as long as we need to between shows. I've seen so many companies start fast out of the gate, and it's too much at once. If you expand too quickly and are too smart to support that kind of ambition, being fast can make you fizzle. Our goal is to do high-quality work.

What we never want, what no theater company should ever want, is the audience to look at us and say, "You haven't proven yourselves yet." Doing shoddy work just to do work proves that audience perception.

I also feel, as acting has been the main focus of our company members, that producing a show very quickly just to produce it is equally wrong. Each production needs time once we are focusing on it. It's good for us to build a show, to mull over what we're doing as we go along, to not rush ourselves. So we aren't focused on doing seasons of work right now. It's more about doing one piece of work, and really focusing on that material, material that turns us on.

For Seth Barrish of the Barrow Group, finding early collaborators who were willing to muck in and sacrifice to stage bold, important work was a watershed for his company. Audiences responded to their hard work and fresh vision. "We really didn't know how to go about doing original shows, so I talked to people who had put up their own work," Barrish recalls.

We were offered the chance to do a one-night presentation at the Perry Street Theatre in the Village—a ninety-nine-seat space.

It rained cats and dogs, but we sold out! We then started doing more—we tackled a four-week run. We put up work at the River West Theatre. We put up work at La Mama and One Dream. We were nomadic, but we kept growing. Since then, we've partnered up with some great producing organizations—Jewish Rep, Daryl Roth, Circle Rep. We also expanded our company to include about twenty resident directors.

AN ASSOCIATION BUILT ON DEVOTION

When those closest to you admire the work you're doing so much, they want to help you realize your dream—you are truly successful. Among Patrick Dooley's most treasured theatrical collaborators: his mom—and she isn't even in the business. Dooley shares his experience, with deep gratitude:

In 2003, I got engaged to my wife Kimberly, also a member of Shotgun Players. We got married, and were living in a house in south Berkeley, and I saw this building for sale five blocks away—a great building, a way to have a 120-seat theater space that would be perfect for the company. It was so cool—rigged up for lights and sound, everything we needed. I thought, "I've got a pregnant wife, how much is this going to be?"

I called the real estate agent—the price was $1 million. I told my mother about it, and I was saying, "What am I going to do about this?" She replied, "I think you should buy it." Then she proceeded to raise the money for me! She got a loan on her own house, and went around to family members asking them to help; she put everything into a trust, so she and our family members became our investors. And we bought the space!

My mom was obviously amazing to do this. What felt great to me was she saw I had figured it out, and slowly gotten this company together. At thirty-five years old, it felt great to know that. So from that point on, things exploded—we suddenly had free parking right there, mass transit nearby, great audience access.

Having our own space cemented the thought in people's minds, "OK, these guys are for real." And the company kept adding things on—a tech director came in, we really started building up our marketing. We started a talk-back program that allowed our audience to tell us about things that they thought had gone well, things that they didn't think had gone well. We continued to grow from this point—and I always appreciate what my mom did to help.

Dooley and his mother believed in the work—ultimately, that mutual belief will allow any partnership you enter in to work. Robert Serrell felt the same way when he met Seth Barrish and Lee Brock of the Barrow Group.

Serrell says, "I trained as an actor, but grew unhappy with a lot of the work I was doing and seeing. Seth and Lee, however—what they do blew me away immediately! In terms of their concept, in terms of this company, it's not about 'me'—this company is about producing great work as a whole. Not so much about any individual artist—which makes so much sense to me."

CEMENTING YOUR DECISION

Here's a ten-point checklist on details to consider before you commit to teaming up with another company, or an artist/artistic team that could truly change your company's creative trajectory (make sure it's for better, not worse). Make sure you're comfortable with the answer to each of these questions.

- Does this entity agree to put the points of your collaboration in writing? Every business point should be in contract form, no exceptions.
- A mission statement for your artistic work created together is a great test to see how well you will collaborate from that point forward. Will this entity work with you on one (again, in writing)?
- How will profits of your association be divided?
- Who will be compensated, and how, in terms of each of your company members (actors, designers, crew)? Will everyone be paid equally?
- How will copyright be assigned for any original work you create together?
- Who is the intended audience for your work? Are you both on the same page in terms of gearing the work toward a niche group, or is the demographic broad?

- What do you like most about this entity's work? Name five things. If you can't right off the top of your head, rethink the collaboration.
- What is the reputation of this entity? Is their work considered to be of real quality?
- Do others feel this entity is filled with folks who are easy to work with? Any enemies with legitimate gripes? Feel free to investigate.
- Do you *like* these people on a personal level? If not, don't make the connection. Your artistic end result won't be what you wished for, and the journey won't be worth the aggravation.

SUCCESS STORY—NATIONAL THEATRE OF THE DEAF, WEST HARTFORD, CONNECTICUT

Founded in 1967 at the impetus of director Arthur Penn and actress Anne Bancroft (out of the knowledge and experience they gained while working on *The Miracle Worker*), National Theatre of the Deaf pioneered the practice of American Sign Language as a descriptive and creative tool in theatrical productions. The company's mission was also to give voice to deaf performers and playwrights, which they've achieved to perfection—its productions have been seen in all fifty states and thirty-three countries, and artists such as Chita Rivera and Peter Sellers have become the company's champions and collaborative partners.

Now in its forty-sixth season, National Theatre of the Deaf continues to push the envelope in terms of challenging material, as well as educating and informing the general public about the importance of disabled artists' talents and work.

Chapter Fourteen
Our Current Profile

Theater companies need to stay very objective about how well they are doing.

This doesn't mean companies need to be relentlessly self-critical. That isn't useful. Yet it's important for a company to step back and take a good look at where it stands from time to time. You don't need to do this on a daily basis. But every six months or so, it can be very helpful to sit down with your season paperwork—your financial records, your reviews, audience surveys and comment sheets, if you have them—and see what's really going on.

It's also very helpful to have regular bull sessions with your staff and company members about how they feel the company is doing. Giving everyone a forum to air their joys and grievances can make for a closer, more productive company.

Perhaps the most important tool in the evaluation process is your gut feelings, though. As a leader, how do you instinctively feel that things are going? If you had to describe your company's current situation to an outsider honestly, what would you say?

Our experts have been frank enough to do just that. In this chapter, they discuss where their companies stand at the moment.

What's the best use you can make of this chapter? Well, read it and enjoy it, of course. Then use it as inspiration. Turn the tables on yourself. Pretend I'm asking you how your theater company stands right this second and you have to answer me right off the top of your head. Answer honestly, then use your own valuable information to feel the pride in your company you know it deserves or to give your company the shot in the arm it needs.

A SENSE OF SECURITY
Post-9/11, many theater companies have had no choice but to reduce staff and/ or freeze hiring, as, unfortunately, attending theater and other entertainment

events has become a less frequent diversion. As people became cost-conscious, many were forced to become more selective about which performances to attend.

The Goodspeed's sterling artistic reputation has, in many ways, given it a unique sense of immunity against audience attendance issues. However, a savvy sense of perspective has also allowed Artistic Director Michael Price to make smart strategic decisions. Price understands that it helps to have a healthy dose of organizational confidence. You have to know exactly who you are and what it is your company does best. For Price's money, that means maintaining a level of supreme staffing excellence. Says Price, "Artistically, we really try to focus our efforts on doing what we want to do, on challenging ourselves in every aspect of every production. To me, the biggest challenge here has been to maintain core competency and that desire for challenge within our team. I always make sure we have the best people working for us—we have the best paint shop, the best tech crews, the best cast members, designers, musicians. To keep these great people, I focus on full employment for them year-round; I'm not hiring for the season or by the show, I'm hiring for longevity. To this end, we've had the same great wardrobe mistress for thirty-five years, just as one example."

CONTROLLING ONLY WHAT YOU CAN

Berkeley Repertory has always been a place ripe with exciting physical and artistic development. Utilizing all of its creative possibilities has meant that the organization has built fresh house space, carefully monitored its audience responses over the years—in short, done everything it can to actively maximize potential. Yet Susan Medak offers us a very sage piece of wisdom. Susan suggests that, as a theater administrator, you should do as much as you can with any given situation, but know when it's time to quit.

"Tony Taccone, our current artistic director, is an artist of the highest caliber," Medak continues.

> You have to know your strengths—I was scared, walking people through changes, but people love [our innovations]! Tony has opened doors even further with his artistic leadership and his complete support of this community. He is not in conflict with anything or anyone.
>
> We all have to let go of control, find a way to manage all sorts of human emotions and opinions. The challenge is to build the organization around individuals' knowledge and strengths.
>
> I think that the greatest challenge for me is learning when to pick my battles—when I should impose myself, and when to step back and pick up the pieces. It's

easier to build a building than it is to run a company. You have to make as many choices as you can up front. You try to fix the things you can control—there's a point at which you have to let go.

BOOSTING AN ALREADY PRESTIGIOUS PROFILE

Steppenwolf has always been a haven for the most brilliant theatrical talent. Collaborating with artists whose sensibilities best fit the company's style of working is really the way Steppenwolf prefers to do things. Former Executive Director Michael Gennaro says,

> We brought on Tina Landau, who is, interestingly, not an actor but a writer and director. I think the first person of that nature—everyone else had basically been an actor. Amy Morton, who has been a longtime actor in the city, who has worked with all these folks, and Martha Plimpton. There've been more women.
>
> I think what we look toward is, people who are actors but also director-actor-writers, so that there's more breadth to what the company can do. I think that one of the things Martha Lavey and I instituted was that we started inviting companies into our studio space. In '91, we built a 511-seat theater. We expanded that [to include] a roughly 200-seat studio space in which we presented some new work, as well as invited companies in, basically local companies, ensemble-based companies who shared the same kind of aesthetic we did. There have been repeatable relationships that have come out of that.

Subsequent Executive Director David Hawkanson honed this approach further, taking extreme care when it comes to using the company's plentiful resources to shepherd the very best material. "The critical thing for us is to sustain a high level of artistry and staff—that's the key priority," he explains.

> Our biggest asset is our people. In terms of theater as a whole, the climate is still as competitive today as when we started. As we are very fortunate in the sense that we have a strong cash and investment position, overall, we can put ourselves as risk, doing work that we want to do as always. *August: Osage County* is a strong recent example of that kind of work.

SOMETHING FOR EVERYONE

LA Theatre Works doesn't simply offer great theater to its many satisfied audience members or great roles for its actors to play. It also produces its work in many different media formats. It truly offers something entertaining and significant for everybody to enjoy.

Such branching out can't occur overnight—you've got to plot out a move into multimedia. Susan Albert Loewenberg has figured out how to pounce on good business prospects when she's seen them. She explains:

We're kind of a hybrid organization. We're not really a radio organization—we're a media organization. We have this very peculiar niche. We're members of the Audio Publishers Association, a very small group, twenty or thirty book publishers. It includes Random House and Simon & Schuster and Time Warner, but it also includes small people; we are the only people who do plays.

We have our own niche—it only works for a nonprofit. It would not be practical for a profit-making commercial organization, because it's too expensive. The sales are modest.

They're limited. It's not like doing Tom Clancy—it's different. But it's an interesting, steady business. It's a great library business—libraries love us.

It's been interesting, it's been difficult, it's been a money-loser, but I think we're seeing the light at the end of the tunnel. We now have recorded hundreds of plays on tape.

We have a unique library—nobody in the world has this library. It's a pretty good representative of the best writing of the American canon in the twentieth century. It's the best state-of-the-art technology. We've done new American operas, we've done several musicals, we've worked with major theaters all over the country. We expanded this project to Chicago for ten years—I did recordings in Chicago under the Doubletree corporate sponsorship, because they had a flagship hotel [there]. I've recorded plays by Steppenwolf, Goodman, Second City, Victory Gardens, and Organic.

Then I started a project in Washington, DC, with the Smithsonian and the Voice of America in working with the local theaters. Basically, I work under the sponsorship of the local theaters, but I'm really bringing in my own production. Those recordings are aired over the local NPR station and the Voice of America.

I did one year in Boston with WGBH and the leading theaters in that area, always bringing in my guest stars from Los Angeles in New York, bringing in my people. We now have a core acting group of fifteen hundred people. Of the thirty-four people who started with us, there have been two deaths, and of those remaining thirty-two, I'd say twenty-eight still work with us on a regular basis.

We've had two really fabulous outreach programs. One is called Alive and Aloud.

We've been in 2,200 schools in every state of the union. Through an initial grant from the NEA, with additional support from a number of foundations and corporations, including the Capital Group company's charitable foundation and Sony, we distribute ten tapes, five literary tapes and five docudramas, and study guides. Teachers use these tapes to teach English and social studies. They really are fabulous teaching tools, much better than video. They're great for concentration and reading skills, critical listening skills. The goal is to get them in all 34,000 public high schools in the United States. We've done teacher training workshops, and we're expanding the program to do a formal evaluation, a lot more interactive stuff, bringing artists into the schools and having the kids come and see a show on a local level.

We've also gotten involved, of course, with the Internet. With a company called Audible.com, and you can download our stuff—you have to pay for it, everybody gets royalties—but you can download about a hundred of our plays.

We're in bookstores all over the country. We were leery—the publishing business is a crazy business and the fact that people can return everything is unbelievable. We were not prepared for that. We did not want to go into the bookstores, we were very cautious about it. We kind of tiptoed in by licensing our stuff to a company called Listening Library, the people who do the Harry Potter books. I was on the phone one day, met this guy on the phone, we ended up licensing various pieces to him so we didn't have any risk, and they did very well with us in bookstores. It was the right thing to do.

We ended up taking the plunge and going with a major distributor in bookstores.

We're in Barnes & Noble and Borders and all the bookstores all over the country and have been working very hard at building our library business, because we knew that was our business. We send 150,000 catalogs a year—very expensive. We're in about two thousand libraries. Some libraries have bought the entire collection— UCLA, Harvard, Princeton, Fordham, NYU—so that's been very impressive. We just went with Books on Tape—they think they can increase our business in libraries tenfold, something we couldn't do on our own. We need to concentrate on individual customer business.

We're learning how to do it. One of the big challenges for us has been, because we have so many products, figuring out how to make them inexpensively enough so the cost of our products wasn't so high, otherwise we could never make any money at it. It needs to be a revenue source, it can't be a losing source. One of the things I did as an administrator was, when we started, we were almost 100 percent dependent on contributed income, as a young organization, and I decided to try to reverse that trend. We did reverse it, so we were going from 30 percent earned to 70 percent earned. That's been very important.

It is very hard to sell radio drama on public radio. It's been basically dead for years, but they have officially closed down NPR Playhouse. Program directors are not interested in ninety-minute formats. They're wrong, they've never known how to market it, it's bad conventional wisdom, it's all of those things, but be that as it may, it is reality.

The good news is satellite radio. They bought eighty programs from us and paid real money for them. We get to our listeners. It also helps us publicize our audio book sales and so on. We're very excited about that. It's a perfect arrangement—our relationship ended with KCRW, which was unfortunate, but this is actually more powerful, puts us on fifty-two weeks a year which is actually better for us.

EXPANDING OUR POINT OF VIEW

The message of cultural pluralism espoused by Mixed Blood Theatre has been long appreciated by culturally aware audiences. Avid fans, plus the Minneapolis community at large, have always been positively affected by the company's thought-provoking work.

So imagine what good could be done if you dropped Mixed Blood's personnel into corporate environments, where issues of social misunderstanding have unfortunately been rampant at times. Jack Reuler thought that prospect sounded like a much-needed infusion of education about social understanding.

He set about making the corporate world aware of Mixed Blood's message back in the 1980s. Now Mixed Blood's corporate outreach work is in high demand in many different fields of occupation. A lot of thinking has been properly adjusted by Mixed Blood's innovative efforts. Jack Reuler explains:

To me, the most interesting part of the organization: in the late '80s, diversity initiatives were everywhere. People looked to us, and we developed, by happenstance, this section of the organization called EnterTraining. It used theater as a voice to address barriers to people succeeding in the workplace.

The people we've worked with over the years of this program have been unbelievable, in terms of what doors it's opened for us. When we do plays at the theater, we hope by osmosis we are able to change the audience's mind. But here, you're actually being invited in to create new works, which is what we like to do, with people saying, "We know that we have issues, and we also have the wherewithal to do something about them."

Through a series of focus groups, we've found out the very specific issues of places.

Some of them were corporations in the earlier years, which were a lot less interesting, but a lot of them are in the legal profession, a lot of them are in health care, in law enforcement. Really interesting areas in which the subtleties and not-so-sublteties of race play a major factor.

We've been able to do some unbelievable theater for some unbelievable audiences with very tangible effects that can really be quantified, and in qualitative ways, measured. I can tell you more success stories from that program than from any of them. You can change not only minds, you can also change policy. It's sort of three-prong—policy, behavior, and attitude. We can change somebody's attitude, but they might not do anything about it. Yet if there's a policy change, they don't have any choice but to do something about it.

Mixed Blood also seeks to expand the audiences for its traditional stage material by extending its production options. "While Mixed Blood has always been focused on and invested in new work, the current era has two trends: continued life and new ways of creation," Jack continues.

As the regional theater movement approaches a post-premiere-itis phase, continued life—second, third, and fourth productions of new work—is very attractive. Whether it's a new play that had its first production at Mixed Blood, or a play that premiered elsewhere, finding subsequent homes for that script is important. In the National New Play Network, of which Mixed Blood is a founding member, there is a continued life fund that now provides $5,000 per theater for three theaters that commit to the production of an original work before its first opening. The playwright gets multiple perspectives—the work of three directors, casts, and creative teams in three different venues.

As creative avenues multiply, however, Jack stays true to his company's humanistic bent. "I currently like to find voices that have been marginalized because of what, not who, they are. For example, we commissioned a playwright to gain invitation into an online subculture of people on the autism spectrum who are waging a new civil rights movement, championing a different model of autism, as opposed to a disorder model. That playwright was commissioned to create stories and composite characters, and take the script back to the online community for response. Once completed, the idea was the play would be virally marketed through online communities, distributed during its run via simulcast, and then on DVD and the web."

GO WITH WHAT YOU KNOW

For established organizations, a creative sea change can reap great rewards—if you're stretching yourself artistically because you genuinely burn and yearn to do so. Don't switch up your programming for completely frivolous reasons, however, it's guaranteed not to work. Lots of times, theater companies tinker away with things that are working well for them already, just because they're bored. Then they live to regret it. It's like having really beautiful long hair, then cutting it short on a whim and realizing you've got big ears that the human race is really better off not being subjected to.

Sometimes changes are essential—you know when it's time to replace an ineffective employee or trim your budget for practicality's sake. But it's always best to avoid change simply for change's sake. Sure, you may have the tools to fix things but that doesn't mean you should use them.

Tried-and-true plans of action are tried and true because they really work. At Wheelock Family Theatre, audiences have come to expect a certain entertainment mix that is altered slightly from time to time but will never be taken for granted and discarded. Specifically, this means producing a certain material balance that fills the demographic needs of all of Wheelock's loyal audience members.

Susan Kosoff believes in giving the people what they want. This attitude has never stopped Wheelock from achieving what it wanted to artistically. Yet at that same time, it's been the attitude that has very deliberately preserved its commercial success. Kosoff reports,

> We tend to do one musical a season and one family drama and one you might tend to think of as being for the older kids. That's pretty much the formula, but there have been years when we've done two musicals, maybe one with a fuller orchestra. There have been years when we've done shows that are more radically different from one another; there have been years when we've done shows that people might feel are more alike.

STAYING TRUE TO OUR ROOTS

For Richard Pletcher, success at the Round Barn at Amish Acres is directly attributed to the loyalty the company has been shown by its traditional, family-oriented patrons. Pletcher returns this loyalty by constantly innovating new routes of connection, which to him means keeping his programming as close to home as he possibly can.

> We've done shows that are so all-American and patriotic we're literally serving apple pie to our audiences! I also work very hard to be sure we've got a strong local link running through our productions whenever we can. For example, David Letterman grew up nearby, so a recent show had jokes about "little Davey Letterman" being in the house with his mom Dorothy—the crowd loved it. We also did a Cole Porter show, and asked his niece, who's from Peru, Indiana, to come by and do a Q&A with our subscribers, which was another big success. I think doing this kind of thing is always lots of fun, but, additionally, it shows our audience that we respect them—that is, of course, very important to me.

KEEPING OUR SKILLS SHARP

Many theater companies feel the best way to maintain their edge involves never taking an eye off the competition. It's never a dumb move to be aware of what the other guy's up to, but if you focus outward too much, your own work will start to suffer. Make this your mantra instead—"We only really compete with ourselves." Focusing on the development of your own organization's strengths will not only bring you big (and obvious) creative and financial gains, it will also make you a more relaxed person. You won't be looking over your shoulder, feeling paranoid, jealous, and pressured 24/7.

Paul Zuckerman makes sure that Chicago City Limits is following this exact philosophy. "Our goal remains the same—to be the best improvisational theater company that's ever been," he says. "We work at our skill sets and try to stretch the envelope onstage." At the same time, though, he's wisely repositioning the company in a changing marketplace. Paul continues,

> We're basically doing what we've always done at Chicago City Limits, but the mix is changing. Our public performances are the icon of our organization, but also the least profitable elements. We've scaled back the number of shows we do. We're reaching out to more companies, working with HR departments to use our skills to help train their staff, [build] speaking skills, create instant relationships, and so on. In terms of marketing, we're relying more on the web, using it to drive interest in the variety of things we do.

LIVING IN THE MOMENT

For Gil Cates, a realistic overview was worth its weight in gold. Cates built the Geffen Playhouse's ongoing success one brick at a time by utilizing his admirable ability to step back and objectively evaluate his company's perspective, position, strengths, and weaknesses at any given moment. Cates felt that it's extremely important to be honest with yourself about where your company stands, and that means knowing exactly why you're doing the work you're doing.

"Ask yourself, 'Who is my audience? Who am I doing this for?'" advised Cates.

> Are you doing this to provide entertainment? Who's going to see your shows—is your demographic a middle-aged audience, or, say, a children's theater or family-based audience? Your theater's physical location also plays a significant role. For instance, we're, of course, located in Los Angeles. If your space is located in the city, offer productions with themes that address your urban audience members' interests

or they won't be interested in coming. Our subscribers are very vocal—they give us an immediate thumbs-up or thumbs-down.

However, when evaluating the Geffen's current position, or any theater's current position, for that matter, Cates didn't put a lot of stock in the power of any reviewers and isn't a proponent of letting critical opinion change the path you're taking. "Critics are another thing entirely," he opined.

> We did a show called *Matthew Modine Meets the Alpacas*. It was a satire that deals with the ridiculous things that people consume their days with. The critics didn't like it but, you know, to me, it didn't matter at all. In terms of the big picture, I always think, "What is success—how do you define it?" The important thing is, did we like the play and like doing it? We did, so it was successful.

Knowing what really matters to you—a great mind-set for any company to adopt, once you know exactly where you stand.

SUCCESS SECRETS: FIVE SURPRISING TRUTHS YOU'LL LEARN AS YOUR COMPANY GROWS

1. Consistency wins you the most fans. Networking with the right people can certainly help when it comes to raising capital or your company profile, but once you meet influential people who can really speed your trajectory, you need to deliver for them, time and again. Walk it like you talk it—always be on time for that conference call. Always utilize a suggestion you like that a donor has made if you said you intended to do so. Never make an empty promise. Be like clockwork—people like it and will stick by you.

2. You'll lose friends as you become more successful. You probably think you'll be the exception to this old adage, because your friends (especially those in the business) are stand-up loyal and want the best for you. If you're lucky, that will be true in many cases, but you will find the last people you thought would move out of your life as your company blossoms will be the first out the door. If you don't have a part or job to give them, they won't stick around. It's OK, though; hindsight is both 20/20 and a great teacher—most likely, replaying your relationship, you'll recall times these folks were not as pleased for you or supportive as they should have been. You'll look back on these folks and thank them for the lessons their disloyalty taught you, so you can read people better in the future and make friends who will be truly happy for your success.

3. Problems will often start to solve themselves without you having to expend as much energy has you have been on them. As your company grows, more folks will

automatically want to help you and make your life easier, and they will tend to pop up with answers just when you need them. Of course, this won't happen all the time, but test out this theory by sleeping on a nonemergency issue or two, and see if a solution doesn't present itself pretty quickly.

4. Great stage managers will start sending you their resumes. Take advantage of this! Stage managers who are truly top of the heap in terms of quality and professionalism keep their ears to the ground, and if they approach you, they've heard your company is well worth their time and skill.

5. You'll stop worrying about setbacks. A show with mixed reviews, a light board failure, a sick actor—what once seemed like a catastrophe will now seem par for the course. Riding out tough spots with ease means you've now got enough experience to know you can deal.

Bonnie & Clyde by Adam Peck
directed by Mark Jackson
Shotgun Players 2013 Season
Pictured: Megan Trout and Joe Estlack
Photo by Pak Han

Chapter Fifteen
A Day in the Life

When you're running a theater company, you don't have a whole lot of time to fritter away. You always have to have your eyes peeled on the many doings and goings-on around your environment. You need to supervise those working for you, watch rehearsals, keep up to date with your supporters, funders, and board (if you have one), monitor audience responses, pay bills, wash dance tights, and refill the Coke machine (at least when you're starting out). You get the picture.

Because there are just twenty-four measly little hours in a day, it's important to pace yourself correctly if you want to accomplish everything you need to accomplish. You need to prioritize correctly. Multitask expertly. Delegate when it's appropriate. In order to maximize your energy and efforts, it can help to hear how the pros manage.

This chapter asks our experts to walk us through a typical day in the life of their respective companies. They explain to us what exactly it is that they do with their work time. This is not only interesting and absorbing information, but also remarkably helpful. This is because our experts have, of course, distinguished themselves professionally long ago, and so they herein allow us individual glimpses of what it means to operate from an advanced position of knowledge, experience, and success. You may be feeling like quite the novice at the moment, overwhelmed about how exactly you should put one foot in front of the other on behalf of your company. These professionals, in letting us in on exactly how they get their jobs done, will clear up some of the mystery for you.

SEE WHAT THE DAY BRINGS

A calm attitude is essential to develop within yourself if you want to ride the waves of an unpredictable business. Our subjects have seen a lot in each of their tenures, the good, the bad, and the unprecedented. What's so admirable about each of them is the way they square their shoulders and face whatever happens to be in front of them head-on.

Chicago City Limits has perfected the art of putting one foot in front of the other business-wise. Paul Zuckerman and company keep up their morale with a healthy dose of optimism. Zuckerman has carefully considered expansion ideas that will take his company to the next level, while simultaneously never losing sight of CCL's ultimate goal—which, at the end of the day, is always to entertain. Paul relates,

> Every day is a new experience. Certain weeks, ongoing projects have continuity, so you're not sitting around going, "What do we do?" I think if there's one thing I can say, over the twenty-some-odd-year history there hasn't been a routine.
>
> There are certain things that are cyclical—the workshops, particularly, have to be cyclically communicated to the public. We change our review twice a year, and twice a year those things are addressed.
>
> There are sort of patterns of work that occur, but, you know, you called me Monday about an interview, so this morning I have an interview. This afternoon I'm looking at silent films for our silent film idea. Have I ever done that before? This is the first week I ever looked at silent films. Those kinds of things change. I guess it's part of what we do—and that's what I like about it.
>
> You have to keep your eyes open, listen to what's going on, and don't take things for granted.

JAM-PACKED DAYS

For the members of the Jewish Theatre San Francisco, there was much variety in the company schedule as well. Sometimes, the group toured its running productions. Sometimes, they were deeply immersed in the rehearsal process for upcoming shows. Then there were fund-raising, administrative concerns, and business meetings to deal with. The activities that happened from day to day were very diverse.

There was just one constant to the company's daily planner—it's jam-packed literally from morning to night. Sometimes, in fact, a typical day at TJT could encompass all of the above activities that the company put its attention to—literally a completely new activity every couple of hours! Each activity is as important as the last, too, so they all must be given equal attention. For this enclave of excellent artists, taking care of business was never a problem.

Corey Fischer says:

> I can give you a quick example what one day was like. We're going to start rehearsal on the first project of the season—I'm performing in it, so I'll be showing up as an actor for the first day of rehearsal. Then we'll all meet at rehearsal. At some point in the afternoon, our playwright is going to arrive and one of us will go with him to an interview at a radio station.
>
> After hopefully a short break, I will have to drive down the peninsula, about forty miles, to do a kind of fund-raising sort of event, an audience development event, at the home of one of the theater's supporters. I'm going to do a report on a recent trip to Israel where I was part of a theater conference. So that's one day!

Back at the company's headquarters, Aaron Davidman was equally busy. "At TJT, as in most companies, I imagine, there was no typical day," he observes.

> A typical week involved a staff meeting during which each department gives the rest of the staff an update. If we were in production, the staff would look at box office numbers and think together about marketing strategies. There were always financial considerations—our finance director was perpetually crunching the numbers and making sure we had enough cash to pay the bills. Our executive director was usually in the midst of writing grants or organizing a fund-raising drive or overseeing our marketing campaign.
>
> I seemed to be in many meetings each week about programming—this could be casting, design meetings, or partnership planning, as we were often looking for coproducing opportunities to share the cost of production. Or weighing in on marketing decisions or grant-writing, or having lunch with potential donors or board members. Or reading plays and seeing other work that might be of interest to the company. In the spring, there'd be a big push to plan the following season with budgeting and scheduling and finding the right lineup for the next year.

GETTING YOUR MIND AROUND IT ALL

TJT's extremely busy days bring an interesting question to mind. You're probably reading such a dizzying list of activity with incredulity, thinking, *How could anybody possibly cope with switching mental gears so quickly, in order to get so much done? And do it so well? And make it look so easy?*

How exactly can you compartmentalize your thinking process correctly, so you're handling everything you need to handle with equal and proper attention? You do this the best when you think in terms of effective troubleshooting.

A good troubleshooter learns to stay on an even keel emotionally at all times, because he or she never knows quite what crisis is about to emerge that will need solving. You have to decide to be unflappable. It's a choice you can make—you don't have to give in to nerves or insecurity, you know. Every problem has some form of solution, and if you apply yourself calmly, you can work most things out faster than you'd ever have imagined.

Rick Lombardo uses a dramatic metaphor to explain this approach, which served him quite well in his work as an artistic head. He doesn't waste time trying to predict what might come his way; he saves his considerable brainpower for what needs attention most when that attention is actually called for.

"I've never had a typical day," Lombardo explains.

> I can best explain why by using the metaphor of directing a play—directing is problem-solving. So doing that, I learned not to plan the day too much. Let the problems emerge.
>
> Rigid people don't do well in this type of job. You can't simply get your cup of coffee at the same time every day, or open your mail at the same time. Like directing a play, running a repertory company is like, first day to the last day at the end of the rehearsal process, what are the issues I'm faced with right now, while I'm keeping an eye on the long-term?
>
> I need a staff that can function in a fluid environment.

Lombardo's former partner and New Repertory Theatre Managing Director Harriet Sheets concurs with that hypothesis. She likes to work with self-motivated individuals herself. Sheets adds, "I agree with Rick's opinion that you have to go with the flow. The staff must work as a team, but it's also important to have people who can move and do things on their own as well within the day, and can handle their own area."

STAY IN TOUCH

Another frequent challenge many companies need to deal with head-on: how to actually stay in regular and productive contact during the day.

This sort of dilemma most often presents itself in situations where a company is made up of a lot of part-time members, who are busy working in a variety of other capacities, many times in far-flung locations away from company headquarters. Most organizations actually struggle with the issue of scattered personnel—actors might be working on more than one project at once in the same city, the office manager might be running errands most of the day, people might have day jobs, you know the drill.

If everybody's running in different directions like chickens with their heads cut off, how do you schedule meetings that people can actually attend at the same time, on the same day? How do you touch base on important decisions that can't be made unilaterally? How do you keep track of how people are handling important duties? How do you coordinate all of this, plus make progress plowing through your own formidable workload?

You must simply accept communication as a top priority within your leadership position. Make a daily communication schedule, preferably on your computer or in your datebook, and stick to it. Plan who you are going to call to say hello to on which days. Figure out who needs to be delivering which project's work when, and check up when necessary.

If your staff sits in one big communal office, make open discussion a way of life. In some professions this is not the norm, but in the theater biz, as you probably already know, it's a common, accepted practice for coworkers to chatter away like magpies. Use this free exchange of conversation as a forum for work discussion, above all else.

If your staff is spread out around the building, walk around frequently to see people.

Encourage people to be able to drop in on you any time as well. (Be respectful, though—neither you nor your employees should intrude on important meetings, phone calls, and the like. This is obvious, of course.)

Gil Cates described how he ran the Geffen Playhouse effectively in this manner while dedicating his time to his essential creative endeavors:

> My typical working day, when I'm directing a show, involves rehearsal from 11 a.m. to 7 p.m., though, of course, during tech, I'm looking at ten- to twelve-hour days. During those times when a show is up or I'm not directing, I get in about 10 a.m. and stay till around 7 p.m. This schedule gives me the chance to see actors as they come in and out of rehearsal, and talk to everyone on staff. My workday consists of lots of phone calls, artistic meetings, financial development meetings, and other theater business with the staff—we employ about fifty people. I often meet donors for lunch, of course, and work a lot on marketing as well.

ART IS WHAT COUNTS MOST

When you're very busy concentrating on the details of your administrative work, your worldview can get pretty small. If you're working hard writing up a budget, it can quickly become all about number crunching in your head, not about the amazing rehearsal that's going on right down the hall right this second. You've forgotten all about art, in favor of calculation. You might as well work at H&R Block, my friend.

Sure, you've got to keep your mind on important technical tasks while they're at hand. We all know that the boring practical stuff is what keeps a company afloat. It's also important, though, that you keep your peripheral vision trained on the beauty your company is creating. Isn't art what inspired you to crunch those numbers in the first place?

Stop often and smell the roses within your organization's walls. Don't allow business concerns to make you uptight and forget all about the reason you're working so hard. Art is what counts most.

Steppenwolf's administration has never forgotten this. Their art is their utmost priority, and it informs every communication transacted within the company. Otherwise, what's the point? Michael Gennaro says:

> I think from the artistic side, a lot of it for Martha is communication with the ensemble. Just saying, "What do you want to do?" Then them thinking about different ideas and who they want to work with. That's part of creating the season. I think one of the things she's been doing more and more of is looking further into the future.
>
> The second thing is, on that side of the operation, they've built up a much stronger base of artistic folks to really hone in on new work, working on new work, and developing local writers. Once more going back to the community—taking the wealth here of people who can write and working with them. That's a typical day over there.
>
> On the administrative side, I think it's probably not unlike most other places. Most of the departments here operate on their own, but they're all hooked together. Communication here, between email and just walking down the hall, and back-and-forth memos, that's probably the most important thing any place can have.
>
> One of the things that sometimes happens, and you have to fight against it, I've seen it everywhere I've been, is the fact that you sometimes can lose the connection between administration and artistic, production in particular. You've got to keep in touch and in contact, and embrace those folks who are making the work every night. If you lose touch with them, you lose touch with what's going on.
>
> All we're doing is getting to the point where we put the show on at night. That's what everybody here knows that it's about. You can never forget that.

You can say, "We gotta get out this subscription brochure, we gotta get out this grant or that grant." But why are you getting it out? If you keep thinking back to that—when someone calls and says, "I've just read your grant, and it's phenomenal because of the explanation of what you're about," then you know you've made sense.

Since beginning his tenure as Steppenwolf's subsequent executive director, David Hawkanson created highly efficient new ways of administrating so he can expend more of his valuable energy on innovative creative efforts. Hawkanson explains,

> We've tried to implement a stronger management model, David Schmitz handling much of the day-to-day management of the theater, allowing me to take significant chunks of time for special opportunities as they come up. It's an incredibly large undertaking to bring a show to Broadway or to international audiences and remount it; those events take up much of my focus.
>
> I also focused on partnership relationships, such as the work we're doing with the Chicago library system. Essentially, we're working on building information services from multimedia, intelligence, humanitarian, and artistic perspectives—how do we rethink a performing arts experience utilizing this kind of informational partnership?

24/7

An artistic organization run by a leader whose brain is always buzzing can't fail. If you take on the mantle of artistic director or managing director, you have to accept, and relish, the responsibility of working, at least in your head, on pushing your company forward twenty-four hours a day, seven days a week.

You may not be behind a desk all that time. Frankly, if you were, you'd be unconscious eventually, and what good would that do your company? Please remember to take care of yourself, no matter how hard you're working. Get lots of fresh air. Eat well and sleep regularly. (Although while you're sleeping, there's the perfect opportunity to dream up fabulous new plans for your company, so feel free). You don't have to be physically present at your theater to work out plans, read plays, and make work contacts.

Keep your mind open to the possibilities of artistic and business inspiration, which can strike anywhere, any time. And use your time well. Kevin Mayes explains the ways he learned to make Bailiwick Chicago operate most efficiently:

On a day a show's about to open, my morning was usually spent on email, getting caught up with other members of the Collective on how various work deadlines are getting met. Our entire company is set up through online project management, which means our workspace is totally virtual. I was running the entire company off the web, which worked really well. So I did a little bit of everything—track progress on a show, plan new projects, work on our calendar. Afternoons were usually taken up with meetings on our current show, plus artistic sessions discussing future work. Then evenings were devoted to rehearsals and/or performances. It's a long day, with a high level of structure each day—this structure allowed me to work six full days a week.

DELEGATE, DELEGATE, DELEGATE

Any theater veteran worth his salt will tell you: you think you can do it all, but you can't. Trouble is, the concept of delegating tasks can be mighty scary to a new theater company head. You probably feel you've got so little wiggle room for mistakes, you're worried about turning over too much work, or even a little work, to staff members who might be inexperienced (and no doubt a number of your hires haven't been around the block much yet).

The solution? Take a deep breath and delegate anyway. Sure, an error could occur, but if you match each employee properly to each task you need covered, working with their strengths, you'll probably be just fine. You can't control every move every employee makes work-wise, but what you can do is inspire. Make a concerted effort to infuse your company's environment with can-do spirit, and verbally encourage your staff as often as possible. Tell them you believe in them, that you're thrilled they contribute their talents to your company, and watch them try their best to deliver for you! Works like a charm.

David Fuller's decades-long career as a theater artist, including his stint as Jean Cocteau Repertory's artistic director, has informed his view of operational tactics as follows:

When you run an organization—I don't care if you're running a small theater company in Queens or running the United States—you really don't ever not work. There's always a part of your brain that's working on something having to do with running your organization. When you're in charge of people and responsible for their livelihoods, that's a big responsibility.

You do wear a lot of hats, but the thing is, when you are tantamount to a million-dollar theater, you have some help, so you don't have to wear so many hats. Sometimes, when you're young, you can do that, but you can only do it for a certain amount of time. Then you burn out.

Just rely on the people you hire. That's the important thing to be able to do. Learning to delegate, I think, is one of the hardest things for young people to understand. It's very freeing to be able to finally say to somebody, "You do that. I don't want to do it."

You have to know what you're good at and know what other people are good at.

SOMETIMES, THINGS ARE JUST CRAZY

A sure sign of success is having more work to do than you think you are humanly capable of doing. The good news is, when push comes to shove, if you're good, you always rise to the occasion and get everything done.

Surprise yourself, and take on more than you think you can handle, as soon as your company is working well on its feet. This trains you and your coworkers faster in the fine art of multitasking than anything else. This is not to recommend you knock yourself out with overwork. But it's OK to take a lot on and have confidence that you'll complete it.

David Zak came to accept during his Bailiwick Repertory days that sometimes things just get crazy. Still, he learned to handle frantic times with finesse and a grain of salt.

David says:

The day-to-day varied during the times of the year. The summer of 2001, for example, there were thirteen full productions during a twelve-week period for the Pride Series. Six of these plays were world premieres. That meant that most days were highly stressed, with lots of production work and pre-production work going on.

STARTING FIRES AND PUTTING THEM OUT

No matter how absorbed you might be at any given task, at any given moment, in order to be a good leader, you must always be planning future endeavors at the exact same time. This is an absolute.

Why? Because for a theater organization, the future is now. Many elements of next year's season need to be locked in now—performance dates, development issues, business details all must be taken care of. You should resist the temptation to procrastinate on such issues or next season will get away from you fast.

Now let's take the opposite point of view. In addition to generating new projects you have to pay attention to what's currently on the front burner at all times. As the head of the company, you have to know what's going on in every corner of your business. Does this mean you have to become obsessive-compulsive, or micromanage like crazy? Not at all.

You simply have to care. Be detail-oriented. Understand how the workings of your organization interlock. In an organization that's running properly, everything is connected on a base level and should be working in tandem.

Susan Albert Loewenberg (LA Theatre Works) gives us a peek into her day, into which she incorporates a detail-driven philosophy in order to manage both present and future concerns.

I usually get up between five and six. I work at home until ten-thirty, even eleven o'clock sometimes. I'm on the phone a lot, with New York, with London. I do a lot of homework at home, I do a lot of thinking at home, I do a lot of reading, because I'm always looking for new material.

Then I come in. I don't take lunch; I'm not a lunch person. I just work until six o'clock at the office. I'm basically doing a lot of things. I have to fill seventeen slots a year at minimum. I'm always looking for plays. I'm kind of planning ahead and dealing with imminent crises.

There are times when we'll book actors and they'll get a movie. That's part of the deal, because we work under an AFTRA contract, but it's nothing. It's basically a very minimal public radio contract, and if you're working with Richard Dreyfuss and he gets a major movie, he's going to ultimately back out, and I'll have to replace him. So there's a lot of forward-planning, six months in advance. You're into one season and you're already planning the next, you're coaxing agents to get them to send you material. You're looking for material frantically all the time; you're trying to book actors.

I have a personal relationship with a lot of people, but a lot of it is also finding new people to work with, working with agents, working with directors, working with other actors, coming up with ideas, coming up with projects. So you're planning the long-term, and dealing every day with a crisis—something fell through, you've got a marketing problem, a play isn't selling well. You've got to deal with all of those issues while you're forward-planning. I'm sort of the new business development person, so I'm always looking for new opportunities.

It's somewhat dynamic, but everybody has their jobs. The positions are pretty well defined. I'm looking over everybody's shoulder. I'm doing the long-term planning on the audio publishing business with my audio publisher person. I'm working with my associate producer, overseeing the season. I'm working with our managing director and our development people. I have my hand in all the development stuff, brainstorming how we approach development challenges. I'm into every single thing, and I try to let people do their jobs, but it's a small organization.

I'm also traveling to Washington to oversee my Washington shows. At one point, I was traveling to Chicago and Washington, and it just became overwhelming. I felt Chicago had played itself out.

You have to be not fazed by multitasking. You have to put one foot in front of the other, and if you've got an immediate problem, just focus on that and don't worry about other things. Those have to wait until you can get to them. At the same time, you can't let them slide too long. So you've got to be comfortable with having a million balls in the air.

GET YOUR SYSTEM DOWN TO A SCIENCE

Your method of operation simply must run like clockwork if you intend for your performances to go smoothly. There's no way around that.

Sometimes, the way a company must be run to maximize what it can do, both creatively and financially, can be grueling. There will probably be precious little downtime for casts and crews. Certainly, there won't be much for you, as you'll be overseeing everything. The way you need to look at handling a tough schedule is realistically. If you want to get anywhere in a profession as difficult as theater, you've got to earn your way. This means long hours and very hard work.

A traditional rotating rep model is probably the most demanding of all theatrical schedules. One show is going up as another strikes, then vice versa. Many of the same actors and crew members, if not all of them, are dually involved with both productions. This mode of performance must be planned to the second, but it can be amazingly beneficial to your company on multiple levels. Your actors will stretch their abilities to their limits; you make more money with two shows running simultaneously; your company will enjoy double the exposure. So if you're up for the challenge, why not go for it?

Michael P. Price has found that overseeing the Goodspeed's stellar seasons works especially well for him when he incorporates fresh outside skill sets. Price explains, "In my working life today, I've sought some assistance from the Yale School of Management. The result has been a wonderful flowering of talent, who've helped so much with management. This has freed me up to be out doing more fund-raising, and I'm able to spend much more time working on the company organizationally."

HAVE HATS, WILL TRAVEL

Another taxing challenge is constant mobility. Some companies really know how to cook with gas. This morning, they're doing a show here, this afternoon another show across town. Tonight, a third show two towns over.

A touring company, or a company that works out of a base of operations but also regularly moves its work into the community, learns quickly how to perform on the fly.

Leadership duties for such a company can be a bit jarring, though. You might feel like you've got mental whiplash, having to zip your thought process back and forth from this show to that show, all of which are being performed this very day. You don't even have the luxury of forward-thinking about next season, while you work on this slot's show! It's all in-your-face immediate stuff.

So how do you deal, if this is your situation? Get into the groove and learn to love it. Train your mind to stay in the present moment as much as possible and put out fires only as they come along. Tell yourself you love the fast pace. You probably do, or you wouldn't have gotten this company together in the first place!

Jack Reuler (Mixed Blood) has always thrived on such fast-paced challenges. "It's the absence of routine that allows each day to be unique," Jack says.

> I try to work smarter instead of harder but end up doing both. I have found that I gravitate toward any opportunity to interface with colleges and universities, hoping to usher in the next generation of theater leaders. However, I have also found that we need to be perpetually adaptable. The new norm is perpetually adapting to new ways of creating connections with ever-expanding partners. That is exciting.

THE BIG PICTURE

Of course, the best way to handle a quick pace is to know it's coming your way. How you avoid surprises—and by now, it's probably clear to you that you can't avoid them entirely but you can control their damage—is by having your season planned meticulously.

This sort of big-picture thinking should cover what's going to happen every single day of your pre-season, active season, and post-season. Sounds elementary, but stunningly, many companies leave lots of their time completely up in the air. This is a very dumb move.

Structured time answers your company members' questions and reassures them.

A good company knows how to perfect a big-picture game plan and encourages their people to learn it like the backs of their hands. Susan Kosoff illuminates a good example:

> Some of the staff reconnoitered August 1. I just put the season brochure to bed with the printer; that goes out mid-August. As soon as I get back in September, we'll have

auditions for the first show. Our fall offerings for classes start in early October, about the same time that we go into rehearsals for our first show.

I've been meeting with the designers for the first show over the summer; the tech people will start working on it. One of the challenges for us is that we build our sets, we rehearse, and we perform in the same space. So we always try to have the basic set ready for rehearsals. That's particularly helpful for the people who aren't as trained. They actually work on the set, and it makes them very comfortable. So we don't have a load-in. It really helps.

All the technical stuff will start in September, and we'll gear up and go into rehearsal in October, when classes start. In a day, they're working on a set onstage, our rehearsals are evenings and weekends, and our classes are late afternoons and early evenings. The show goes up in early November and it runs through the month of November. In addition to weekend performances on Friday, Saturday, and Sunday, we have student matinees, we have as many as seven shows in a week. While the show is up, we're beginning to work on the second show. Meeting with the designers, we'll have auditions in November, early December, for our February show. We try to give everybody a little time off for Christmas. Then we come back, and we go right back into rehearsal first of January for the next show.

The first session of classes ends in December. We started intense, one-week classes for young people and teenagers over school vacations that we run in February and April. In February, we open our second show, and that comes down at the end of February. During that time, of course, we're starting to work on the next show. The turnaround time between the February show and the next show is faster than in the fall.

In March we start our second session of classes. Then in April, we open our third show. We're working in schools all the time—we have partnerships. Although we do some programs within the schools themselves, and we have two satellite sites—one in Newton, MA, one in Framingham, MA—we also try to work with teachers. We're not necessarily just doing classes ourselves for kids in the schools, we're helping teachers learn how to do it.

What makes us different from other educational programs is that we are a professional theater, one that is connected to productions. We have Q&As with the partner schools. In July we have hundreds of kids. It's a pretty intense schedule. We're never out of good ideas!

DO WHAT FEELS RIGHT TO YOU

There are practical ways to manage a day that you can always use, as we've learned. Still, theater is a business with a lot of wiggle room. If you eschewed professional freedom on principle, after all, you'd probably be working on Wall Street.

If you're like most artists who've chosen to blend their love of creativity with making a living, though, you like to keep a few options open. You should, definitely. Do what feels right to you, in terms of time management. Work out the system that you like best and that your company members like. Discover your best working hours. Be a little abstract at times. It's OK. It might just spark a surge of more creative thinking.

Base your system on a structure, but add your colors and you can't go wrong. Jack Reuler further discusses what makes up his working day at Mixed Blood:

> I think it really varies. I remember when that Rodney Dangerfield movie *Back to School* came out, and he was saying, "Here's how you really do business. You grease the palm of this politician, and you talk to that inspector."
>
> I had the opportunity to teach a class called "The Artistic Director" at UCSD's MFA program. It was really good for me to realize I've learned something in my twenty-odd years of working. I brought in some of the artistic directors from San Diego to talk to this class. They sort of did it by the book and understood the value of directors and artistic directors. These students were around thirty, they weren't right out of undergraduate school, and they really did sort of buy into my live-life-on-your-own-terms approach to artistic directorship. To not be, for lack of a better term, starfuckers, by really wanting to be like the Globe or the Playhouse or the San Diego.
>
> I'd say that one thing that differs about me, I've never had a managing director, in terms of classic relationships between artistic directors and managing directors. I don't know if that's right or wrong, but I never have a managing director saying, "We can't afford this," and I never have an artistic director saying, "We need to do something bigger." By being both, it's actually worked for me pretty well, but I think the art, I've done less, because I've been both.

YOU GOTTA LOVE IT

A spontaneous attitude toward what may happen in the life of your company, on any given day, will get you farther than anything.

Also, remember this: If you're not enjoying your day, something isn't right. Figure out what it is that's bothering you about your work and fix it. You have lots of control. You work for yourself, remember? That's a lot of responsibility, sure, but it's monumentally rewarding.

Strike a balance between the work you have to do and the joy you've got to experience. Mitzi Sales did this in her days at Berkeley Repertory, and she's never regretted it.

As in most jobs, and certainly in a managing director's, there are certain routine things that have to be accomplished in any given week. One of the great appeals of a job as working as managing director in a theater company is, there are also unexpected things that come every week, sometimes every day.

One of the reasons I was able to stay in the job as long as I did was because it was fun. It was challenging. There were unexpected things that happened, and it was engaging. What is my worst fear? Being bored. I was rarely bored!

Mutt
A coproduction between Ferocious Lotus Theatre Company and Impact Theatre in
Berkeley, CA
Photo by Cheshire Isaacs

Chapter Sixteen
The Process of Planning

In order to get to where you want to go, you have to adopt some sort of long-range planning model. This is accepted conventional wisdom in most corners of the business world.

Usually, this planning model is broken down into manageable time increments. Frequently, you have a one-year plan for what you hope your company will accomplish and/or a five-year plan. So does this type of traditional model work for the sometimes very nontraditional business of theater?

Some of our experts speak from a very calculated, strategic point of view. They are using traditional business practices and thinking to realize their company's intentions for the immediate future. Other subjects are a bit more apt to see where events will take them and have always operated quite successfully from keeping a looser hold on the reins.

I've come to believe that both of these approaches are right on. Why? Because planning is a totally individual process. How you do it best depends completely upon who you are, as an organization and as a human being (business people are, after all, human beings first).

Planning scrupulously and effectively is a talent. So is eyeballing a situation and trusting yourself and your company enough to go with the flow. Both of these mind-sets have merit. My advice on how you might plan your company's future? Figure out who you are and use that to dictate the steps you wish to take.

To be in charge of a theater company means you are automatically following some kind of "yellow brick road." Either it's a road you've carefully constructed inch by inch yourself, or it's a road you're happy simply to wander along and see what comes up ahead of you. No matter what, you're in forward motion. It's up to you how to pace your steps.

CREATIVE GOALS

By nature, most companies actually employ a one-year plan without even realizing it. They do this by setting their next season in advance. Even if the choosing of material and announcement of slotted offerings seems like a necessity rather than a careful plot, it instantly determines a company's direction in the shorter term. Your next season's selections speak volumes about where your company currently aspires to be—to your audience, funders, and, especially, those who work within its structure, whose professional futures are tied intricately to these selections.

There is no greater factor in where your company will be within one year as what you intend to do creatively. Examine what plays are calling your name, and you may find out more about where your company is headed than you ever consciously considered. Have you chosen a particularly controversial work for next year? Maybe, without coming right out and saying so, you've felt your company is playing things a little too safe, and now is the time to push the envelope, to open up the possibility of a bolder future.

The nature of Chicago City Limits and its performance work, as we know, is completely spontaneous, not preset in a traditional season slot format. Yet Paul Zuckerman makes a perfect example of this point of creative goals:

> I honestly don't believe in the business plan model so much as kind of knowing what you want to do. Maybe that sounds contradictory—right now, our business plan is probably clearer than it ever was. That is, to diversify the offerings of the theater. That is going to happen, or we'll go out of business making it happen, one way or the other.

COMPANY COHESION IS KEY

Good planning should also involve collaboration and showing off your company's creative assets. That's why many organizations, with an established, permanent troupe of actors to utilize, seek out material that can include as many of those individuals as possible. Other times, a repertory company will select material that showcases the strengths of its personnel, such as the chops of a particularly fabulous actor, or a musical that will highlight the vocal talents of its best singers. Company size, too—either bountiful or limited—plays a role.

Lots of companies go after the dream projects of its pet directors or actors. Sometimes, frankly, these are vanity projects that should have been left well enough alone (and we've all seen a production or two to prove that). Other companies know their members know best and can safely trust the artistic judgment of its movers and shakers to come through with a great take on their favorite material.

It's always a good idea to take your actors' preferences into consideration when picking a show. This is not because you need to indulge their whims foolishly. It is, however, a wonderful expression of trust you show the people you've selected to create with you and for you. Actors are not your personal workhorses; they are, in fact, your collaborators. They're out there onstage, making you look good every night. They're your ambassadors, in a sense. So if you respect them enough to hire them in the first place to represent you, respect them enough to listen to their thoughts on the plays they want to do and think they can bring some genius to.

You and, in many cases, the directors you are working with do have the final say, of course, but it's a wonderfully inclusive gesture to touch base with your actors regarding their opinions about your season choices. It creates a sense of casting cohesion, of a democratic collective. Some of the greatest theater ever produced was based on this belief system.

This includes the legendary work produced by Steppenwolf. The ensemble mind-set is what Steppenwolf is all about. It's always been an important priority and company touchstone to respect the artistic impulses of the ensemble, and to work in every aspect as a fully fused team.

Michael Gennaro explains the ways in which Steppenwolf's 2001 to 2002 season, as one example, reiterated the ensemble aesthetic by bringing it boldly full circle:

> That season is interesting, because it returned to a very specific agenda, specifically on the mainstage of work. You look at *Mother Courage*—it's driven by an ensemble member, Eric Simonson, who's done a number of things with Steppenwolf, wanting to work with Lois Smith in the lead. That drew a lot of ensemble members to want to become involved in that. And repeating a relationship with T-Bone Burnett, who wrote the music for it.
>
> Next piece, obviously, is *Glengarry Glen Ross*, which is right up Steppenwolf's alley. Directed by Amy Morton, with some of our ensemble members, and a guy named Mike Nessbaum, who was in the original cast, now playing one of the older parts.
>
> *Maria Art* came out of Tina Landau working with a couple of ensemble members; it's an obscure German piece she found. *The Royal Family*, perfect for our company, directed by Frank Galati.
>
> Finally, a new work, with a writer we've been working with for years, Bruce Norris, with Laurie Metcalf, directed by one of the resident people, in the fifth slot.

All of those choices come out of an ensemble directive. Somebody wanted to do something. So it's one of the strongest seasons, I think.

It doesn't have a kind of apparent "blockbuster," in some ways. You look at *One Flew Over the Cuckoo's Nest* with Gary, it kind of makes sense. You look at *The Libertine*, Malkovich, it makes sense. But we have the good and the bad. People take shots and say, "You're gonna do a play with Gary Sinise? Of course you'll sell tickets." . . . If it is good, that's how you get to Broadway and get a Tony Award.

People call Steppenwolf and say, "How'd you like to do this play? We'll put together this cast, blah, blah, blah." [The company] never does that. The first musical Steppenwolf ever did, *The Ballad of Little Jo*, which is so noncommercial—at the end, everybody dies. It was kind of rewarding to me. I was at a conference and a couple of my peers who regularly do musical work said, "You are the only people who have the resources and the guts to take that on." I doubt Steppenwolf's going to do *South Pacific*.

STRIKING A BALANCE

Goals can't be completely artistic, of course. You no doubt take the finances of your company seriously. Even if you don't adhere to a sophisticated money management plan, if you didn't think ahead about dollars and cents, you ultimately wouldn't have any dollars and cents to think about.

I'm a strong proponent of financial planning in the longer term. This may seem like a ridiculous thing to focus on if you've just started your company and you don't have two nickels to rub together. But windfalls in theater tend to occur when you least expect them. Say that grant you apply for suddenly comes through. Or your new musical opens and is an unexpected smash. Money is suddenly sitting in your lap. How are you going to handle it correctly if you've done no preparation for its management?

Kevin Mayes, formerly of Bailiwick Chicago, observes,

> In terms of the recession affecting theater, Chicago did not see the same impact as the West Coast or New England, but for a theater like this, it's still important to ask, "Where do we lie in the order of our audience's priorities?"
>
> You have to identify your strengths, strengthen your sense of identity, and get to know your audience in terms of having a two-way conversation. It's really an issue of engagement; if you're going to be competitive, what's distinct about your competitiveness? To answer that question, we planned a whole series of programming to help us engage in conversation about our works and increase our development of new works. We recognized how extremely bright our audience is and want their ideas and input.

As it should be, if you want your company to stay alive. But you know this already, so I won't say it twice. Just do yourself a favor and never forget it. Always, always, always be sure your company's making its best effort to strike the proper balance between commerce concerns and artistic concerns.

PEOPLE LIKE IT WHEN YOU KNOW WHAT YOU'RE DOING

Another strong argument in favor of formulating some sort of solid plan: it's professional. People admire professionalism, even in a creative field.

It's always very important to back up what you say with facts, knowledge, and dependability. Be verbally organized about your company's endeavors and goals, and how you intend to achieve what you want. When you're organized, it's reassuring to others you may do business with (like actors and directors), or who may move to hold a stake in your company (like funders and donors).

Think about it: Would you want to involve yourself business-wise with a dippy slacker wearing a T-shirt emblazoned with the logo for his college production of *Pippin*? A dreamer who can babble on for hours about that mesmerizing experimental production he once saw performed in Chinese during a vicious hailstorm, but who hasn't the foggiest idea what he, himself, is going to do with his own theater company? (The very same theater company he's asking you to back financially, I might add). Bet you wouldn't touch such an endeavor with a ten-foot pole.

Honestly, now, are you giving off the most professional impression possible when you speak about your company's future? If not, it's time to get serious if you ever want to be taken seriously. Being able to articulate what your company's stake in the future is as clearly as possible is extremely important.

This isn't to suggest you need to start faking business acumen you simply don't have familiarity with, or start tossing off million-dollar SAT vocabulary words to dazzle people. Just make sure you can discuss where your company is going in the longer term with simplicity, clarity, and a sense of command. Make sure you can both verbalize this and write it effectively, as no doubt you'll need to do both.

Corey Fischer (The Jewish Theatre San Francisco) explains his feelings about this issue of clear expression:

> As anyone working with a new company will quickly find out, you're probably going to want to become a nonprofit as soon as possible—you almost have to. And you're probably going to want to start applying for funding. To do that, funders want to know you are thinking beyond the day-to-day and that you have at least a three-year plan. That's not only important for the funders, it's an important tool for decision-

215

making. It becomes a rough guide, not written in stone, but you need to have a sense of, what do you want things to look like in a year, two years, three years.

CONFIDENCE COUNTS

Having the confidence to enact your twelve-month goals is as vital as how well you can understand what exactly you want to do and express that understanding.

Self-confidence in business is, to a great extent, earned. You screw up your courage and set out to achieve something worthwhile with your company; you work hard against tough odds, get kicked in the head, make mistakes, learn from them, make a few more. You finally enjoy the fruits of your labor. Build up enough experience, and success, and you've earned your stripes—the right to feel proud of what you've achieved, and self-assurance that you can do it again.

Even before you've really set the world aflame, though, having faith in yourself and your company is essential. You can feel more self-assured by not simply having your goals clearly outlined, but outlining a solid idea of how you are going to meet them. Always have a command of your situation. The best way to get that sense of power is to fact-find, do your homework, and pinpoint your particular strategies, till you have mastered a theory of how you will go about getting what you want.

Terrence Dwyer (La Jolla Playhouse) sets a strong example:

> Building on the educational contributions we can make with programs is very important. So again, building upon our human resources, continuing and continuing our staff development. Plus strategic thinking—revising the long-range plan. Understanding we have to spend money to make money.

THE BEAUTY OF A BACKUP PLAN

In setting one-year goals, the great upside is that the more control you have over the elements of your plan, the faster you can hope to achieve it. A five-year goal can of course be planned very smartly and achieved, but its distance can make it seem unreal.

The further away a goal is, as well, the more likely it is you might get caught up in the details of its planning and lose sight of the bigger picture of its achievement. You may even have difficulty focusing on exactly what you're working so hard for, at times. This sort of tunnel vision can happen in terms of achieving a short-term goal, too, but it's a bit less likely. Michael P. Price (Goodspeed Musicals) wisely observes:

> I think it's very important that you don't become isolated within your company. It would be easy to do that in this little hamlet here, but I fight complacency by always

looking around for new ways to do things. I want very much to hear ideas from my staff. I consider the staff itself to be our chief administrator. I really feel I'm a dreamer, and a better fireman than I am a planner. So what works well for us is that my staff tries to harness me while I try to push them in new directions. Everyone reports directly to me. If you fuck something up, come into my office and say, "I screwed up." I won't get upset till the third or fourth time it happens! I want my staff to feel comfortable, to know their voices are wanted, and I want no one to fear they're going to hear the words "you're wrong" unfairly.

So what may be more likely to befall a one-year plan? Oh, you name it. If you're not getting so wrapped up in some details you're ignoring others, your financing sources could fall through. You could lose key staffers on whose skills you were counting to realize your goals. Even though you have a somewhat wider margin of control over shorter-term planning, you just never know for sure. Anything can happen; such is life.

What can you do to protect yourself? Always form a backup plan.

The beauty of a backup plan is that you'll probably never have to use it. Just knowing there is another option gives you peace of mind, and peace of mind frees your energies so you can focus on the tasks you have at hand. And if you do have to use your backup plan, you may not be getting exactly what you set out to get, but you will not be left holding an empty bag.

A backup plan must be unfailingly practical and always your safest, most boring bet.

This is good for a couple of reasons. One, it'll be sure to work. Two, if you are unfortunate enough to suffer a shocking setback, believe me, safe and boring will feel pretty darn good to both you and your company members.

A VIEW TOWARD STABILITY

The two schools of thought that divide the professional outlooks of some theater professionals—either an inclination toward structured thinking, or a more fluid approach to the twelve-month planning cycle—are interesting to analyze.

The issue of stability from a purely strategic business angle is clear and sensible. Nobody wants their company to be on the edge of a precipice. Beyond that obvious point, there's a very strong psychological boost that a sense of stability provides you and your company as a whole.

Oftentimes, if your goal is creating a more secure, solidified plan for your company in a one-year period, the novelty of scrambling has worn off. You're ready to leave constant struggle in the dust. You're no longer an amateur, a kid wet behind the ears. You're a professional with a business to run.

The psychological relief that accompanies true stability will carry you far. When you have a bit of money set aside in case you need it, a staff you can count on, and actors who take their work seriously (they stick with you, cheerfully doing the same role over and over for months, happy for the steady gig), then you have an organization that's matured and stabilized.

WHEN IT'S WISE TO STAY FLUID

There are a number of extremely good reasons not to seek too much stability at the wrong point in time, however.

Sometimes, it's simply not in the makeup of a company to work from too rigid a point of view. If a company is very young and very based on collaborative thinking, there isn't that much to lose yet. So that's why making decisions in a fluid, groupthink, brainstorming kind of way may serve the organization best. As this company grows, it will eventually pay off to appoint a theoretical "head" to deal with more structured decision-making and to be a liaison to the outside world (i.e., funders, press, and the like).

Remember, too, that circumstances completely out of the realm of your personal control can change your ideal timetable. Because of this, it's essential that you don't lock in any ideas you can't change if necessary. David Fuller, former artistic director of Jean Cocteau Repertory, observes: "I am by nature a very patient human being. Because I happen to be patient, my ideas, I know, can't happen overnight. It's just a question of having a vision and moving forward. It took me over two years to assemble the staff that I wanted [at the Cocteau], and that's normal."

LEARN THE LANDSCAPE

It's also very important to take your time when you're faced with conditions you're unfamiliar with. Say you've just moved into the business of running your theater company from a completely different occupation. Until you've completely researched what your new work will entail, spoken to others in the field for insight, eyeballed your environment, and seen firsthand how things really work, making your own innovations can wait. Based on his ultimately fruitful experience taking over a long-established organization, Ralph Remington, formerly of the Living Stage, advocates feeling out any new artistic position carefully: "I think it's foolhardy to go into a situation that's existed for thirty-five years and just start making new judgments."

It's also crucial to keep up on developments in the theater business as a whole. Network, read, stay in touch with trends, and try to anticipate changes that could impact your work. "The food chain of the American theater has needed changing," observes Mixed Blood's Jack Reuler.

Smaller, nimbler theaters with skills in producing new work can commission, develop, produce, and disseminate new work in exciting ways, reversing the decades-old trend of regional theater artistic directors looking to last year's small off-Broadway hits for fare because of a box office track record and pedigree. Commercial producers have become the arbiters of taste for nonprofits, when it's our role as heads of nonprofits to lead audiences to where they do not yet know they want to go.

THE SPECIFICS OF GOOD ONE-YEAR PLANNING

The specifics of a one-year plan for your company are, of course, going to depend largely upon your company. Its size, what you want and need, why you need it, and by which specific date you need it are all factors that must be taken into consideration.

Dona Lee Kelly, former managing director of Jean Cocteau Repertory, offers up some excellent advice on how the size of your organization can determine, in some ways, your future success. Kelly explains,

> Midsize companies and middle-class companies are probably the most difficult companies to manage. A small company doesn't have the overhead; they can cut really fast. A big company can absorb any losses in earned income. A midsize company—you have expenses. No matter how you cut them, you have them. There's a certain amount of staff you need to run the company well.
>
> Midsize companies are in the most dangerous position. Cash flow is always a problem. You can never get enough money fast enough.

Much-needed 411, in general, but should it daunt you completely? Nope. You steer your own organizational boat and control your own future no matter what size your company is. It's wonderful to learn from those who have walked before you, but it's equally important you don't imitate anyone too precisely in setting your goals. What worked for one company might not work for you.

You never want to measure yourself by any predetermined yardstick, profile-wise. Don't let anyone else's standards define what your company can do. Make your own choices, not simply in terms of one-year goals, but in terms of whatever decisions you must make for the health of your company.

DO YOUR OWN THING

Jack Reuler learned the dangers of trying to fit an institutional model when he was putting together his early organizational planning. His experience has made him determined ever since to operate on his terms.

Says Reuler,

I really took things for granted. In 1984, 1985, things were humming along.

You've got to understand that the maturation of the philanthropic world sort of matches the history of the regional theater movement. There was a major IRS tax change in 1964 that really changed giving across the country; that's about the same time as the regional theater movement is recognized as beginning. But there was a lack of sophistication in the giving world.

There's this notion of an institutional model: if you look like this, we know how to evaluate you. For one year, I pandered into that and got certain administrative staff I'd never had. In 1980, we went from one to two, then in 1984, I think, we went from two to five.

The problem wasn't that we got these people; the problem was that for that one year, I found myself pandering to what someone else wanted, not to what I wanted. Within a year, I was back down to three.

The NEA had this advancement program. We applied and got in. We really said, "What we really want to be is the best Mixed Blood we can be, not the best institutional model by somebody else's definition."

We worked with a good consultant they provided and developed a three-year plan.

It came with $75,000 that we strictly used as a cash reserve. Before that, zero meant zero. Suddenly, zero meant $75,000. To me, it was quite freeing. Up until then, if the show was a bust, we had zero and went out of business. I still, to this day, have never had a deficit. Not because of any great wisdom—I just don't know how to spend money we don't have. I think one time, in the years we've had that money, we have dipped into it just for cash flow purposes.

In that year that we had that staff of five, instead of saying, "I can relax, I did ten shows." Which was just nuts. We'd do three shows in one night. I just got zealous. I forgot that rule of producing in the nonprofit world—the more you do, the more you lose. So by doing ten shows, you're losing not only technically and artistically, but also financially.

The key thing that came out of that was to do things on a long-term. To be the best Mixed Blood we can be. I don't care how the rest of regional theater does it. I don't care what funders think. Let's do good work. Do it well. When we went through that advancement process, I think it reminded us of something we probably knew but had let other people talk us out of.

STRATEGIES THAT SURPRISE

Long-term planning can be very useful in preserving the artistic freshness of your organization. You can, and should, actually strategize the creative curveballs you intend to pitch to the public. In addition to planning for practical matters,

La Jolla Playhouse's major strategy seeks to prevent its artistic reputation from being pigeonholed in any way.

Terrence Dwyer says:

> Longer term, [La Jolla Playhouse] wants to enhance its name in the field nationally. [The company] wants to be building an endowment as well, and to utilize a new building. A certain sense of artistic unpredictability is also a priority—doing a different set of productions than people expect so that [the company] defies description.

ADMINISTRATION ADJUSTMENTS

Sometimes, a five-year plan is based primarily on one facet of a company's growth. Maybe you don't have a long-term eye toward material choices, for example, as much as you are precisely transitioning an aspect of your administration, such as staffing, by utilizing specific methods of intention.

At Berkeley Repertory, Susan Medak wisely thought from the start about the beneficial ways her gifted staff would move the theater forward and is working hard to prepare the theater for future achievements. "Our heightened profile and the opportunities that has created for the theater, as well as the financial constraints of this economy, really changed my workday," Susan explains. "I spent much less time actually producing theater, and much more time working on projects that will benefit the theater in the future. I thought of myself as creating the architecture for projects that will eventually be 'managed' by our very capable senior staff."

TWO SMART AND OPPOSING VIEWPOINTS

You can be extremely successful following a long-term model as well as going in the exact opposite direction.

Here are two differing opinions about whether a five-year plan can work. First up, Susan Albert Loewenberg. Experience has shown her what isn't right for LA Theatre Works.

> I'm not a five-year planner. We've done a couple of those things, but basically, it's a year ahead. But there's a vision—like the vision of the audio publishing business, we've realized the vision.
>
> Unfortunately, the reality of a small arts organization is, it's just not going to happen. People telling you to do five-year plans—it's a big waste of time. It's nonsense. You don't have the resources. It's not possible, and it's certainly not possible in the arts.

You can't spend all that staff time doing that. These corporations and foundations come with their lofty ideas—they're overstaffed, they're underworked, and they're telling you to make five-year plans, and you're wondering where your next dollar's coming from!

It's unrealistic. It actually makes me mad, because I think that they don't realize how much we put out, and how much we do, with very few people. It's absolutely unrealistic.

It's very fluid, but at the same time, there are some basic rules. You have to learn to delegate. You have to think big. You have to learn how to diversify. You have to learn very quickly how to build your revenue. You cannot be dependent on the whim of a corporation or foundation, because nothing is forever. Nobody's going to fund you forever. Your best funder is going to disappear one day. You can't be dependent on a single source.

You have to be in constant motion, and you do need to have an idea where you're going, and you have to have some goals. But you can't be thinking that you've got to act like a major corporation thinking five years out. Not gonna happen.

Sheldon Epps, on the other hand, is a believer in strategic visualization. He has employed it in every aspect of his career, including within his work as the Pasadena Playhouse's artistic director. He says, "It's only by dreaming that you come up with the plans to do things. To get there yourself, allow for a bit of trial and error. Try a little forward-planning. If it doesn't work, focus primarily on the more immediate. Or mix up your strategy and try a little of both."

Bottom line: Evaluate your own specific situation while weighing the sage advice of others. Then, follow your gut.

SUCCESS SECRETS: FIVE TOOLS TO KEEP HANDY AT ALL TIMES

1. Batteries. Double AAs, 9 volts—every type you can think of. Batteries solve equipment failures, power that extra flashlight at tech, and much more.
2. An old-school X-ACTO knife. This is such a useful item when it comes to quick adjustments on any set, and it is really useful in your office for everything from physically cutting hard-copy scripts in a pinch before handing out text changes to repairing your desk lamp's frayed wires.
3. Disposable cell phones. Always keep a few on hand for cast and crew to use if needed, and use one yourself to conduct long-distance business calls that might add too much cost to your regular phone bill. (Both the phones and their plans can be incredibly cheap and pleasantly dependable.)

4. Bottled water. It's the least you can offer your actors and crew as they toil away on a hot stage in July—or any time, for that matter.
5. Your sense of humor. But you knew that.

Baal by Bertolt Brecht; adapted by Patrick Dooley
directed by Patrick Dooley
Shotgun Players 1996 Season
Pictured: Richard Reinholdt and Richard Silberg
Photo by Patrick Dooley

Chapter Seventeen
Our Ultimate Goals for the Future

You have to earn your legacy in life.

Our experts will all have legacies admired by many people, that's certain. Yet here's an interesting question: How do they perceive their own achievements and the achievements of their companies?

Considering all of the changes, successes, battles, disappointments, and issues each of our subjects' companies have faced, what are their ultimate goals for the future? Have these goals changed from those envisioned at the company's origin? How would these theater personnel like to go down, reputation-wise, in history?

In short, what is each subject's definition of complete success?

Here's what they think.

WHAT'S GOOD FOR THE GROUP

Michael Gennaro, former executive director of Steppenwolf, says: "The seamless integration and harmony of the staff, board, and ensemble means a lot.

> I was the one who got to go up and get the Tony Award for *Cuckoo's Nest*. It was very moving for me. More important to me were the feelings and emotions of the staff, board, and actors, and what that meant.
>
> Personally, for me, not only have I had staff members leave and come back, but I have had staff members who continually return here to visit their friends and just hang out. That is an important thing, because it means people are happy. These are people who are making choices to do this kind of work for not a great financial reward. If we can be leaders in that regard, in terms of, "This is a good place to work, and they pay as well as anybody," if people can go, "I get a chance to really explore," that, to me, is what it's all about.

IDENTIFYING NEW VISIONARIES

Gennaro's successor, David Hawkanson, equally committed to infusing the company with the very best artistic sensibilities. He explains.

> Steppenwolf has really moved into an identity as an actor/director/playwright-driven theater company. Playing off our ensemble has also given us great success, and our group continues to regenerate itself by adding new skill sets. We've been working with wonderful playwrighting talents like Tyler McCraney as part of an increased focus on new works. We also want to do a wide range of scale, in terms of the plays we produce—smaller productions are a newer focus, and Polly Call, who became our director of artistic development, changed so much for us in terms of bringing new playwrights to our attention.

NO REGRETS

Paul Zuckerman, speaking of Chicago City Limits, states,

> In terms of defining success, I think that's a multileveled question. I've often thought, "Gee, I've had a pretty good run." We came out to New York in a little van, nobody knew us, and created New York's longest-running comedy review. So in some sense, if it all ended today, I'd have lots of regrets that it ended, but I'd also have a sense of accomplishment that, we did it. It was a fun job. I can't think of anything I'd like to do more than this sort of thing.

BLAZING NEW TRAILS

"Looking toward the future, I'm very proud of our collaborations with playwrights like Neil LaBute, Donald Marguiles, and Jane Anderson," the late Gil Cates of the Geffen Playhouse reflected. Gil's goal was also . . .

> . . . to develop more material for the canon. After all, somebody was the first to do *Hamlet*! We have not had the luxury of operating on a three- or five-year plan, but I am now looking forward to expanding our outreach program, doing potentially ten plays a year, doing a Christmas or holiday event. That's how I think; not that three- or five-year plans aren't helpful, they are, as long as you're not slavishly committed to them.

His visionary thinking, and legacy, lives on at the Geffen to this day.

MAKING OUR MARK

Rick Lombardo, associated with New Repertory Theatre, has this to add:

I'd like to know that New Repertory Theatre can grow, through civic discourse and the art produced. That it is the Boston area's finest midsize theater. That New Rep's impact reaches a very large segment, and that its art serves its audience.

MORE GROWTH

Terrence Dwyer shared his dream for La Jolla Playhouse: "That it continues to grow and expand, in both an artistic sense and a business sense simultaneously." Personally, he has high hopes for playmaking as well. "My dream project? A great production of *Hamlet* or *Richard III*."

FREEDOM TO MAKE OUR IMPACT

Corey Fischer's hope for the Jewish Theatre San Francisco was, "Artistically, to continue to create works of theater that are unique and create a deep need within the audiences and within ourselves.

> In terms of audience, it's never about sheer numbers with theater. You're really limited by the nature of the event. You're never going to reach as many people as with film or video. But the impact has to do with how you're received and how you can inform other work that's being done, what people go and do with it—the depth with which you impact people's lives.

ENCOURAGING PROGRESSION

Fischer's colleague at TJT, Aaron Davidman, stated proudly,

> We programmed seasons that have a variety of plays speaking to a wide spectrum of the audience in the Bay Area. Our audience was largely Jewish, but the company has seen itself as a bridge to other cultures, and people of other cultures found our work meaningful and important.

KEEP AIMING HIGH

Richard Pletcher's ambition for the Round Barn at Amish Acres is to continue collaborating with the theater's brightest and most enduring talents:

> We wanted to do *The Baker's Wife*, a lesser-known show that hadn't been produced in the past decade, but needed a director. Joe Stein said, "What about Scotty?"— meaning Scott Schwartz, Stephen Schwartz's son. Scott did a great job, as Joe of course has always done with us. In fact, we dedicated our stage to Joe in 1996. Three years ago, the York Theatre in New York City staged a revival of three Stein shows,

227

Plain and Fancy included, so my wife and I got to travel to participate in that. I can say I finally made it to Broadway!

THE PRESENT DETERMINES OUR FUTURE

For Kevin Mayes, protecting the legacy and future success of the reconfigured Bailiwick Repertory meant staying in the moment:

I'm all about thinking and brainstorming about where we want to be in three or five years, and I believe a five-year plan at macrolevel is very valuable. The first years of our regenerated company, though, have to be about learning how to work together, how to make decisions together, and how to operationalize, all of which will move us toward our ultimate goals.

TRAINING THE NEXT GENERATION

For the Barrow Group's Robert Serrell, the company's ultimate success is greatly reflected in the new actors it trains.

To attract great students to our school, we bring in top-tier teachers with sterling reputations, who work consistently and closely with those students. These students master the specific acting approach perfected by Seth and Lee, and through this theater training, have the tools to realize huge artistic potential. That starts with beginning acting classes right on through to the most advanced instruction levels.

ARTISTIC EQUALITY IS CRUCIAL

For Lily Tung Crystal, infusing Ferocious Lotus with new works and new collaborators will bring the company's goals full circle.

My vision over the next few years is to expand our yearly offerings. Eventually, it would be wonderful to do three shows a year, plays, or musicals. We also want our company to include many quality artists, not simply Asian American artists. We just want to work with good playwrights! Our mission has changed in this way: evolving from working with just Asian American artists, we want to give voice to others as well. To promote reality, that a theater company should represent all cultures and gender parity.

THE MANY FACETS OF SUCCESS

Susan Medak, of Berkeley Rep, says,

I don't mean to sound Pollyanna-ish, but complete success for me is to do work of the highest caliber. Our production of *Orstea*, which was the opening show of our new theater, is an example. What I mean by this example, too, is artists have been able to do their most ambitious work here—not always their best, but that will come later. To get them there, you can support them, you can help them.

Complete success for me as well is when audiences can see great artists producing great work and feel engaged, respected, and challenged by that. Complete success is when an audience feels they've been well served.

You learn from the people in your life, too. I've been able to grow within this job and as a human being, because I have a family and a full life away from the theater.

STAYING ALIVE

Susan Albert Loewenberg of LA Theatre Works opines,

I would love to leave LA Theatre Works intact with an endowment, I've realized from the audio publishing business. I would like to build that business. LA Theatre Works would never be able to raise endowment money—it's too small. But I've always had the dream, since I started this business, that the audio publishing business would become so successful that we could endow ourselves.

Then I could leave it with a small endowment and really leave the organization and allow it to continue. Whether it continues in the same form, or altered, is not important to me. I would love to be able, when I leave, to have it go on and to be able to leave it in good financial shape. Leave it to someone, or a group of people, who could carry it forward with the same degree of excellence and do better than I. Much better than I, do a better job than I do, because at a certain point, there'll be younger people who can do this better than I can do it, who can see other exciting things and other directions to take it in.

ENCOURAGING EXPRESSION

Mitzi Sales no longer works for Berkeley Repertory, but she has this to say about the goals of that theater and all theaters:

I've always felt like the principal goal of any managing director is to find the audience for the artistic output, for the artistic director's vision. I think that we were able to do that over the years.

It's that situation where, let's do some theater—what do people want to come to? Well, you don't do theater like that! Hello?! You find somebody who needs to say something, and then you find people who want to do that. I think, largely, that was my goal. That was my role, and I think that we were able to do that.

I would like to take credit for knowing when to leave. I think that it was one of the smartest things I ever did, because with Susie Medak and Tony [Taccone] and Sharon [Ott], this fresh new creative energy was able to get this new theater built. I'm not saying it wouldn't have happened if I'd stayed, but it might not have. I was very wise to leave when I did for the theater as well as for myself. The theater deserved to have somebody who was completely engaged and not feeling unchallenged.

So I take full credit for knowing when to leave and doing it.

HOPE FOR THE NEXT GENERATION
Susan Kosoff's wish for the Wheelock Family Theatre:

I think ultimate success for me will be that it continues. Part of the impetus for a strategic plan was the knowledge that Jane Staab and I are not going to go on forever.

Part of what we looked at is, how do we look at the leadership for the future? How is that going to work?

For me, the tale will be told in whether the theater continues and continues with the same general mission. That's not to say there can't be changes, adjustments, and new ideas. I think that's healthy. My hope is that the theater will be stable enough and not dependent on me and on Jane to continue.

NEVER KNOW IT ALL
The Goodspeed's Michael Price feels that his company's ultimate glory means staying curious:

There is nothing more exciting to me than watching an audience rise to its feet at the end of a performance here, or for a patron to come up to me and say, "You really blew it!" All feedback is of equal value, because as I look back on my career, I think the most important thing I've learned is what I know. I'm still learning. If I'd figured that out years ago, I would have saved myself a lot of grief. I think the most important message is to be open to learning what you don't know at every stage of your career, and to accept the fact that you'll always be learning.

KEEPING CORE VALUES IN MIND
Shotgun Players' Patrick Dooley believes that realizing his ultimate goals for the future depends upon an unwavering commitment to the philosophies that he's held throughout his life.

I think that ultimately, success really has a lot to do with the following combo: you knock on that door, but then you have to be there and ready when it opens.

Our success, and the success of any theater company, I think, has lots to do with persistence. Raising money from people, they know I'm there—I've been doing this for years, it isn't just some flight of fancy. I've always known success was gonna happen for our company; I trusted myself and the people I work with, and other people pick up on that.

My grandpa was such a great influence on me, in terms of teaching me how to really make this thing work. He was a crazy-successful businessman, and I watched him make things happen—if he knew someone had money they owed him but wouldn't pay, he'd literally take their clothes. And wear them! He taught me how to negotiate!

And another important thing I've learned: to be successful, you have to treat people right. You have to take care of the people who work for you—they're giving you the best of themselves, so they deserve this. I'm happy to write a letter of recommendation, for example, that allows a member of our company to create elsewhere. I'm thrilled when our people get successful and move on, sometimes to work in a larger venue—it's a great sign of success to me when this happens. We're proud of that—it's like, who's the next hungry, hardworking person we're going to find who will go on to major individual success? The best thing is, these artists come back to work with us—we have successful long-term relationships built with them.

MISSION ACCOMPLISHED
On the other hand, Jack Reuler hopes the need for Mixed Blood will diminish in the coming years:

We'll be ultimately successful when we're no longer necessary. If you have a mission, you've got to be aspiring to realize it. The Polio Society, when it existed, its purpose was to find the cure for polio, and when it found that cure, it no longer needed to exist. I think it still existed to help people who had polio get through life. I sort of see us that way, perhaps farther and farther away all the time. When people, both audiences and other arts organizations, have embraced what it is we're trying to do more intelligently than we do it, all we can be is another theater doing good work, or maybe there's enough theater doing good work that we don't need to be.

Closing our doors because we've realized our mission would be the greatest thing that could happen, not a sign of failure.

AS FOR YOUR LEGACY . . .
It will be whatever you choose to make it. Hopefully, it will be glorious. To give you a head start, I'm going to clue you in to something. Here now, I will impart

to you the ultimate secret to achieving total and complete success in the theater. Get ready—it's Holy Grail time!

Here comes the secret . . . Is your seat belt fastened? Good.

The secret is . . . always have fun.

Have fun as you work in the theater. It's why Carol Channing has been smiling constantly for the past eighty years. It's also contagious. That's why audiences have had such a good time watching everything from Shakespeare to Blue Man Group. It's also why you never noticed you'd gotten fleas until that performance of *Cats* was over.

Great theater is great because it's infused with joy. Those who make it work directly from the truth that they love what they do. Whether onstage or backstage, they have fun. I once read a quote attributed to Paul McCartney—he said that doing music should never feel like work. You always want to make it play, and, therefore, it will be great. This is one of the best nuggets of wisdom I've ever heard. Creativity springs from our imagination. The same imagination that we developed as kids, playing and having a good time. That sense of fun is the purest resource of success a theater professional can draw upon.

A life in the theater is rough, right? So don't make things any more difficult than they have to be.

Stay loose. If your work feels like fun, trust that you're onto something. Other people are going to respond to it.

At all stages of building your company, work as hard as you can. Learn as much as you can. Allow each and every accomplishment to inspire you onward to future achievements. But never forget to have fun.

Enjoy the ride as you go along. Make yourself some great memories. You'll be successful then, no matter whether the show makes you rich and transfers to the Winter Garden or closes opening night.

Don't get me wrong. I wish you millions of dollars and hundreds of Tony Awards. (If you apply the information you've learned from this book, hopefully you're well on your way). It's just that you can't measure success materially, not really. You can only measure it through self-satisfaction, creative fulfillment, friendships, and peace of mind.

So make happiness your goal as you build your own successful theater company.

Break a leg, and always have fun.

Appendix A

Physical Production Details for the Theater Companies Profiled within *Building the Successful Theater Company*

Steppenwolf Theatre Company
Mainstage space: 510 seats. Thrust stage setup.
Studio space: 299 seats. Black box structure.
Garage space: 100 seats. Black box structure.

The Geffen Playhouse
Mainstage space (Gil Cates Theater): 512 seats. Historic building space, constructed in 1929; newly renovated for performances in 2005 with state-of-the-art acoustic/lighting upgrades.
Second space (Audrey Skirball Kenis Theater): 149 seats. Full production venue.

La Jolla Playhouse
Mainstage space: 492 seats. Proscenium stage setup.
Second stage: 398 seats. Thrust stage setup.

Chicago City Limits
Mainstage space (Jan Hus Playhouse): 150 seats. Cabaret-style seating.

Berkeley Repertory Theatre
Mainstage space (Roda Theatre): 600 seats.
Second stage: 400 seats. Thrust stage.

Goodspeed Musicals
Mainstage space (Goodspeed Opera House): 398 seats. Proscenium stage setup. Second space (Norma Terris Theatre): 200 seats. Modified proscenium stage setup.

Mixed Blood Theatre Company
Mainstage space: 200 seats. Adjustably structured stage. The company also tours productions at a variety of venues.

Wheelock Family Theatre
Mainstage space: 650 seats. Proscenium stage setup.

LA Theatre Works
No permanent set performance space.
Records and performs at various venues.

Bailiwick Chicago Repertory
Flexible stage space.

New Repertory Theatre
Mainstage space (Moseian Theater): 340 seats.
Second space: 90 seats. Black box theater.
The company also tours productions at a variety of educational venues across Massachusetts.

The Round Barn Theatre at Amish Acres
Mainstage space (Joseph Stein Stage): 400 seats. In-the-round seating.

The Barrow Group
Mainstage space: 99 seats. Flexible stage space. Proscenium stage setup.
Studio space: 40 seats. Flexible stage space.

Shotgun Players
Mainstage (Ashby Stage): 100 seats. Raised stage space.

Ferocious Lotus Theatre Company
No permanent stage space.
Presents at various venues.

Appendix B

National Associations and Organizations

Here is a listing of some national theater arts assistance organizations you may wish to contact for resource information and advice as you establish your own theater company. Arguably, your first stop should be the Foundation Center for grant/funding information.

Alliance of Resident Theatres/New York
www.art-newyork.org
questions@art-newyork.org

Americans for the Arts (New York City)
(212) 223-2787
(212) 753-1325
www.artsusa.org

American Theatre Wing
www.americantheatrewing.org

Black Theatre Network
Contact through email: *president@blacktheatrenetwork.org*

The Broadway League
www.broadwayleague.com

Appendix C

Regional Associations and Organizations

Austin Circle of Theatres (Texas)
www.austincreativealliance.org

Baltimore Theatre Alliance
www.baltimoreperforms.org

Greater Philadelphia Cultural Alliance
www.philaculture.org

League of Washington Theatres
info@lowt.org
www.lowt.org

NYC Mayor's Office of Film, Theatre, and Broadcasting
www.nyc.gov

Portland Area Theatre Alliance
(503) 241-4902

Stage Source (New England)
info@stagesource.org
www.stagesource.org

Theatre Bay Area
www.theatrebay.org

Foundation Center (New York—National Headquarters)
www.foundationcenter.org/newyork

Atlanta:
www.foundationcenter.org/atlanta

Cleveland:
www.foundationcenter.org/cleveland

San Francisco:
www.foundationcenter.org/sanfrancisco

Washington, DC:
www.foundationcenter.org/washington

Institute of Outdoor Drama
outdoor@unc.edu
www.unc.edu.depts/outdoor

National Endowment for the Arts
1100 Pennsylvania Avenue NW
Washington, DC 20506

Performing Arts Resources
Contact through website: *www.performingarts.net*

Theatre Communications Group (TCG)
(212) 609-5900
www.tcg.org

Theatre Development Fund
(212) 912-9770
www.tdf.org

United States Institute for Theatre Technology
(315) 463-6463
www.usitt.org

3 University/Resident Theatre Association
www.urta.com

Volunteer Lawyers for the Arts
(212) 319-2787 (information directory)
(212) 319-2910 (legal matters line)
(212) 752-6575 (fax)
www.vlany.org

Appendix D

Unions

Actors' Equity Association (New York City—National Headquarters)
(212) 869-8530
www.actorsequity.org

Actors' Equity Association (Chicago)
(312) 641-0393

Actors' Equity Association (Los Angeles)
(323) 978-8010

Actors' Equity Association (Orlando, Florida)
(407) 345-8600

American Federation of Musicians
Contact through website: *www.afm.org*

American Guild of Variety Artists
(212) 675-1003

Association of Authors' Representatives
(212) 353-3709

Dramatists Guild of America
www.dramatistsguild.com

Society of Stage Directors and Choreographers
www.sdcweb.org

Appendix E

Talent Banks

Here is a listing of resource organizations that you may find helpful in terms of locating qualified professional performers for your theater company and for filling administrative staff positions.

ArtsSEARCH
www.tcg.org

Breakdown Services
www.breakdownservices.com

Nontraditional Casting Project
www.ntcp.org

Appendix F

Audition Resources

The following organizations sponsor audition conferences for professional theaters or offer networking opportunities that connect talent with theater companies.

Florida Professional Theatres Association
(561) 848-6231

National Dinner Theatre Association
ndta@aol.com

New England Theatre Conference
www.netconline.org

Princess Grace Foundation
(212) 317-1470
pgfusa@pgfusa.com
www.pgfusa.com

Southeastern Theatre Conference
(336) 272-3645
www.setc.org

Appendix G

Publications/Web Resources

Consult the following publications for consistently helpful information about the business of theater. Web info is listed below; also check newsstands for a number of these titles in hard-copy versions.

Academy Players Directory (Actors' Directory)
www.visualnet.com

American Theatre Magazine
www.tcg.org

Backstage
www.backstage.com

Black Talent News
www.blacktalentnews.com

Broadway.com
www.broadway.com

Call Board/Pointe Magazine
www.pointemagazine.com

Curtain Up
www.curtainup.com

Dramatics Magazine
www.edta.org

The Hollywood Reporter
www.hollywoodreporter.com

Performing Arts Magazine
www.performingartsmagazine.com

Ross Reports (union, TV, and movie coverage)
www.backstage.com

Stagebill Magazine
www.avant-rus.com/stagebill

Stage Directions Magazine
www.stage-directions.com

Variety/Daily Variety
www.variety.com

Appendix H

Theatrical Supply Resource List

Here is a listing of supply companies that may be able to provide you with specialized equipment for your company via shipping. Most have full catalogues available upon request.

All Pro Sound (sound and lighting)
(800) 925-5776
www.allprosound.com

Atlas Stageworks Lighting, Ltd. (lighting instruments)
1100 Capital Blvd.
Raleigh, NC 27603
(800) 334-8353
https://atlasstageworks.com

Charles H. Stewart Scenic Design (curtains and backdrops)
115 Flagship Drive
North Andover, MA 01845
(978) 682-5757
www.charleshstewart.com

City Theatrical (multiproduct stock)
752 East 133rd Street
Bronx, NY 10454
(718) 292-7932

Columbus McKinnon (rigging)
140 John James Audobon
Amherst, NY 14228
(800) 888-0985
www.cmworks.com

Eartec (headsets)
145 Dean Knauss Drive
Narragansett, RI 02882
(800) 399-5994

Kryolan (theatrical makeup)
132 Ninth Street
San Francisco, CA 94103
(415) 863-9684

Pacific Northwest Theatre Associates (multiproduct stock)
333 Westlake Avenue North
Seattle, WA 98109
(206) 622-7850
www.pnta.com

Premier Seating (audience seating units)
4211 Shannon Drive
Baltimore, MD 21213
(888) 456-SEAT

Sapsis Rigging, Inc. (safety inspections)
233 N. Lansdowne Avenue
Lansdowne, PA 19050
(800) 727-7471
www.sapsis-rigging.com

Stagelam (theatrical flooring)
173 Glidden Road
Brampton, Ontario, Canada L6W3L9
(800) 361-1698
www.stagelam.com

TicketMaker (box office software)
(888) 397-3400
www.ticketmaker.com

Tools for Stagecraft.com (a huge selection of theatrical hand tools and more)
(877) 80-TOOLS
www.toolsforstagecraft.com

Tracy Theatre Originals (costumes and props)
(800) 926-8351
www.tracytheatreoriginals.com

Index

Books from Allworth Press

Business and Legal Forms for Theater, Second Edition
By Charles Grippo (8½ x 11, 192 pages, paperback, $24.95)

The Business of Broadway
By Mitch Weiss and Perri Gaffney (6 x 9, 292 pages, hardcover, $24.99)

The Business of Theatrical Design, Second Edition
By James Moody (6 x 9, 304 pages, paperback, $19.95)

Careers in Technical Theater
By Mike Lawler (6 x 9, 256 pages, paperback, $19.95)

Fundamentals of Theatrical Design
By Karen Brewster and Melissa Shafer (6 x 9, 256 pages, paperback, $27.50)

The Health and Safety Guide for Film, TV, and Theater
By Monona Rossol 6 x 9, 288 pages, paperback, $27.50)

Leadership in the Performing Arts
By Tobie S. Stein (5½ x 8½, 252 pages, paperback, $19.99)

Movement for Actors, Second Edition
Edited by Nicole Potter (6 x 9, 304 pages, paperback, $19.99)

The Perfect Stage Crew, Second Edition
By John Kaluta (6 x 9, 272 pages, paperback, $19.99)

Performing Arts Management
By Tobie S. Stein and Jessica Bathurst (8½ x 11, 552 pages, paperback, $50.00)

Running Theaters
By Duncan Webb (6 x 9, 256 pages, paperback, $19.95)

Singing in Musical Theatre
By Joan Melton (6 x 9, 240 pages, paperback, $19.95)

Technical Theater for Nontechnical People, Second Edition
By Drew Campbell (6 x 9, 288 pages, paperback, $19.95)

To see our complete catalog or to order online, please visit *www.allworth.com*.